COMPUTER MEDIATED COMMUNICATION

COMPUTER MEDIATED COMMUNICATION

SOCIAL INTERACTION AND THE INTERNET

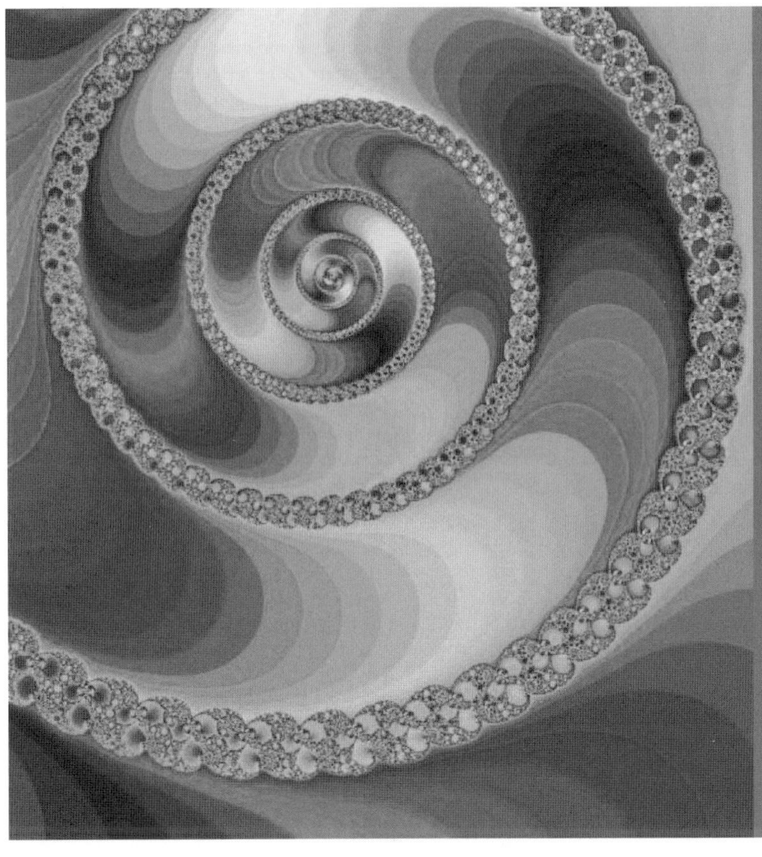

CRISPIN THURLOW
LAURA LENGEL
ALICE TOMIC

Los Angeles | London | New Delhi
Singapore | Washington DC

First published 2004
Reprinted 2009, 2010, 2011, 2012

SAGE Publications Ltd
1 Oliver's Yard
55 City Road
London EC1Y 1SP

SAGE Publications Inc.
2455 Teller Road
Thousand Oaks, California 91320

SAGE Publications India Pvt Ltd
B 1/I 1 Mohan Cooperative Industrial Area
Mathura Road
New Delhi 110 044

SAGE Publications Asia-Pacific Pte Ltd
3 Church Street
#10-04 Samsung Hub
Singapore 049483

British Library Cataloguing in Publication data

A catalogue record for this book is available from the British Library

ISBN 978 0 7619 4953 4
ISBN 978 0 7619 4954 1 (pbk)

Library of Congress Control Number available

Typeset by M Rules
Printed and bound in Great Britain by
CPI Group (UK) Ltd, Croydon, CR0 4YY
Printed on paper from sustainable resources

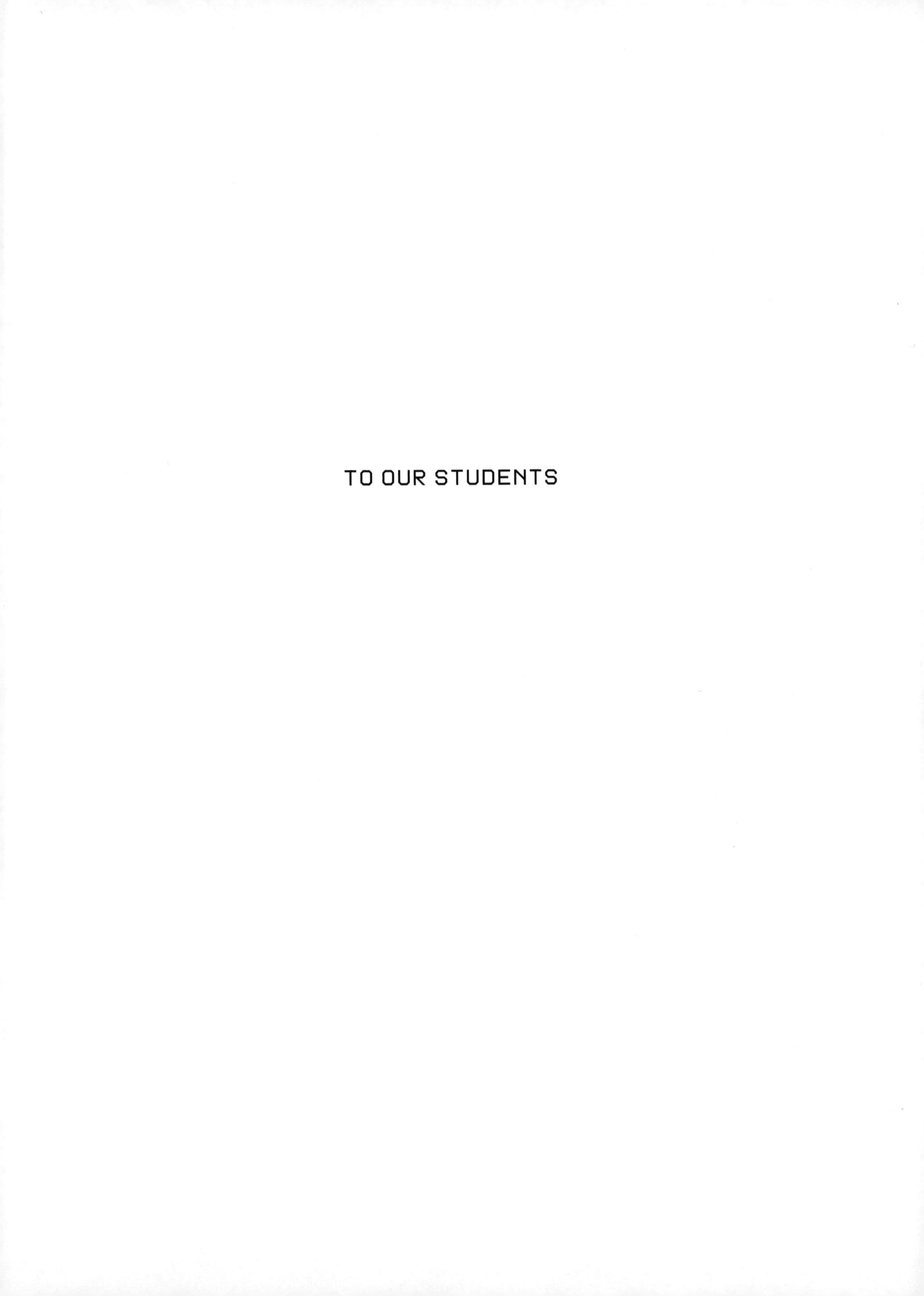

TO OUR STUDENTS

CONTENTS

STRAND 4 EXPLORE: FOCUS AREAS 197

LIST OF ILLUSTRATIONS

ACKNOWLEDGEMENTS

No act of creative, intellectual activity is ever achieved in isolation. All work is collaborative. For us, this book project was an adventure and a challenge, particularly as we were writing from three different countries, sometimes FtF, usually via CMC and often LOL. There is also always an infinite web of family, friends and colleagues who give support, either knowingly or not. First and foremost, we want to thank our families, without whose support this book project and the rest of our working lives would not really be possible. It was David Rogers at Stacklands and Judy Thurlow who helped secure our writer's retreat in the Kent countryside of West Kingsdown towards the final stages of the book – we thank them for that. We are also very grateful to Suzette D'Cruz and Daniel Fedak at VPT, for weaving our ideas and design concepts into a lovely website. Thank you to Calvin Sweat at Digital Fractal Images for permission to use his inspirational fractal. Thank you also to Katya Bahkmetova, Silke Kirschner and Andy Gault for their valuable assistance. Laura also thanks Victoria Newsom for exchanging ideas, reading drafts assisting with the editing of the manuscript. Finally, we definitely want to thank Julia Hall, Jamilah Ahmed and the production editors at Sage UK, especially Fabienne Pedroletti, for being so supportive of our pedagogical and conceptual visions for this book, as well as our proposal reviewers for their incredibly useful comments and ideas.

Crispin Thurlow
Laura Lengel
Alice Tomic

November 2003

INTRODUCTION 1

FOR STUDENTS: GETTING INTO CMC

FRACTALS AND SPIRALS: PATTERNS IN NATURE

> *Fractal images are shapes showing self-similarities at smaller and smaller scales. Before magnification, the size of the fractal image here was much, much smaller than a grain of sand. In fact, if your computer monitor [or the page of this book] were magnified by the same amount, it would fill the solar system! (Fractal Digital Images)*

> *You see spirals every day. They are the natural growth curves of plants and seashells, the celebrated golden curve of ancient Greek mathematics and architecture, the optimal curve for highway turns. Peer into a flower or look down at a cactus and you will see a pattern of spirals criss-crossing each other. (Wilson, 1999)*

We've chosen to use a fractal on the cover of this book because we think it's a powerful metaphor for computer mediated communication (CMC) ◎. As you may already know, fractals are images and shapes where an identical pattern is repeated over and over and over. What's really amazing about these digitally created, visually detailed images, however, is that exactly the same thing happens in nature. We find fractals in the formation of trees, coral or even a branch of broccoli – wherever a design or structure just keeps repeating itself. So, even though an image like the one on our cover may seem very synthetic and mechanical, it's also incredibly natural and lifelike. Fractals are digital and new-age, but simultaneously organic and prehistoric. The same is true of the internet. Sure, it's a pretty new, sophisticated technology, but what's really interesting about it is the way it's being used to do the same old totally natural thing: communication.

◎ We are very grateful to Fractal Digital Images for permission to use this image. Their website has many more great images like this one: <http://fractal-digital-images.com/>.

But why a *spiral* fractal in particular? Well, the spiral is an ancient symbol occurring across many cultures and throughout history. This is because it too is both a natural pattern and also a mathematically precise pattern. Some people consider spirals to be almost mystical in their perfection. There's certainly something captivating about them. (To see a range of spiral images, just run a quick search for 'spirals' in Google's image bank.)

www For weblinks and resources visit the CMC website at <www.sagepub.co.uk/resources/cmc>

Spirals like the one on our cover are made up of a seemingly infinite repetition of exactly the same angular turns – again and again and again. In fact, they're one long curve made up of an endless number of minute twists and turns – appearing to start from nowhere and going on forever. This is also similar to the internet. However revolutionary it may feel, it's actually just the next step in a very long line of technological and cultural changes. The reality is that great social changes like these usually happen incrementally – like the gradual turns in the spiral, one small step after another, and with many, many more to come.

THE INTERNET AS CULTURAL TRANSFORMATION

Throughout history, adventurous types have pushed against the boundaries of knowledge to explore the unknown and to make sense of what appeared to be mysterious and unfathomable. The early map makers found out that you couldn't, after all, fall off the edge of the earth. The first space travellers in the 1960s found out that humans could explore space, a journey only dreamt of earlier. In many ways, at this point in history, cyberspace has replaced space as the great unknown. As such it's a topic surrounded by myth and reality, assumptions, suppositions and unanswered questions. It's one of our societies' great talking points at this moment in history.

As a book about CMC, this book examines the social and cultural transformations being brought about by computers and, more precisely, the internet. It goes further than this, though, by focusing on social interaction – how *identities*, *relationships* and *communities* are being changed or influenced by the internet. In our book we also do this from an international perspective. Even though a lot of the theory and facts and figures come from Western scholarship and US experience, we think it's really important to explore beyond the familiar and taken-for-granted. Whether you own a computer or not – and billions of people don't – these days everyone's lives are transformed by new media like the internet, sometimes positively and sometimes negatively.

Have a look at this statement by the educational scholar Muhammad Betz (quoted in Henrickson, 2000), who recognizes that we're all undergoing a historical shake-up of some kind:

> Our behavior away from our tools will probably be influenced by the tools that we use . . . [and] will probably show some of the learned characteristics we have acquired from the time spent with our tools. I still wonder what the long term effects of information technology can have on our character, psychological and physical, when the artifacts of technology are in flux.

What he's saying is that there's more to technology than technology. It's human communication and what we do with our technology that really counts. What's more, it's all about the transformation of our patterns of social interaction – how we live and work through, with and around the technology. The trouble is, however, we don't always know what the outcome of these transformations will be, and that can be quite unsettling.

YOUR ROLE IN IT ALL: GETTING INTO CMC

> *My generation of students is very upbeat. They're all interested in new technology and innovations. I believe we'll probably be the ones to make a difference in the world. (First-year undergraduate, 2003)*

Imagine you're looking at a hand-held kaleidoscope. As you hold it against the light, an orderly pattern of pieces of colored glass creates a pleasing design. But when you give it a shake, the design changes completely. The colors are still the same but the design has reconfigured itself into a different pattern. In the same way, at strategic points in time, history shakes up the world and our perceptions of it. This is what's been happening with the internet. But it's a bit of a paradox: everything changes and nothing changes. In French there's a great expression for this experience: *Plus ça change, plus c'est la même chose* ('The more things change, the more they stay the same'). As a scholar and as a human being, your challenge is to at least try and make some sense of it all.

You've probably felt this yourself: a sense of the rapid pace of technological change around you. It would, for example, be difficult to give an accurate number of mobile telephone and internet users in the world today, since today's figures will undoubtedly be superseded by tomorrow's. In fact, the tough reality we've faced in writing a book like this is that many of the figures we give will already be out of date by the time you read this sentence. It's also really hard for people to get their heads around the volume and speed of transmission of information and communication these days.

All this makes defining and understanding the changes even harder. As international globalization expert Anthony Giddens (1999) reminds us, however, the changes are happening not only 'out there', but also 'in here' – in our homes and inside our heads, in how we see the world and our place in it. We all have a responsibility, therefore, to think about and debate our experiences of these cultural transformations. The fact is, it's impossible to remain neutral to their consequences. This is why it's important to see how all the changes are affecting everyday human interaction. What's more, anyone entering the world of work these days needs to have an intelligent opinion about the internet.

PORTALS: NEW TECHNOLOGIES, NEW WAYS OF LEARNING

One thing's for certain: the internet and web have brought about whole new ways of learning. This is not to say that they've totally replaced the old ways, but your experience of being a student is undeniably different from ours. We certainly know that our experience of being teachers and academics is not the same as it was before. You may not be completely wired to the web, but as a student in the twenty-first century you're a 'cyber-student', if only because your writing practices are actually *typing* practices, and because the internet is one of your major information sources.

New ways of learning also demand new kinds of books. This is why, in preparing this book, we've tried really hard to put together something which we hope responds better to the way you need to read and research nowadays – even if it means our book is a bit unorthodox. In this sense, the *portal* has been our inspiration and framework. In an age of overwhelming and easily accessible information, we don't believe students want to have a book which provides all the answers and which dictates your learning. Like most students, we imagine you'll also want to search out materials and answers of your own.

BOX 1 WHAT IS A PORTAL?

Portal: an entrance, gateway or doorway, especially an imposing or awesome one. (Chambers' *Twenty-first Century Dictionary*)

By the spring of 1998 a new bit of vocabulary had entered the media world: 'portal' or 'web portal'. Companies that had formerly been known as search engine companies or web directories started to call themselves by, and be referred to as, this new term. The idea of a portal site is that all your web journeys should start here. (Miller, 2000: 117)

As a portal, therefore, this book is meant to be a doorway to understanding, but also a gateway to further investigation and first-hand experience. Portals are always starting points, never end points. However, we don't want it to be a portal like the one Vincent Miller describes above, where, for commercial self-interest, your freedom to search and surf on the internet is narrowed and restricted. For us, this is what happens when gateways become *gatekeepers* – monitoring and controlling who stays out and who passes through. Our portal is rather an invitation to independent inquiry. This is why, throughout the book, we've identified ideas for further discussion and investigation. There are also '◎Links' at moments in the text when we'd like to direct you to additional information, to help clarify something or cross-reference ideas discussed elsewhere in the book.

Studying CMC is all about thinking for yourself in a rapidly developing field in which, you could say, the goalposts are forever moving. This definitely makes things more challenging. Someone once described researching the internet as like trying to take a sip from a fire hydrant! Even though the landscape is always changing, however, the scholarly equipment used for exploring it remains the same. The main 'equipment' we promote in this book reflects the four qualities of intellectual pursuit laid down in 1998 by the internationally renowned scholar Pierre Bourdieu. In fact, we think Bourdieu's ideas offer such a good framework for studying CMC that we've used them as slogans for each of the main sections in this book, and we'll be explaining them as we go along.

BOX 2 THE PILLARS OF INTELLECTUAL LIFE

- The demolition of simplistic either-ors.
- The critique of received ideas.
- Freedom with respect to those in power.
- Respect for the complexity of problems.

LOOKS LIKE A BOOK, FEELS LIKE A BOOK . . .

The idea of this book is to develop your intellectual skills in approaching CMC as a scholarly field. We would, however, just like to get two things straight:

- **Number 1:** You don't really have to know anything about how computers work. You will, of course, need to learn some new computing skills, but this is *not* a book about computers; this is a book about communication. In fact, many of our students start by declaring that they don't even like computers! We don't believe it's necessary to know how the mechanics of technologies work to think critically about their influence in our lives.
- **Number 2:** This book is not the last word on CMC and the internet. No book ever is. Our book raises as many questions as it answers and no single section offers the final word on the area it covers. It's like we say above: we can only highlight the things which we think are important, suggest some good questions to keep asking, and then recommend things to read and places to look. The rest really is up to you.

Practically speaking, the book is organized into four *strands*, each of which highlights the core academic activity which we think is most relevant.

- **Learn: basic theory.** In the Basic Theory strand, we begin by examining the nature of CMC. In each of the six units we therefore do some defining, some theorizing, some explaining, and so on. The idea here is that you will probably need to *learn* the concepts, arguments and theories covered in order to build an adequate base from which to move through the rest of the book.
- **Critique: central issues.** In the Central Issues strand we give you a chance to consider some of the major issues in CMC more generally – especially in terms of identity, relationships and communities online. In moving through the seven units in this strand, we hope that you will be able to draw on what you've learned in the Basic Theory units and, more importantly, use this understanding to *critique* the popular and academic ideas in each area.
- **Apply: fieldwork.** In the Fieldwork strand of the book we've designed six tasks so that you can actually do some CMC and *apply* the knowledge and critical perspectives you acquire from elsewhere in the book. Some of this will be familiar territory, some of it will be new to you – and may create quite a steep learning curve.
- **Explore: focus areas.** In the Focus Areas strand we've identified a series of nine topics which open things up for independent research. Each topic briefly sketches the connection between CMC and another important area of communication scholarship. Depending on what your course leader or instructor decides, we recommend that you get going on one of the Focus Areas units as soon as possible – either on your own or in groups. We've put together a few notes for each topic so that you can then go and *explore* further.

In more ways than one, this is meant to be an *interactive* text. Neither the separate strands nor the individual units, topics and tasks are meant to be taken in isolation of each other. Nor does the book have to be read in any particular order.

To clarify what we mean, we'll offer just one final metaphor for understanding how the book's supposed to work. It's also a way of taking our fractal/spiral/portal motif one step further. We're thinking here of the 'coil' or 'helix' – essentially, a two-dimensional spiral in endless motion. Once again, the coil or helix is also a structure or pattern found in nature – most famously in the shell of a simple garden snail. Even more famously, however, the helix is also the base structure of DNA – the material of all human life. For us, what's interesting about the shape of the DNA helix is that it's actually made up of two interwoven, spiralling coils. The reason this is useful to us is because it's how we've looked to structure our book. The underlying aim is to encourage you to use the book in a lateral, open-ended way rather than a linear way, creating a pattern like a helix: separating, interconnecting, diverging and coming together again.

FIGURE 1

The coil or helix

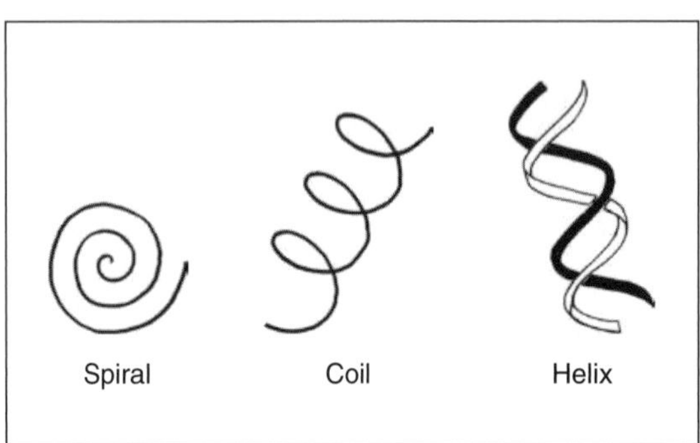

The thing about spirals, coils and helixes is that, unlike circles, you also *never* come back to the same spot again – it all just keeps on going. So, as with hypertext on the web, where you choose to go next is more or less up to you. You can stay and read more (e.g. using our ideas for further discussion and investigation) or you can jump to somewhere else and maybe return later for a more thorough read.

READINGS, REFERENCES AND RESOURCES

Although our book is grounded in an extensive and diverse literature, we know from our own experience that students are easily put off by endless citations and long lists of theoretical approaches. In fact, they hate it! Because of this, we've chosen instead to keep the references and readings to a minimum. In each unit, for example, we recommend no more than four stimulus readings, intended either for further study or for more detail. We've also deliberately chosen a mixture of more contemporary (i.e. post-2000) and 'classic' (1980s and 1990s) readings to give a feel for how the academic field of CMC started and how it's been developing since. In addition to this reading, in the Resource Materials section on the book's website we also direct you to hundreds of online resources and other materials: electronic journals, key books, movies and television programs.

WEBSITE AND WEBLINKS

Last but by no means least, we come to what's probably the most interactive feature of our book: the CMC website. In preparing this book about CMC, we felt strongly that the only way for it to make any sense was for us to provide you with an online support like our clearly designed, easy-to-use website. This is our online gateway for you. So, as well as the internal ◎ Links mentioned above, we have hundreds of ' **www** Weblinks' throughout the book. These occur wherever we think you might go online and click through to external webpages and websites which clarify, exemplify or demonstrate whatever we're discussing in the book. For example, as a way of helping you get to grips with the field, there's an interactive directory of 'Who's Who' in CMC. Remember, we want to offer you valuable concepts to debate and different perspectives to explore, but more than anything we want you to have plenty of hands-on experience with the issues the book sets out to critique.

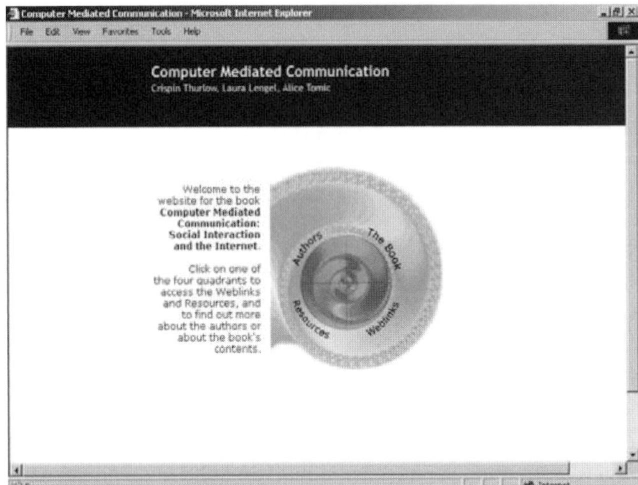

FIGURE 2

Your online gateway to support www.sagepub.co.uk/resources/cmc

INTRODUCTION 2

FOR COURSE LEADERS: TEACHING CMC

CMC AS A DYNAMIC AND CREATIVE FORCE

> *It is a constant idea of mine that behind the cotton wool (of daily reality) is a pattern: that we – I mean all human beings – are connected with this: that the whole world is a work of art: that we are parts of that work of art. (From Virginia Woolf's* A Sketch of the Past, *quoted in Fletcher, 2001: 260)*

As we explained in our introduction for students, we have chosen a fractal for the design of our book cover for a reason. Whereas some fractals have a beauty springing from their mathematical precision and self-similarity, others are the result of random factors and have their own sort of beauty. Computers usually have a built-in chance mechanism, a kind of electronic dice that allows this element of chance. It's this combination of a dynamic force, the potential for creativity, the element of unpredictability, which seems to us such a fitting metaphor for Computer Mediated Communication (CMC) where both orderly patterns and random developments provide an engaging focus of study.

Evidence suggests that, since computers were first introduced into schools, colleges and universities, teachers have had to devise by trial and error ways of using all the related technologies and incorporating them into their pedagogy. This book looks to address the deficit of support which teaching professionals have experienced in mediating for their students the impact of the cultural revolution brought about by the internet. It sets out to give badly needed support to instructors in a range of disciplines as they engage with their students in the study of this dynamic field of inquiry. Our focus is specifically on the impact of the internet on social interaction: the ways people construct their identities, make relationships and build communities. While the critical theory informing this text is primarily Western in origin, we want to encourage both teachers and students to look at issues from international perspectives – after all, this is one of the most powerful opportunities opened up to us by 'new' communication technologies.

www For weblinks and resources visit the CMC website at <www.sagepub.co.uk/resources/cmc>

MANAGING CHANGE IN THE CLASSROOM

Instantaneous electronic communication isn't just a way in which news and information is conveyed more quickly. Its existence alters the very texture of our lives. (Giddens, 1999: 3)

There is no doubt that those of us who are involved in education are facing the management of change. With the expansion of computer technology, we are witnessing dramatic changes in teaching and learning which, on the one hand, can be exciting but which, on the other, can be threatening and unsettling to the teaching profession. Will the internet, we ask ourselves, lead to a radical transformation of learning or merely to better and different ways of doing the same things? How can we best help our students to engage with a force that is clearly significant in their present and future lives? Even if the computer is 'just a tool', how might its capacities alter the way that we interact with each other? What social structures is it replacing or changing? What opportunities does it offer us for endorsing, changing or expanding our sense of our own identities? This book attempts to steer a critical and constructive path for both teachers and students through some of these unanswered questions.

The management of change has been seen in the past as something special that occurs intermittently against a background of stability. Postmodernist theory sees the management of change quite differently. Turbulence and stability can coexist and the skill lies in learning how to live and operate in this ambivalent, contradictory and unpredictable environment. As Stacey (1992) put it, how do we 'manage the unknowable'? For our students, as well, the speed of change and its repercussions are a bewildering scenario. Partly because of this, we have anchored our book to Bourdieu's four hallmarks of intellectual pursuit which, we believe, provide clear and guiding principles for approaching the study of CMC (see p. 4). Above all we want to encourage in students a spirit of intellectual inquiry, of open-mindedness and critical thinking.

THE RATIONALE FOR THIS BOOK

Technology challenges people's assumptions about what it means to be educated. (Morrison and Oblinger, 2002: 2)

Many would acknowledge that, to some extent, we are dealing with 'the unknowable', since the impact of the new media 'revolution' remains immeasurable and hard to define. What will be important in the future is how teachers and students negotiate and create their own meanings in the context of changes wrought in the classroom. National and institutional directives to incorporate communication technologies into the classroom constitute a strong rhetoric but the realities are often confusing and demoralizing. We sense that it is fitting for us to address in the classroom the impact of CMC on the lives of our students, but it is not always easy to see how.

Those who qualified to teach more than a few years ago may often have had little or no training to incorporate the use of computers into their teaching, and many will have had 'hit and miss' experiences finding out what 'works' and what 'doesn't work' in the classroom. We hope that this book will reduce this risk factor by providing a series of effective teaching and learning strategies. We firmly believe that encouraging students to examine and explore the everyday communicative dimensions of the internet is one of the best ways to engage them in a critical debate about new media and social change.

CHANGES IN PEDAGOGY

> The Digital Disconnect, *a 2002 report by the Pew Internet and American Life Project on middle and high school students, states that 'educators often don't know, don't want or aren't able to use online tools to help [students] learn'. (Levin and Arafeh, 2002: iii–iv)*

Part of the exploration of a changing social landscape requires us to revisit our role as educators. For example, teachers who are trained in linear writing need to learn how to value multimedia expression. Educationalist Gunther Kress (2003) reminds us that 'the world shown' is a very different world from 'the world narrated'. Even the meaning of the term 'literacy' is being subverted by the dominance of the visual image in our students' lives. Students who cannot remember a single quotation from a canonical book have little trouble at all in 'reading' film text and understanding concepts like 'genre' and 'iconography'. Their visual literacy often leaves us in the shade. Discussions surrounding 'computer literacy' in the 1980s and 1990s (focusing on practical skills like word-processing) have been dislodged by the growing realization that we need to ask our students to engage differently and much more critically with communication technology and to start getting them to ask some difficult questions.

Contrary to the traditional model of stand-up-in-front-and-talk (the 'sage on the stage' syndrome), teachers in classrooms using communication technology will often find a dramatic change in classroom dynamics. The power shifts incontrovertibly and we are required to re-examine our attitudes to risk and control. The instructor in the CMC classroom does not always know better. More than a few of us will no doubt have experienced occasions when our students knew more than we did about the potential of the computer. An essential spirit of collaboration between teacher and learner in the computer classroom often means that the teacher also becomes the learner. Understandably, many teachers find it hard to relinquish their perceived authority, but this very state of affairs can create a new and exciting synergy in the learning process. The emphasis on process (exploration, evaluation, collaboration, discussion, reflection, and formulation of individual and shared meanings) requires our participation as learners alongside our students. Our main role is as guides and mediators, facilitators and mentors. With CMC and the internet, we do not need to be techno-experts; we need merely to steer students towards a critical engagement with a powerful force in our lived realities.

Educators also need to get inside the heads of those we teach. They need to explore what students will find meaningful in the course material we offer them. The sociologist Felix Geyer, in his 1996 study *Alienation, Ethnicity, and Postmodernism,* claims that students in the postmodern era have been caught in the throes of a complex and rapidly changing society (quoted by Newton, 2000: 12) The consequence of large-scale systemic change, when a chain of familiar patterns is disrupted, is the potential for individuals to become alienated and lose sight of purpose, become empty of meaning, and operate without a standard ethos. Coherence is lost. Students can re-discover coherence by establishing a personal worldview, an organizing structure, which helps them make sense of the complexity of their lives.

> Students can develop this structure through a variety of means, including the process of primary group socialization, the prescription of societal rules and guidelines, and more recently, extensive exposure to electronic media, which has opened up a myriad of additional worldviews that would have seemed remote to a previous generation. (Newton, 2000: 12)

Fred Newton, an expert on undergraduate attitudes, takes Geyer's proposal further by suggesting that an additional feature to promote for students is 'manageability'. For students this 'manageability' connects the learning experience with future utility. It also means not being overwhelmed by all the surrounding influences but being able to acknowledge selectively what is within one's reach and capability. In this sense, Newton's comments have a direct relationship to our topic and to the way we have designed this book. Students' attitudes to learning are increasingly pragmatic and they often have an instinctive understanding of course material that is of value to them in their later lives. We have tried to make the material in this book resonate with all three of the features Newton describes, because teaching about CMC seems to offer a very particular opportunity to engage the interest of our students.

OPPORTUNITIES FOR 'DEEP' RATHER THAN 'SURFACE' LEARNING

It is often useful to recall our own first encounters with computers and the routes we took. In many ways the implementation of computer-based learning follows the same patterns as our own discoveries of the potentials of cyberspace. We started with mastering the computer and exploring its potential on a practical level and then moved to a more critical awareness of the way it enabled us to participate in social interaction using other than traditional channels. But it is one thing to find out these things ourselves and quite another to integrate them successfully into our pedagogy. What is the nature of the learning we can encourage? Most of us initially focused on practical applications of the computer for our students: to explore the potential to improve their writing, use graphics, contact others via email, join chat rooms, create their own websites. But, as many people still ask, what was actually being learnt apart from 'surface learning', practical skills equivalent to using a glorified typewriter or riding a bike?

We are confronted here with an opportunity rich in potential for 'deep learning', for a radical transformation of learning about ourselves, about others, and about the world we live in. In response to this opportunity we have set out to develop teaching and learning strategies which focus on a critical awareness of CMC as a powerful force in everyday social interaction.

HOW IS THIS TEXT DESIGNED TO HELP?

Far from laying everything down for the student reader, using a deliberately accessible, conversational tone, we frame this book to move students from declarative knowledge (basic theory and central issues units) to procedural knowledge (Focus Areas Topics and Fieldwork Tasks). The focus is on getting students to research *about* the internet *on* the internet. With this in mind, the book offers students a task-based, critical exploration of the nature of CMC and the impact of the internet on social interaction.

BOX 3 THE LEARNING GOALS OF THIS BOOK

The CMC book is designed to help students learn in three different ways:

- By engaging them in key theoretical issues central to understanding CMC.
- By directing them to a range of important learning outcomes.
- By equipping them with online research and technical skills.

THE 'PORTAL' STRUCTURE OF THE BOOK

The 'Introduction for students' (p. 5) gives a detailed breakdown of the structure of the book. The material is designed to be adaptable to more than one level of study and can be used as a course book by undergraduate students or as a resource book for graduate students and secondary school teachers. The broad perspectives remain common to all levels, but the desired level of extended study via readings and practical application is left very much to your discretion. There are clear learning outcomes for each section and, as assessment of such courses is often problematic, the organization of the material enables those teaching to measure effectively the learning taking place.

With an emphasis on learning-by-doing, the book is designed not only as an introductory resource for academic and theoretical content, but also as a stimulus for independent inquiry and research by students. We have designed a website specifically for users of this book where we can keep materials updated and create a sense of the dynamism of this field. The book also encourages students to apply what they learn about CMC theory and issues to a selection of applied research areas in communication and internet studies: for example, new media developments, instructional communication, organizational communication and visual communication.

We hope that, for instructors, our book will offer some reassurance and support, hitherto sparse, in addressing this important area of scholarly exploration. With many decades of teaching experience between us, in different countries and cultural backgrounds and at different academic levels, we hope that you will gain from the book new insights, new teaching ideas and, perhaps also, some coping strategies for 'managing the unknowable'.

> Ultimately, the information technology is not about technology; it is about what happens to people as a result. We have to remember that education is a very human endeavor and that students are terribly important people. Although technology plays a central role, people still come first. (Morrison and Oblinger, 2002: 5)

STRAND 1

LEARN: BASIC THEORY

'THE DEMOLITION OF SIMPLISTIC EITHER–ORS'

As the heading of this strand suggests, this first part of the book introduces you to some of the essential theoretical ideas in computer mediated communication. This is a way of introducing you to CMC as a field of scholarly study. While reading the units in Basic Theory we think it's worth remembering from p. 4 the first of Pierre Bourdieu's four pillars of intellectual life: the 'demolition of simplistic either–ors'. What he means by this is that we should not oversimplify things and put them in binary opposition to each other – in other words, not judging things as either right or wrong, either good or bad.

We know that theory can be scary, but you'd be surprised at how much CMC theory actually connects with everyday communication and things you may already take for granted. After all, theory is just a way of trying to explain the world around us. Rather than making assumptions about what CMC is like, however, we do need you to *learn* some of the basics of what scholars have already discovered so that you are in a stronger position to *critique* the Central Issues, *explore* the Focus Areas, and *apply* all this knowledge in the Fieldwork tasks.

The book has been designed to allow you maximum flexibility in moving between different strands, units, topics and tasks. However, in laying a theoretical foundation and giving you the concepts you need in the rest of the book, each Basic Theory unit builds on the one that went before. Because of this, we recommend you follow the units in the order in which they are presented here.

UNIT 1

DEFINING CMC: AN INTRODUCTION TO THE FIELD

OVERVIEW

KEY TERMS

communication
mediation
computer
field/discipline
internet studies

MAIN OBJECTIVES

- Examine ways of defining what computer mediated communication entails.
- Understand the core concepts *communication*, *mediated* and *computer*.
- Identify the connections between CMC and Internet Studies.
- Appreciate the potential diversity and range of CMC as a scholarly field.

WHAT IS COMPUTER MEDIATED COMMUNICATION?

Technically speaking, computer mediated communication (or just CMC as it's commonly known) has been around since the first electronic digital computer was invented (some time during World War II), or at least since the first recorded exchange of prototype emails in the early 1960s. ◎ From these moments on, people have been communicating about, and by means of, computer technology. Either way, the history of computer mediated communication is little more than fifty years old. For most of us it's hard to imagine a time when computers where not such an integral part of our lives, and it's only really been in the last twenty years that computers have gone from being highly technical and specialist to being personal and popular.

◎ If you'd like to find out more about the history of computers and the internet, we recommend you visit the US-based Computer Museum History Center [**www** BT1:1]. For a more detailed history of the internet, you could also look at the Internet Society's account [**www** BT1:2].

Certainly, by the 1990s, personal computers had sprouted like mushrooms on the desks

www For weblinks and resources visit the CMC website at <www.sagepub.co.uk/resources/cmc>

of office managers, schoolteachers, college students, doctors, home makers, and so on. Prior to the early to mid-1990s, however, academic interest in the way that people interacted with, and communicated through, computer technology was still fairly exclusive and restricted mainly to practical concerns such as information processing, data transfer, hardware design, and what is known more generally as Human-Computer Interaction (or HCI). However, it's only really been since the mid-1990s that the fast-growing popularity and ubiquity of personal computers (especially for emailing, chatting and surfing the web) has caused CMC to become so attractive to scholarly attention. As odd as it may seem, it's possible to regard CMC research and writing from the 1980s and especially 1990s as being 'classic' in the sense that this was an important foundation period when the scholars really started identifying the main topics of study and issues for debate in CMC. By being one of the first course books in the area, this book is itself just another stage in this gradual process of establishing CMC as a scholarly field.

So what exactly is it that we look at in CMC? This may seem like a pretty obvious question but it's worth being clear about what we as the authors mean by the term right from the very start. Although in this book we will want to narrow our focus a little, the label 'computer mediated communication' essentially refers to any human communication achieved through, or with the help of, computer technology. For example, this is how Gerry Santoro (1995: 11) has put it:

> At its broadest, CMC can encompass virtually all computer uses including such diverse applications as statistical analysis programs, remote-sensing systems, and financial modelling programs, all fit within the concept of human communication.

Or there is this slightly more enigmatic definition from John December (1997): ◎

> Computer Mediated Communication is a process of human communication via computers, involving people, situated in particular contexts, engaging in processes to shape media for a variety of purposes.

◎ John December is someone who's been associated with CMC for a long time, having founded and edited the widely cited website *CMC Magazine* [**www** BT1:3].

Yet another 'classic' definition is proposed by Susan Herring (1996: 1), a scholar who's also been associated with the field for some time (see Central Issues: Units 4 and 5):

> CMC is communication that takes place between human beings via the instrumentality of computers.

As well as looking to see how scholars define CMC in theory, another good way of learning what the term encompasses is simply by looking at scholarly publications to see what actually gets researched and discussed in the name of CMC. Especially with a relatively new field like CMC, it's always worth remembering that all intellectual knowledge and all scholarly disciplines only ever exist by convention. In other words, we choose to label academic work in certain ways and we choose to pursue agreed-upon agendas of work. So, for example, we could say that psychology is what psychologists do; alternatively, psychologists are people who study psychology! For the most part, however, the field of psychology is very wide and defined in many different ways, depending on the particular interest of the individual psychologist concerned. Nonetheless, at the end of the day, to know what a field is about is really only to know what people who describe themselves as members of the field are actually doing.

It's for this reason that, as far as CMC is concerned, one of the best places to start is simply by reviewing the wide range of topics covered in the *Journal of Computer-Mediated*

Communication (*JCMC*) [**www** BT1:4] which was founded in 1995. For example, a quick look at its index shows the following kinds of themes:

- electronic commerce
- law on the electronic frontier
- studying the net
- virtual organizations
- online journalism
- CMC and higher education
- electronic commerce and the web
- health and new media

Already you'll notice that, by referring to terms like net, web and online, it's not just any kind of computer technology and digital activity which is covered by the *JCMC*. In fact, another closely related academic forum for CMC researchers is the *Journal of Online Behavior* [**www** BT1:5]. Founded in 2000, *JOB* describes its field of interest much more clearly as follows:

> The *Journal of Online Behavior* is concerned with the empirical study of human behavior in the online environment, and with the impact of evolving communication and information technology upon individuals, groups, organizations, and society.

We could go on by looking at any number of related journals, but instead we'll show you just one more: *Computers in Human Behavior* [**www** BT1:6]. This is a journal which has been running for twenty years and focuses specifically on CMC from the point of view of psychology.

> *Computers in Human Behavior* is a scholarly journal dedicated to examining the use of computers from a psychological perspective. The journal addresses both the use of computers in psychology as well as the psychological impact of computer use on individuals, groups and society. The latter category includes the psychological effects of computers on phenomena such as human development, learning, cognition, personality, and social interactions. The computer is discussed only as a medium through which human behaviors are shaped and expressed.

So, although CMC is defined by Santoro, December and Herring as being as encompassing as the applications and impacts of computer and digital technologies are wide, in practice CMC is usually concerned more specifically with human interpersonal communication on, through and about the internet and web. (We'll return for a more careful look at these two terms in Basic Theory: Unit 2.)

So far, we've recommended just two strategies for identifying the key principles and issues which define the field of CMC: scholarly definitions and scholarly discussions. Perhaps the most effective way of pinning down CMC is, we believe, to try and pin down the core concepts. In the case of CMC, and however obvious it may seem, this means spending a bit of time considering its three constituent terms: communication, mediated and computer.

EXAMINING THE CORE CONCEPTS

CORE CONCEPT 1: COMMUNICATION

If you've studied human communication before, or if communication is currently your main subject, you'll already know that communication is itself something of a slippery fish to define. Even though it's something we all do all the time, deciding what communication is and how it works has kept scholars busy for a very long time. In fact, one of the things that new technologies have done – and have always done – is force people to reconsider what the essential nature of communication really is. This is partly what makes CMC such a fascinating field of study for communication scholars: in some ways, it's almost as if we are experiencing communication anew, and yet in other ways, nothing's changed. This is precisely what we're hoping you'll be able to decide for yourself as you move through the book, asking yourself what's the same and what's different about communication when people use technology to do it.

We haven't the space to delve too deeply into defining and explaining communication, but we do think it's important to ground CMC in a proper understanding of the basic principles of communication. ◉ To start with, it should be said from the outset that this book is essentially concerned (1) with human communication rather than media or mass communication or communications technology *per se*, and (2) with social interaction. Beyond this, it's possible to clarify our position a little further by means of a series of brief, interrelated statements about how we understand the nature of communication.

◉ For a more thorough introduction to the field of communication, we recommend Rob Anderson and Veronica Ross's *Questions of Communication* (2002) and Daniel Canary, Michael Cody and Valerie Manusov's *Interpersonal Communication* (2003).

Communication is dynamic

One of the most well known ways of thinking about communication is the idea of a sender, a message and a receiver – often represented in the way shown in Figure 3. Unfortunately, this model oversimplifies communication to the rather static exchange of information – what, in computer terms, might be regarded as an 'information-processing' perspective. Instead, communication is better understood as a process which is much more dynamic. The meaning of messages does not reside *in* words, but is much more fluid and dependent on the *context*, shifting constantly from place to place, from person to person, and from moment to moment. To see this, you have only to think of the way the meanings of words like 'wicked' and 'gay' have changed over time. Another example is the word 'kiwi', where, without contextual information, it's impossible to know whether this is meant to mean a bird, a fruit or a New Zealander.

FIGURE 3

A simple model of communication

Communication is transactional

Even though people still sometimes like to think of communication as the exchange of messages between senders and receivers, communication is really about the *negotiation* of meaning between people. Individuals are both speakers and listeners and these roles switch back and forth all the time in any one conversation. Once again, this also means that communication is constantly changing as two (or more) people interpret each other and are influenced by what the other says. In other words, it's a *transaction* between them. Most theorists would agree that communication simply cannot happen outside human social interaction. It is really only when someone recognizes and/or responds to something you say or do that communication can be said to have occurred.

Communication is multifunctional

Consciously or unconsciously, communication serves many different functions and usually serves more than one function at any given time. For example, communication may be used to influence people's behavior or attitudes, to inform people, to seek information, to exert control over people, to befriend or seduce people, to entertain and please people, and so on. Although for the sake of analytical convenience, scholars do sometimes distinguish between the interactional (or relationship-focused) and informational (or content-focused) domains of communication, it's usually impossible to separate the two. Think about famous chat-up lines like 'Can I buy you a drink?' or 'Do you have the time?' Although both *appear* to seek information, the intention is clearly relational!

Communication is multimodal

However important it may be, language is of course just one of many ways we have of communicating. Verbal messages always come packaged with other messages (or 'metamessages') formed by different ways of making meaning – what are usually called nonverbal *modes* of communication. In fact, more often than not it is these other modes of communication which are relied on more than the verbal mode. The best example of this is when someone is lying to us: 'Look me in the eye and tell me you didn't do it!' The range of nonverbal codes is vast and accounts for much of the social information we glean: vocal (e.g. tone of voice, accent, volume, pauses), movement (e.g. facial expression, gestures, posture), physical appearance (e.g. height, weight, skin colour), artefacts (e.g. lighting, décor, fashion), and use of space (e.g. body orientation, touch, distance).

Each of these statements about communication clearly overlaps with the next. Communication is transactional and so must be dynamic; similarly, because it's multimodal it's also bound to be multifunctional, and so on. What all four have in common, however, is that they are also central to understanding how communication works and how it's used to express our identities, to establish and maintain relationships, and eventually to build communities – three of the most important themes in CMC. In fact, identity, relationships and community can only ever be achieved in communication, which is to say through the *multimodal*, *multifunctional processes* of *social interaction*.

CORE CONCEPT 2: MEDIATED

Depending on how much you already know about human communication, you will more than likely know that *all* communication is mediated to some extent or other. According to Chambers' *Twenty-first Century Dictionary*, the verb *to mediate* means to convey or transmit something or to act as a medium for something. In turn, *a medium* is something by which, or through which, an effect is produced. In other words, **mediation** is simply the process or means by which something is transmitted – whether it's a message, a feeling, a sound, or a ghostly apparition! In the case of communication, we've already indicated that communication is always channelled by, and dependent on, its context for meaning. Communication is therefore mediated through our interactions with people and by means of any number of different verbal and nonverbal modes. Communication can never exist in a vacuum.

You will probably have heard about the phrase 'channels of communication'. These can be social (or cultural), psychological (or mental), linguistic (or symbolic) or material (or technical). It's in this way that scholars usually identify several layers of contextual variables which influence – or mediate – communication. Broadly speaking these fall into three main categories:

- *psychological*, e.g. our perceptions, mental maps, and prototypes;
- *social*, e.g. our relationships, stereotypes, and individual experiences;
- *cultural*, e.g. the myths and ideologies of whole societies of people.

These are what some communication scholars refer to as 'structures of expectation', by which they mean the knowledge, experience and cultural background which enable people to make sense of the world around them. So, for example, any communication between a lawyer and a client will necessarily be mediated through contextual filters such as the professional nature of their relationship, the client's perceptions of lawyers generally, and the often powerful status of lawyers in society.

In the case of CMC, of course, another, more material layer of mediation is added, namely *technological* mediation. It's at this point that another common meaning of the word *medium* comes into play – or more correctly its plural form *media* – as 'the means by which news and information are communicated' (Chambers' *Twenty-First Century Dictionary*). In most instances we recognize the technology involved here to be things like televisions, radios and the press. But what is technology exactly and where does one draw the line between media technology, telephones, cars, microwaves and other artefacts?

Arguably, and not forgetting the types of contextual mediation just mentioned, communication has been technologically mediated for centuries. In some senses, for example, putting pen to paper (or stylus to wax tablet) mediates speech by means of a tool. Returning to the dictionary for the last time, technology is really nothing more than the practical application of 'scientific knowledge in industry and everyday life' – a pretty vague definition. Once again, however, CMC usually restricts what it means by technology to the machinery designed, built and used for the purposes of information exchange and communication. This is what is usually referred to as 'Information and Communication Technologies (or ICTs) and brings us nicely to the last of CMC's core concepts.

CORE CONCEPT 3: COMPUTER

Having confronted the relative complexity of the terms 'communication' and 'mediated', it may disappoint you to know that even the term **computer** cannot be taken for granted. Almost everything nowadays involves computers in some way or other, and, consequently, almost everything we do is in some way or other mediated by computers. Think, for example, of the digital technology which drives our telephone exchanges, brings television channels into our homes, tells us the time, and so on. What's more, with such things as video conferencing, webcams and voice recognition, technological changes are taking us nearer and nearer to the kind of face-to-face (or just FtF) communication we've been used to all along. It's in this way that the computerization, which drives so many areas of our lives, is becoming more and more invisible. Indeed, Pixy Ferris (1997) previously proposed that CMC should also be broad enough to include office automation, electronic boardrooms, teleconferencing, Computer Supported Co-operative Work (CSCW), and Computer Assisted Learning (CAL). ◎

◎ If you choose to pursue Focus Areas: Topic 3 or Topic 7 you'll probably find it useful to look further into these last two specialized applications.

For this reason, we need to be a little more specific about what we – and other CMC scholars – tend to mean when referring to 'computer'. Bearing in mind that the two may never be straightforwardly separated, what we've decided to do in this book is prioritize relational communication and to deprioritize communication activity which is more exclusively informational. In computer jargon, this is what might be called 'informatics' – the storage, manipulation and retrieval of data. Under this category one might look at things such as management information systems, computer networking, library resources, CD-ROM databases, and so on. However, instead, our perspective will be focused on that computing technology which more explicitly facilitates human communication defined in the terms we introduced above. In other words, we are more interested in the 'C' of ICTs than the 'I'.

While the *Journal of Computer-Mediated Communication* legitimately covers work in such diverse areas as e-commerce, online journalism and virtual learning, in this book we're primarily focused on the ways people make conversation, build communities and construct identities through, and by means of, new communication technologies – or what might more accurately be described as 'technologies *for* communication'. In particular, like most CMC scholars, we're specifically interested in the ways this is all being done via one of the newer and more exciting of communication technologies: the internet.

IDENTIFYING ALLIED APPROACHES AND PERSPECTIVES

Just as the users and uses of 'new' communication technologies have grown rapidly in the last twenty years, so too has academic interest which has also become increasingly formalized and covers a wide range of writing and research. As we mentioned at the beginning of this unit, scholarly interest in the field now known as Computer Mediated Communication is itself barely more than ten years old. Not only has academic interest been sudden, but it has also been diverse. By its very nature, CMC is a multidisciplinary or multiperspective effort. As such, CMC is best regarded as a scholarly **field** of study rather than as a neatly defined **discipline** (see Box BT2:1).

BOX BT1:1 DISCIPLINE OR FIELD?

Communication scholars Rob Anderson and Veronica Ross (2002: 331) draw the following distinction:

A discipline is a branch of learning that possesses its own content and relatively distinct curriculum, and that prepares people for well defined career responsibilities (e.g. engineering, physics, or accounting).

A field may be defined as a loosely associated group of scholars working on similar problems, but not unified by consistently defined concepts and not necessarily tied to particular career responsibilities (e.g. cross-disciplinary areas like International Studies or Women's Studies).

In fact, for many people CMC is more accurately thought of as *sub-field* of a far broader field known as **Internet Studies**.

BOX BT1:2 CENTER FOR INTERNET STUDIES, UNIVERSITY OF WASHINGTON [www BT1:7]

The Center for Internet Studies is an interdisciplinary research and teaching unit for the study of the internet's global impact on economic, political and social systems.

BOX BT1: 3 OXFORD INTERNET INSTITUTE, UNIVERSITY OF OXFORD [www BT1:8]

The Oxford Internet Institute is a leading multi-disciplinary academic centre focused on furthering understanding of the economic, political, institutional, scientific, legal and other social factors shaping the internet and its implications for society.

Two well known centers for internet research are to be found at the University of Washington in the United States and at the University of Oxford in Britain, where, as you can see from Boxes BT1: 2–3, the field of research activity is described very broadly. As the internet becomes a bigger and bigger part of many people's lives, so the implications of the internet become wider and wider. At the same time, the overlap between the internet and the web has also been getting greater and much of what people do on the internet these days involves the web. It's for this reason British media scholar David Gauntlett (2000) suggests it's probably even more appropriate to talk about Web Studies than Internet Studies. Certainly, even though some writers occasionally talk about them as being distinct, Web Studies and Internet Studies are these days largely synonymous. ◎

◎ This is an important consideration and raises the issue of technological convergences which we've chosen to discuss in more detail in Basic Theory: Unit 2.

Just as there's a lot of overlap between these two wide-reaching fields, there are also a number of other related approaches to the same general field of interest covered by CMC. Most notably, there are internet-focused contributions coming from traditional academic disciplines such as Geography, sometimes using the label *cybergeography* [www BT1:9], Sociology, or *cybersociology* [www BT1:10], and Psychology, or *cyberpsychology* [www BT1:11]. In fact, it seems there are as many 'cybers' as there are subjects! Media Studies obviously has a stake in the field too, as does Cultural Studies, which, not surprisingly, tends to describe its main interest as being with cyberculture. The fact is that CMC is a *very* interdisciplinary affair, with useful contributions being made by scholars from many different backgrounds. If you think again about the topics covered by the *Journal of Computer-Mediated Communication*, you'll begin to see how there are any number of points of contact between new communication technologies and traditional academic disciplines, such as:

- media studies/journalism
- linguistics
- sociology
- anthropology

- psychology
- law
- computer science
- education
- politics
- economics/commerce
- medicine/health care

Some of the main concerns and interests which unite all these different perspectives and approaches are the very same things you are likely to cover in Strands 2, Central Issues, and 4, Focus Areas, of this book. So, for example, scholars and professionals examine commercial topics such as online shopping and advertising, social topics like inequality and prejudice, legal topics like copyright and pornography, and psychological topics like addiction and mental health. Media scholars are obviously also interested in all communication technologies and especially changes brought about by more recent technological developments such as mobile phones, webcams, digital radio and digital television.

It would certainly be very wrong of us to imply that the study of CMC is in any way a tidy business, with nice sharp boundaries and a clearly defined agenda of topics. Nonetheless, CMC scholars have been trying hard to organize themselves around their key, shared interests. In fact, one way scholars often start to organize themselves and to formalize their field of study is by writing books like this one to help introduce newcomers to the field. In terms of CMC, another obvious manifestation of this process of academic formalization has been the establishment of organizations like the Association of Internet Researchers (AoIR) [**www** BT1:12]. Here for example is the 'blurb' from the association's first conference in 2000 entitled 'Internet Research: The State of the Interdiscipline':

> Despite great interest, knowledge-building in internet research is hindered by a lack of international, centralized opportunities for scholars from different disciplines to interact. This international conference, the first meeting of the Association of Internet Researchers, will focus on the internet as a distinct interdisciplinary field for research.

A very common part of this process of academic formalization rests in simply demarcating your particular areas of specialization – saying what it is that you are mainly interested in. The truth of the matter is that no one can do everything – even though some try hard to. This is why we've spent some time defining CMC in this first unit. To summarize our position, we would say that this book is based on the psychology, social psychology and, to an extent, sociology of online communication. Furthermore, we're specifically concerned with (1) patterns of linguistic and communicative practice, and (2) processes of social interaction such as identity, relationship and community. Having said all of which, we still believe that a healthy, robust field of academic life is one where overlap is not seen as a threat and where interdisciplinarity is seen to be a strength. Only the insecure and the fanatical feel compelled to define and guard their boundaries strictly.

REVIEW

In this unit we introduced you to the field of computer mediated communication – usually known as just CMC. We offered a few scholarly definitions and recommended looking also at relevant journals. We then outlined the core concepts of *communication*, *mediated* and *computer* which constitute CMC. We ended by considering again the diversity of CMC with reference to the broader field of Internet Studies, as well as other disciplinary areas which share an interest in many of the concerns of CMC.

STIMULUS READINGS AND RESOURCES

These four classic readings from the *CMC Magazine* give an insight into the way CMC was first formalized as a scholarly field:

December, J. (1995). Transitions in studying computer-mediated communication [**www** BT1:13].

December, J. (1997). Notes on defining computer-mediated communication [**www** BT1:14].

Ferris, S.P. (1997). What is CMC? An overview of scholarly definitions [**www** BT1:15].

Murray, P.J. (1997). A rose by any other name [**www** BT1:16].

The next three readings are examples of some of different approaches to the field, from Cultural Studies, Psychology and Media Studies respectively. Each author gives an overview of how they think scholars should be studying the internet.

Escobar, A. (2000). Welcome to cyberia: notes on the anthropology of cyberculture. In D. Bell and B.M. Kennedy (eds), *The cybercultures reader* (pp. 56–76). London: Routledge.

Joinson, A.N. (2003). Chapter 7: A framework for understanding internet behaviour. In *Understanding the psychology of internet behavior* (pp. 163–84). Basingstoke: Palgrave Macmillan.

Wakeford, N. (2000). New media, new methodologies: studying the web. In D. Gauntlett (ed.), *Web.studies: Rewiring media studies for the digital age* (pp. 31-41). London: Arnold

IDEAS FOR FURTHER DISCUSSION AND INVESTIGATION

1 Have a look at the most recent issues of the *Journal of Computer-Mediated Communication* [**www** BT2:4] to see what's been researched and discussed. Alternatively, visit the website of *Wired* Magazine [**www** BT2:17] to get a more popular perspective on current interest in the internet and web. One way to keep up with current new media developments is to subscribe to *Wired*'s email update list [**www** BT1:18].

2 Have a look at the online texts listed above. These are early examples of the ways in which CMC was defined as a field, the basis of which remains largely unchanged. Can you identify ways in which they might seem outdated, especially in the light of the material covered towards the end of Basic Theory: Unit 2?

3 One of the really exciting online resources available to scholars and learners is the Resource Center for Cyberculture Studies (RCCS), founded and maintained by David Silver at the University of Washington [**www** BT1:19]. Spend some time browsing around the RCCS, looking at the books being discussed, the conferences listed and the many different courses being offered to students around the world.

4 Track the publicity for the last few conferences of the Assocation of Internet Researchers (AoIR) to see how the Internet Studies agenda is being redefined each year. You might start, for example, with the fourth conference, which was held in Toronto in October 2003 under the theme 'Broadening the Band' [**www** BT1:20], or look for the next one via the AoIR website [**www** BT1:12].

UNIT 2

SITUATING CMC: TECHNOLOGIES *FOR* COMMUNICATION

OVERVIEW

KEY TERMS

technology
convergences
internet and web
cyber-space/society/culture
sub-systems and genres

MAIN OBJECTIVES

- Consider the main technological antecedents of the internet.
- Understand what is meant by the term 'new communication technology'.
- Sketch the history and ongoing development of the internet and web.
- Identify the main sub-systems and communication genres of the internet.

A QUICK TRIP THROUGH COMMUNICATION TECHNOLOGY HISTORY

In discussing the core concept 'computer' in Basic Theory: Unit 1, we considered the possibility that the notion of **technology** can, in principle, be very far-reaching. For example, here's how the International Technology Education Association in the United States (ITEA, 2000: 2) defines technology:

> Broadly speaking, technology is how people modify the natural world to suit their own purposes. From the Greek word *techne*, meaning 'art' or 'artifice' or 'craft', technology literally means the act of making or crafting, but more generally it refers to the diverse collection of processes and knowledge that people use to extend human abilities and to satisfy human needs and wants.

www For weblinks and resources visit the CMC website at <www.sagepub.co.uk/resources/cmc>

We are all of us surrounded by technology. Different types of technology, it's true, but technology nonetheless. If you're at home, stop reading for a moment and just walk around the place where you live, making a note of all the different technologies you can see. (You can always just do this in your mind's eye instead.) We think it'll be surprising how much you actually do see. It's quite likely that you'll have spotted things like an oven, a fridge, a camera. What about less obvious technological innovations like a doorbell, lights, a vacuum cleaner, clocks, heaters? How about knives and forks, toothbrushes and razors – electric or otherwise? Thinking more specifically about communication technologies, are you able to see a telephone or mobile phone (or both), a television, a video recorder, a fax machine? What about pens and paper, or Post-it notes and paperclips?

Even though we often think about technology in terms of such modern innovations as space shuttles and DVD players, technology is also as old as the wheel and writing, and as simple as handwriting. However novel and exciting, the internet too is just one of the more recent developments in a long line of technologies. (Recall our discussion on p. 6 about the endless twists and turns of the helix.) Historically speaking, major developments in technology have found communication being mediated in a number of revolutionary new ways. This is why, in trying to understand CMC and new communication technologies, it's really helpful to have a sense of their historical antecedents. Such major technological developments include the printing press in the mid-fifteenth century, the telegraph in the 1840s, the telephone in the 1870s, and the television in the 1930s. At each point, communication was transformed in some way by, for example, enabling mass publication (in the case of the printing press) and far greater speed and distance (in the case of the telegraph and telephone). ◎

◎ The prefix of the words 'telegraph' and 'telephone' is in fact the Greek word *tele*, meaning 'far off'. Where the one introduced long-distance text (hence *graph*), the other brought long-distance sound and voice (hence *phone*).

There are, we think, two very important points to be made about such technological innovations. The first is the way that, over time, they often come to be associated strongly with a single, and traditionally male, inventor. For the printing press it was Johannes Gutenberg, for the telegraph Samuel Morse, for the telephone Alexander Graham Bell, for the television John Logie Baird. We'll come on to newer communication technologies in just a moment, but the same is true say of Tim Berners-Lee, who is commonly hailed as the 'father' of the world wide web. What's more, individual countries (usually from the industrial West) also like to tell how it was one of their own citizens who should be credited with each wonderful invention. The fact of the matter, however, is that no technological progress in the history of humankind has ever been this straightforward. As a famous show-tune once put it, 'Nothing comes from nothing, nothing ever could.'

All human endeavor, all human knowledge, science and invention are always collaborative. A brief look at the history of any one of the key technologies listed above will show this to be true. In almost every case, the 'discovery' of new technology represents the aggregation in one place, in one moment, and perhaps by one person, of technologies which have been emerging for many years, if not centuries, and in many places, and by many different people. More often than not, it is also ordinary people like you and us who really make the difference. By this we mean that there is always a distinction to be drawn between what technologies are *supposed* (or designed) to do and what people *actually* do with them. In other words, whatever the intentions and goals of the designers and inventors of different communication technologies, 'ordinary' people inevitably make their own decisions about *whether* they want to use the technology, and, more importantly, *how* they want to use it based on their own needs and values.

Perhaps one of the best case-study examples of all this is the telephone. Although attributed to Alexander Graham Bell in 1876, it is a communication technology which had arguably been emerging at least from the time that electricity and magnetism were first put to use in the form of batteries at about the beginning of the 1800s. Furthermore, Bell was by no means alone, as Mary Bellis (2002) explains:

> In the 1870s two inventors, Elisha Gray and Alexander Graham Bell, both independently designed devices that could transmit speech electrically (the telephone). Both men rushed their respective designs to the patent office within hours of each other, Alexander Graham Bell patented his telephone first. Elisha Gray and Alexander Graham Bell entered into a famous legal battle over the invention of the telephone, which Bell won.

What is even more interesting about the telephone is that, from Bell's now famous first telephone 'call' to a colleague in the room next door, it took another seventy years before it became the kind of technology *for* communication which we recognize today. ◎ Telephone cables were laid first across London in Britain, then between Washington DC and Baltimore in the United States, then across the United States, then across the Atlantic, and eventually around the world. In spite of this growing telephonic network, however, it was not until the 1950s that the telephone was revolutionized from being an information tool for war or business, to being a tool for communication. Only once consumers realized the telephone's chat potential did ordinary folk take it up, ensuring the phone its popularity, its ubiquity and its eventual integration into the very fabric of our daily lives. It's largely immaterial that the telephone was initially intended as a practical technology for information exchange; it seems that technology invariable buckles under the pressure of our human impulse to converse and socialize.

◎ Not realizing at the time that his words were actually being transmitted, Bell is supposed to have said, 'Mr Watson, come here. I want you.' Not the most exciting phone call by any means!

But what about newer communication technologies? Generally speaking, communication technologies have simply continued the same drive towards covering greater distances, at even greater speeds, carrying even greater amounts of information, and involving even greater numbers of people. Of course, more than anything else, it's been computerization and digital technology which have made this possible, with a convoluted history of key moments like Charles Babbage's development of a mechanical calculator in the 1820s, Alan Turing's contribution of code breakers in the 1940s, and the Apple Corporation's use of microprocessors in the late 1970s. ◎ Without doubt, we've all been catapulted into the so-called Information Age, through the relatively rapid digitization of just about every technology we have. Communications Technology Update [**www** BT2:2] looks at recent developments in a range of communication technologies and offers a fairly long list of current technologies – most of which have been, or are in the process of being, digitized. A handful of these are shown in Box BT2:1.

◎ For a quick history of computerization, see the *Jones Digital Century Encyclopedia* [**www** BT2:1].

BOX BT2:1 DIGITAL COMMUNICATION TECHNOLOGY

- cable television
- pay television services
- digital television
- streaming media
- radio
- satellites
- multimedia computers
- video games
- the internet and the web
- internet commerce
- office technologies
- virtual reality
- home video
- digital audio
- telephony
- wireless telephony
- broadband networks
- distance learning

Although not a totally satisfactory solution, in this book we regard a communication technology as 'new' if it's digital and computer-based. By the time you read this book, however, we can only imagine what other corners of our lives will be digitized and driven by computer technology. In the meantime, it's one of the most well known and 'revolutionizing' examples of this ongoing process of computerization which interests us more than anything else: the internet.

THE INTERNET: CONVERGENCES IN CYBERSPACE

There are so many accounts online of the history of the internet and web that it hardly warrants discussion. (Once again, our recurring fractal motif is there to remind you that this book, like all such books, is merely a portal – an opening to further exploration and learning.) Having said which, it is worth knowing just a little bit about what they entail so that we can also point you to some significant developments and convergences in cyberspace before moving on to think about the interactive technologies within the internet. (By **convergences** we simply mean the coming together and/or overlapping of different aspects of something.) First, we would just like to note one other important fact about this book. People interested in studying CMC come from all sorts of different backgrounds and have various different levels of experience and expertise. If you're one of the people who already know a lot about cyberspace, please bear with us while we cover some of the basics. Besides, in our own experience – even as senior scholars – there's usually always something new to be learned.

THE INTERNET – OR 'INTERNET' OR JUST 'NET'

Put simply, the **internet** is an almost global network connecting millions of computers. Using a number of agreed formats (known as *protocols*), users are able to transfer data (or files) from one computer to the next. For more information, *A Brief History of the Internet* is offered by the Internet Society [**www** BT2:3]. ◎ In terms of our discussion above, however, it's worth noting that, according to the almost mythical history of the internet, it was originally envisioned in the 1960s by the US Department of Defense as a means of securing information exchange in the event of nuclear war. It was later taken up by academics, again mainly as a means of information exchange – in this case, exchanging details about their research. However, one major application of the internet from the start was also the sending and receiving of emails, and, much like the telephone, email was rather unexpectedly taken up by users as a way of doing things social rather than things scientific – and the rest, as they say, is history! Well, almost . . .

◎ If you're really keen and want to know more about the development of the internet, Robert Hobbes has a very detailed, well maintained 'timeline' [**www** BT2:4].

THE WORLD WIDE WEB – OR 'WWW' OR 'W3' OR JUST 'WEB'

Also developed initially as a means of scientific information exchange in the 1990s, the **web** is a system of computer servers connected through the internet, and which supports the exchange of files (or *webpages*) formatted mostly in a simple programming language known as HTML (HyperText Markup Language). With the help of *browsers* (e.g. Netscape Navigator and Internet Explorer), these files can be translated from dull programming language ('plain text') into colorful, formatted webpages ('rich text') and links can be followed between documents by directing the browser to 'addresses' (other files) on other computers elsewhere on the web. Technically, web addresses are known as URLs (Uniform Resource Locators), although, in this book we've chosen to label them *weblinks*. You will also probably know that nowadays other programming languages (e.g. Java) and animation technologies (e.g. Flash) are used to write (or 'build') much more elaborate webpages which contain graphic, audio and video files adding movement and sound to written text. ◎

◎ If any of the technical terms leave you cold, we recommend you use Matisse Enzer's straightforward *Glossary of Internet Terms* [**www** BT2:5].

Importantly – and this has been stressed time and again by CMC scholars – the internet and the web are *not* technically synonymous. Strictly speaking, the web is a technology within a technology; it is just one part of the internet which also hosts the transfer of other types of documents or files, the best examples of which are emails and discussion group postings. But saying that the web is 'just' a part of the internet is rather like saying that a motorbike is *just* a bicycle with an engine! In some ways, therefore, the web is to the internet what language is to communication: it cannot account for everything we do, but it is unquestionably a major element in the larger system. In fact, there's been a seemingly unstoppable convergence happening since CMC first started to establish itself as a field of study, and that is the convergence of the internet and the web. (We recommend you see the stimulus reading by Nina Wakeford in Basic Theory: Unit 1.) Currently, the web is *the* most important and most dominant component of the internet. Fewer and fewer things done on the internet these days are not actually hosted on the web – email, chat, bulletin boards and so on are just about all web-based these days.

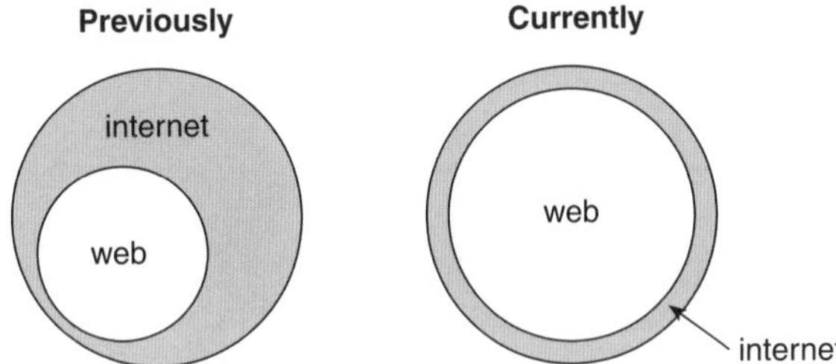

FIGURE 4

Convergence of the internet and the web

CYBERSPACE, CYBERSOCIETY AND CYBERCULTURE

> Sure, internet communication involves information exchange in its raw sense, as much as talking via the phone involves vibrating carbon particles. But there is something more to internet-based CMC than data exchange. (December, 1997)

Without wishing to minimize the wonder of either, the internet and web are really 'just' the technology – the hardware if you like – behind what's really going on in CMC. **Cyberspace**, on the other hand, is where it's really at. Cyberspace is about the people who use the internet and the different uses they put it to. This is why CMC scholar Steven Jones (1995) prefers to talk about **cybersociety** – a term which perhaps describes better the way that communication mediated by the internet is all about social life: people, interactions, relationships, identities and communities. It's for this reason that we're less interested in the technology *per se*, than in its human users and uses.

Another noticeable convergence related to the internet has been the one between cyberspace and 'real life'. Previously, cyberspace was the exclusive domain of relatively few people. (In fact, given the worldwide inequality of access to the internet, it still is.)

For this reason also, the academic study of cyberspace was also quite restricted. However, as we noted at the start of Basic Theory: Unit 1, what's been increasingly happening is that more and more people in the richer countries of the world have been coming online. As a result, the overlap between life online and life offline has been getting greater and greater for many of us.

Nowadays, cyberspace is just an added dimension in the lives of many people and it's hard to imagine many people living in isolation from the internet and web (see Central Issues: Unit 1). Just think of how everything has a web address on every magazine advert, online banking and shopping, chat and messaging. As Figure 5 suggests, the overlap between cyberspace and the 'real world' is great – so great in fact that the difference between what's *cyber* and what's *real* is sometimes impossible to tell. This is the kind of issue which keeps scholars in Cultural Studies very busy, not least because they recognize better than most how fluid culture is and how everything we do is about cultural identity and cultural practice – whether it's ballet or bingo, fine art or fly-fishing, and so on. Just as communication scholars see computer-mediated communication as an extension of everyday communication, for cultural critics **cyberculture** is merely another domain or expression of cultural life more generally. Their preference for the term cyber*culture* is also similar to Jones's preference for 'cybersociety'; it's intended to reflect their primary interest in the human, social and creative aspects of internet use.

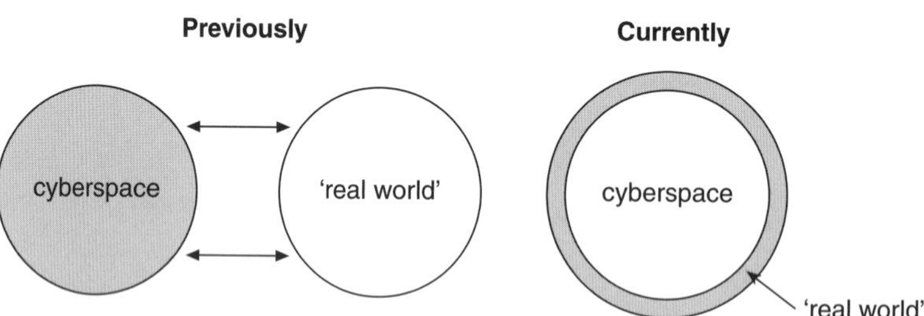

FIGURE 5
Overlap of cyberspace and the 'real world'

NARROWING THE FIELD: INTERACTIVE GENRES OR SUB-SYSTEMS

As Susan Herring (1996) rightly notes in her definition in Basic Theory: Unit 1 (p. 15), what interests scholars of CMC first and foremost are the ways computers and the different communication technologies or **sub-systems** of the internet impact on human communication (e.g. language practices and patterns of social interaction). In turn, CMC is also interested in the extent to which people simply bring existing ways of communicating to these new technologies of communication. In other words, those of us studying and learning about CMC want to know *if* and *how* communication is different when it's mediated by the internet. Of course, it's also interesting to see how patterns of communication are being influenced by other new technologies like cellphones and to see, for example, how mobile communication compares with internet communication.

In these terms, therefore, it's safe to say that, in this book, we are specifically interested in what Jiri Weiss and Michelle Nance (1997) used to characterize as 'beyond the browser' technologies. 'It's out there, beyond your browser, where a lot of people find the real value of the internet – namely, the ability to communicate directly with practically anyone in the world' (Weiss and Nance, 1997). Of course, as we've just suggested, there's not much these days which is actually beyond the reach of the web browser. What's more, we would certainly consider personal homepages on the web important forms of communication and social interaction – as you'll see from Central Issues: Unit 2 and Fieldwork: Task 6. Nevertheless, what Weiss and Nance meant was that the really interesting communication activity is not to be found in the masses and masses of data and information contained in the 3,307,998,701 pages of the web. ◎ On the contrary. According to CMC scholars Joseph Walther and Malcolm Parks (2002: 3), it's only really in the *interactive* spaces where 'the real give and take of social life' on the internet occurs. In fact, we could go even further and say that we have a particular interest in the largely text-based **genres** of CMC which psychologist Patricia Wallace (1999) describes as the 'bread and butter' of cyberspace. Once again, however, the story is more and more complicated because everything is becoming more and more multimodal and so less easy to define in these simple terms. However, following all these directions, the technologies of the internet which tend to interest CMC scholars the most are these:

◎ This was the number of pages being searched by Google when we were putting the book together. Have a look at the figure published on the bottom of the Google homepage to see what it is now.

- emails, listservs and mailing lists
- newsgroups, bulletin boards, and blogs
- internet relay chat and instant messaging
- metaworlds and visual chat
- personal homepages and webcams

These are all 'technologies within technologies' which facilitate interaction. To use spatial metaphors, these are the 'places' in cyberspace where people hang out together and the 'niches' where they are sociable. There are of course other specialist contexts (e.g. business teleconferencing) or more informational exchanges (e.g. online shopping and MPG music downloads) which might reasonably fall under the scope of CMC. The boundaries we are drawing here are fairly specious, and in the Focus Areas topics you'll find it necessary to open up your investigations to include specialist and more information-oriented examples of CMC (e.g. in the areas of health and medicine, business and education). You'll also see references made in some of the recommended readings and elsewhere to other internet technologies like FTP, Telnet and, especially, MUDs. For the most part, however, we won't be covering these in this book, partly because they are fast becoming supplanted by web- or browser-based technologies. A good example of this is the way visual chat is becoming increasingly popular compared with text-only, virtual reality environments like MUDs. In much the same way, a traditional chat technology like IRC (Internet Relay Chat) has been seriously challenged by popular chat technologies like ICQ and the kinds of web-based and even audio chat offered by Yahoo!, AOL and other major content providers. Which is not to say that more traditional spaces like MUDs and MOOs don't continue to have their avid supporters – they do.

As you can see, the internet is not a single communication technology but rather a collection of different technologies for communicating. For this reason, it may be better to think of the internet as a system comprised of many sub-systems, and each sub-system has its own genre or type of communication. There is certainly no single way of communicating on the internet. Indeed, new ways of communicating through the internet are evolving and emerging all the time in response to both technological *and* social changes. What we intend to show you in the Basic Theory units which follow is that any discussion about CMC must therefore always take certain contextual factors into account.

Perhaps the most important of these contextual factors is simply the type of internet technology actually being used. Think about it for a moment. The way people communicate is quite likely to be different if they're using email compared with, say, instant messaging, just as personal homepages may serve different communication goals from the type of CMC that happens in newsgroups. In fact, communication on the internet will always be heavily influenced by some, or all, of the following contextual factors:

- the type of channel (e.g. email or webpages) and the modes of communication it enables (e.g. text-based, graphics-based or audio-visual – or all three);
- the participants (e.g. male or female, young or old) and the number of participants (e.g. one-to-one, one-to-many, many-to-many);
- the length (e.g. long-term or fleeting) and the nature of people's relationship (e.g. personal or professional);
- the topic (e.g. medical advice or romantic date) and purpose of the exchange (e.g. scholarly, private or commercial);
- whether the interaction is synchronous (i.e. in real time) or asynchronous (i.e. not in real time, with delayed interactions);
- whether it's public or private (e.g. interpersonal, small group, or mass communication) and whether it's moderated or unmoderated (e.g. under the direct or indirect supervision of someone or not);
- what the general attitude of participants is towards communication on the internet (e.g. enthusiastic or sceptical, half-hearted or committed) and how long they've been doing CMC (e.g. are they newcomers or are they really experienced?).

CONCLUSION: HOW TO SHOOT A MOVING TARGET

Evidently, there's a lot of variety on the internet – in terms of different technologies, in terms of different users, and in terms of different ways of communicating. It makes the internet a much more complex field of study but also a much more interesting field of study for scholars. The truth is, that even by the time you come to read this book, the field will already have undergone important changes. Here's how the Internet Society puts it:

> One should not conclude that the internet has now finished changing. The internet, although a network in name and geography, is a creature of the computer, not the traditional network of the telephone or television industry. It will, indeed it must, continue to change and evolve at the speed of the computer industry if it is to remain relevant. [**www** BT2:3]

In fact, trying to pin CMC down is like trying to shoot a moving target at a funfair. Only relatively recently have scholars begun to start doing more research and writing about the impact on CMC of more recent technologies like webcams and visual chat, for example – not to mention the interface of the internet and other communication technologies like mobile telephony. In fact another major convergence in terms of communication technology is the way so many 'old' and 'new' media technologies are being brought together into cyberspace, driven for the most part by the commercial interests of large media conglomorates. Two significant examples of this is have been (1) the now taken-for-granted presence of print newspapers on the internet, and (2) the popularity of web-based radio and the use of chat sites and online information resources by television companies. ◎ As old communication technologies become ever more interactive, new communication technologies like the internet also become more and more multimodal (e.g. with videos, webcams, moving graphics and sound). Even though it may be the bread and butter of CMC, less and less of what happens in CMC is merely text-based. These are all changes which you need to bear in mind as you learn, critique, explore and apply your way through this book.

BOX BT2:2 IT'S ALL JUST COMMUNICATION SOUP

New inventions can change the world in unimagined ways. In the case of the telephone, for example, it introduced new ways of thinking about communication, new social practices, and new ways of talking. And this is true for a wide range of communication technologies. But the other thing [to remember] is that communication technologies don't tend to replace each other completely but rather they blend together in a sort of communication soup. (Chris Dillon in *Cybertalk* – see [**www** BT2:9]

REVIEW

In this unit, we started by looking at the historical context of new communication technologies and technologies like the telephone and telegraph. We then briefly described the internet, the web and cyberspace, before turning to identify the major interactive technologies on the internet which concern scholars of CMC. We also considered how genres of communication will vary not only from technology to technology (or sub-system to sub-system), but also in accordance with a range of other contextal factors. We ended the unit by recognising how quickly the field covered by CMC is changing.

◎ If you're interested in trying out internet radio, you could try VirtualTuner.com [**www** BT2:6]. Meanwhile, a good example of the television-internet convergence is the BBC's 'Communicate' page [**www** BT2:7] as well as its 'interactive service' known as BBC-i [**www** BT2:8].

STIMULUS READINGS AND RESOURCES

Cyberatlas [**www** BT2:10].

Nua Internet Surveys [**www** BT2:11].

Internet Society's *Brief History of the Internet* [**www** BT2:3].

Berners-Lee, T. (2002). *The world wide web – past, present and future:Exploring universality*. The Commemorative Lecture 2002, Japan Prize. Available (2 November 2003) online at <http://www.w3.org/2002/04/Japan/Lecture.html>.

Burnett, R. and Marshall, P.D. (2003). Chapter 3: The web as communication. In *Web theory: An introduction* (pp. 45–60). London: Routledge.

Guice, J. (1998). Looking backward and forward at the internet. *The Information Society*,14(3), 201–11.

Sterne, J. (1999). Thinking the internet: cultural studies *v.* the millennium. In S. Jones (ed.), *Doing internet research: Critical issues and methods for examining the net* (pp. 257–88). London: Sage.

IDEAS FOR FURTHER DISCUSSION AND INVESTIGATION

1 Visit the following websites to find out more about the history of key communication technologies such as the printing press, the telegraph, the telephone, the television and cinema: the Media History Project [**www** BT2:12], the Virtual Museum [**www** BT2:13], the Inventors Museum [**www** BT2:14] and About.com's pages on Historical Inventions [**www** BT2:15].

2 Spend some time online reviewing and making notes about the most recent reports published by Cyberatlas [**www** BT2:9] and Nua Internet Surveys [**www** BT2:10] – two well known commercial organizations producing the latest figures about the internet. What emerging demographic and usership trends are there which look set to impact on CMC?

3 Use resources on the web to find brief descriptions or explanations of the different genres of CMC such as email, mailing lists, instant messaging, MUDs, bulletin boards, newsgroups, personal homepages, virtual reality environments, internet relay chat. In addition to Webopedia.com [**www** BT2:16], you might also like to try the following online resources: the Living Internet [**www** BT2:17], Learn the Net [**www** BT2:18], About.com's Internet for Beginners [**www** BT2:19], or the Internet Tutorials [**www** BT2:20].

4 In Focus Areas: Topic 9, you can choose to research and explore further some of the latest technological developments in CMC. However, from what you already know, which new media (as in new modes of communication and also new broadcast media) are currently being incorporated into CMC most rapidly? Of those mentioned here in the unit, which do you think will be most popular among young people – and why? Based on your own experience, what impact is WiFi (i.e. wireless internet) having on CMC? (See **www** BT2:21 for more information about WiFi technology.)

UNIT 3

THEORIZING CMC: TECHNOLOGY AND SOCIAL INTERACTION

OVERVIEW

KEY TERMS

invisible technology
hype and hysteria
technological determination
social constructivism/realism
technical affordances

MAIN OBJECTIVES

- Review the major pattern of technological development.
- Examine dominant myths about technology and social change.
- Describe and critique the notion of technological determinism.
- Consider the alternative 'social constructivist' and 'realist' perspectives.

HUMANS AND THEIR MACHINES

Whether it's radios, televisions or computers, much of what is written about communication technologies has to do with people's underlying beliefs about the nature of the relationship between human beings and their machines. In fact, CMC concerns itself with a range of different ways of thinking about this relationship by asking questions like:

- How do people interact with, and in the presence of, technology?
- How do people incorporate technology into their social interactions?

www For weblinks and resources visit the CMC website at <www.sagepub.co.uk/resources/cmc>

- How do people interact through, or by means of, technology?
- How do people represent and talk about technology?

The first question is one which is usually dealt with in the more specialized area of Human-Computer Interaction (HCI), an area we've decided not to cover in detail this book. In the same way, the last is the kind of question which is of greater interest to writers in Cultural Studies. This is not to say that we're not interested in these issues ourselves; it's just that our main areas of interest in CMC lie with the middle two questions. We're more interested in the relationship between the forms of communication technologies and patterns of social interaction and interpersonal communication. In particular, we want to know whether, and how, communication mediated by computers is different from communication which is not. Related questions for us are: How do people adapt their communication to technologies? How do they appropriate the technologies to suit their everyday communication needs?

To find out more about HCI, look at these two websites: the Human-Computer Interaction Lab [**www** BT3:1] and the Graphics, Visualization and Usability Center [**www** BT3:2]. You'll want to think about HCI in more detail if you select Focus Areas: Topic 8.

And why is all this interesting? Well, as we suggested in Basic Theory: Unit 1, one very good reason for studying CMC is that we can learn more about the nature of human communication when we look to see how it is affected by technologies. By the same token, we can also learn more about communication technologies when we observe the ways they transform – and are transformed by – human social interaction.

TECHNOLOGICAL DEVELOPMENT: BECOMING INVISIBLE

BOX BT3:1 NEWSFLASH! HOT OFF THE PRESS . . .

A new communications technology has been developed that allows people to communicate almost instantly across great distances, in effect shrinking the world faster and further than ever before. A worldwide communications network whose cables span continents and oceans, it has revolutionized business practice, given rise to new forms of crime, and inundated its users with a deluge of information. Romances have blossomed over the wires. Secret codes have been devised by some users, and cracked by others. Governments and regulators have tried and failed to control the new medium. Meanwhile, out on the wires, a technological subculture with its own customs and vocabulary is establishing itself.

Does all this sound familiar? In fact, it is more or less how British writer Tom Standage (1999: 1) cleverly describes the impact in the nineteenth century of the telegraph – what he refers to as *The Victorian Internet*. As Standage goes on to say, at a time when there were no planes, no televisions, no spacecraft, no mobile phones, the telegraph was a new communication technology which 'ushered in the greatest revolution in communications since the development of the printing press'. Like the internet, what was so revolutionary about the telegraph was the speed of message transfer it enabled. Previously, messages between people could really travel any distance only at the speed of horses, carriages or trains – perhaps with the odd exception of smoke signals or semaphore! With the advent of the telegraph, however, messages could be sent and read just about simultaneously.

We've already commented in Basic Theory: Unit 2 on the fact that the internet comes from a long line of technologies for communication, including the printing press, the telegraph, the telephone, the radio and the television. In point of fact, humans have been creating ways to transmit, store and manipulate information and messages for centuries – if not millennia. However, in thinking again about the technologies in your own home, think now about the kinds of changes which each one has provoked. How has each piece of technology helped or hindered our lives? More specifically, what kind of impact has it had on our social lives? For example, while wandering around your home looking for technologies, it's more than likely that you came across a washing machine. Well, some commentators have suggested that, more than any other single factor (i.e. social, political or economic), the development and popularization of the washing machine in the 1950s were responsible for the empowerment of women in Western societies. The washing machine, so the argument goes, meant that women were finally liberated from one of the most time-consuming of household chores and therefore free to pursue work outside the home as never before. ◎

◎ Not everyone would agree with this. In her book *More work for Mother: The ironies of household technology*, Ruth Cowen argues that the washing machine has in fact served to create more work for home makers because we simply wash more clothes than before! [**www** BT3: 3].

Whatever the eventual impact they have on our lives, according to Ursula Franklin (1990), all technologies (and not just communication technologies) appear to develop in two distinct stages (Box BT3:2).

BOX BT3:2 STAGES IN THE DEVELOPMENT OF TECHNOLOGY

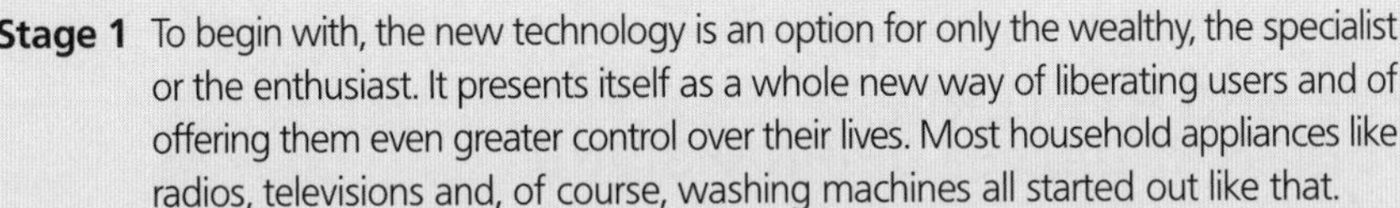

Stage 1 To begin with, the new technology is an option for only the wealthy, the specialist or the enthusiast. It presents itself as a whole new way of liberating users and of offering them even greater control over their lives. Most household appliances like radios, televisions and, of course, washing machines all started out like that.

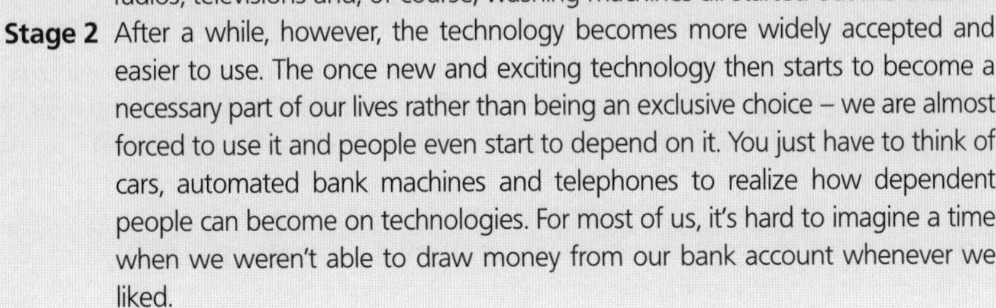

Stage 2 After a while, however, the technology becomes more widely accepted and easier to use. The once new and exciting technology then starts to become a necessary part of our lives rather than being an exclusive choice – we are almost forced to use it and people even start to depend on it. You just have to think of cars, automated bank machines and telephones to realize how dependent people can become on technologies. For most of us, it's hard to imagine a time when we weren't able to draw money from our bank account whenever we liked.

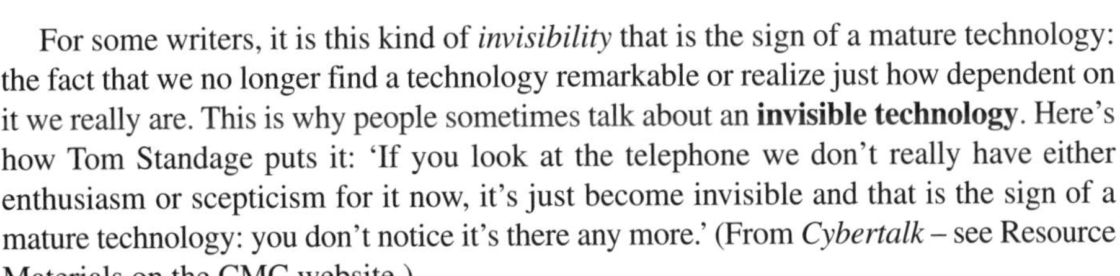

For some writers, it is this kind of *invisibility* that is the sign of a mature technology: the fact that we no longer find a technology remarkable or realize just how dependent on it we really are. This is why people sometimes talk about an **invisible technology**. Here's how Tom Standage puts it: 'If you look at the telephone we don't really have either enthusiasm or scepticism for it now, it's just become invisible and that is the sign of a mature technology: you don't notice it's there any more.' (From *Cybertalk* – see Resource Materials on the CMC website.)

BOX BT3:3 PERSON OF THE YEAR 1982: THE HOME COMPUTER

Although they see dangers of unemployment and dehumanization, nearly 80 percent of Americans expect that home computers will be as commonplace as television sets or dishwashers – solid majorities feel that the computer revolution will raise living standards and improve the quality of children's education. In a larger perspective, the entire world will never be the same. Prophets of high technology believe the computer is so cheap and so powerful that it could enable underdeveloped nations to bypass the whole industrial revolution. [One commentator], who believes the computer's teaching capability can conquer the Third World's illiteracy, says: 'It's the source of new life that has been delivered to us.'

Jane Gackenbach and Evelyn Ellerman (1998) present the more detailed case study of the radio as an excellent example of this pattern of technological change and development, whereby the radio moved from being a specialized military tool, to being part of a subculture of enthusiasts, to being taken up for commercial, educational and purposes. Of course, in many parts of the world there's little doubt that computers too have long since become a mature technology and it's hard to imagine that back in 1982 *Time* magazine famously voted the personal computer 'Person of the Year' because it was such a novel, remarkable phenomenon [see Box BT3:3 and **www** BT3:4].

◉ Made in 1998, the film *You've Got Mail* is considered something of a turning point because, for the first time, it represented in such a mainstream way how the internet can be used for building strong interpersonal relationships.

HYPE AND HYSTERIA: UTOPIAN AND DYSTOPIAN VISIONS

The dialogue in Box BT3:4 is taken from the opening sequence of the 1998 movie *You've Got Mail*. Have a look at the exchange between the characters Frank (a journalist, played by Greg Kinnear) and Kathleen (a bookstore owner, played by Meg Ryan). ◉

BOX BT3:4 THE END OF THE WORLD AS WE KNOW IT?

Frank: Listen to this. The entire force of the State of Virginia has to have solitaire removed from their computers because they hadn't done any work in six weeks.

Kathleen: That is so sad.

Frank: You know what this is, what we're seeing here? It's the end of Western civilization as we know it. Technology. Name me one thing – one! – that we've gained from technology.

Kathleen: Electricity.

Frank: That's one. (*points to her computer*) You think that machine is your friend, but it's not.

This is a good example of another striking aspect of the development of technology. With each new technology, there's almost always an associated period of social and cultural reorganization and reflection – and sometimes even anxiety and conflict. Almost always there is also a lot of talk as journalists, scholars, politicians and ordinary folk try to make sense of what they know and hear about these new technological developments. Often popular myths about new technology can be very extreme, tending to exaggerate the negative or positive impact they believe technology will have on society, social interaction and individual psychology. (By using the term 'myth', we don't mean to say that there is no truth at all behind the ideas, just that these are stories we like to tell as a society.) Although it seems absurd nowadays, people were once genuinely concerned that the body would disintegrate if they drove over twenty miles an hour, or that you could go deaf from excessive telephone use!

As you can see from the wording of the *Time* magazine feature article about its 1982 'Person of the Year' (Box 3:3), it's not just in the movies or on the streets that people prophesize wildly about the impact of new technologies. Nor is it all bad news. In fact, more often than not, what tends to happen is that public and scholarly opinion about the cultural and social impact of new technologies is initially polarized into extreme positions. On the one hand, there are those who create a lot of **hype** about the wonderful, unique advantages of the technology; on the other hand, there are those who appear more **hysterical** about the terrible effects they foresee.

Thinking more specifically about the internet, John Kling (1996) sets out what he sees as the basic tenets of the 'utopian' and 'anti-utopian' visions people tend to have regarding the effects of computerization on human interaction and social life. These two extreme positions are characterized in Box BT3:5.

BOX BT3:5 THE UTOPIAN AND DYSTOPIAN POSITIONS

The utopian vision emphasizes the life-enhancing, exciting possibilities of computing technology with claims for global connectivity, democratization, and the opening of the frontiers of human experience and relationship. (Do you recognize this from the *Time* magazine article?)

The anti-utopian (or dystopian) vision concerns itself with people's enslavement to digital technology, their growing dependency, as well as the relentless, unstoppable growth of technology which brings with it information overload and the breakdown of social structures and values.

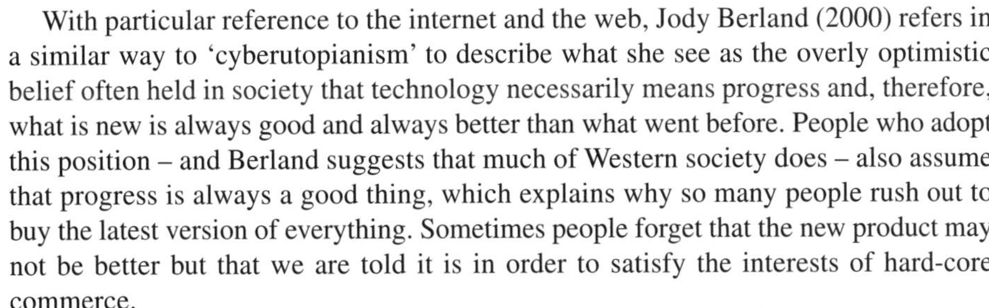

With particular reference to the internet and the web, Jody Berland (2000) refers in a similar way to 'cyberutopianism' to describe what she see as the overly optimistic belief often held in society that technology necessarily means progress and, therefore, what is new is always good and always better than what went before. People who adopt this position – and Berland suggests that much of Western society does – also assume that progress is always a good thing, which explains why so many people rush out to buy the latest version of everything. Sometimes people forget that the new product may not be better but that we are told it is in order to satisfy the interests of hard-core commerce.

Whether you agree with Berland or not, what we always see with new technological

FIGURE 6
Rorschach inkblot

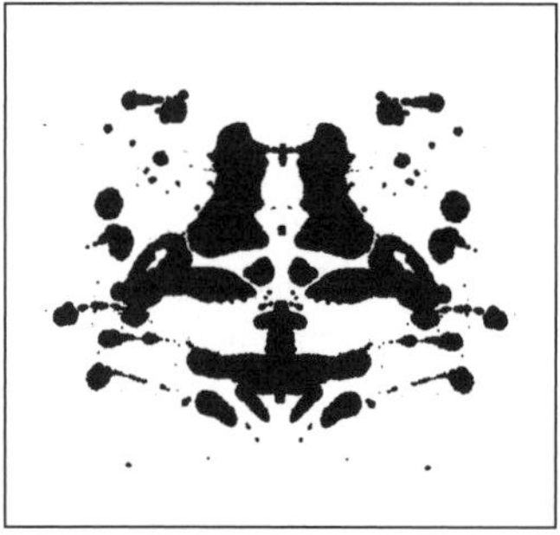

developments is a mixture of hype and excessive optimism, on the one hand, and hysteria or fierce scepticism on the other. In her well known discussion about 'life on the screen', Sherry Turkle (1990) introduces the notion of the 'subjective computer'. What she means by this is that people tend to project on to computers and digital technology their own individual fears and aspirations. As such, the computer and the internet end up being treated like a Rorschach inkblot (Figure 6). In psychology, therapists sometimes ask people to imagine what they see when looking at an image similar to the mock one here. The idea behind this is that the things people say they see reveal important clues to the therapist about how the person is feeling and what's really on their mind. And so, in much the same way, how people talk about technology often says more about them than it does about the technology itself! As further evidence of this, Daniel Chandler's essay *Imagining futures, dramatizing fears* (1998a) shows how our relationship with technological innovation is also a common theme in books and films – evidence again of how much we love to tell stories about the relationship between our technological creations and our lives.

FRAMING THE MYTHS: TECHNOLOGICAL DETERMINISM

There's one key concept which offers a really useful framework for understanding the relationship between technology and human communication: **technological determinism**. In fact, it seems that no paper, chapter or book about communication and technology is complete without mentioning this concept – and for a very good reason. Basically, the term indicates an extreme position in explaining the relationship between technological change and social life. In another excellent essay, Daniel Chandler (1995) offers a clear definition (in Box BT3:6).

BOX BT3:6 TECHNOLOGICAL DETERMINISM

Technological determinism is the assumption that technologies are the *primary* cause of:

- major social and historical changes at the macrosocial level of societal structures and processes;
- subtle but profound social and psychological influences at the microsocial level of the regular use of particular kinds of tools.

Technological determinism therefore sees technology as the big 'mover and shaker' behind major social transformations at the level of institutions, social interaction and individual cognition (i.e. ways of perceiving and thinking about the world). In order to adopt this perspective, technological determinists must make a number of important assumptions. Chandler (1995) identifies these assumptions one by one, although, for our purposes, the four main ones are listed in Box BT3:7.

BOX BT3:7 CORE ASSUMPTIONS OF TECHNOLOGICAL DETERMINISM

- **Reductionistic.** Technological determinism reduces the relationship between technology and culture to one of straightforward cause and effect.
- **Monistic.** Rather than being multi-causal, technological determinism oversimplifies an otherwise complex relationship to the effects of a single factor.
- **Neutralizing.** Technological determinism represents technology as neutral or value-free and therefore absolved of 'responsibility'.
- **Technological imperative.** Technological determinism presents technological 'progress' as unstoppable, inevitable, and irreversible.

Although few scholars nowadays would feel comfortable taking such an extreme position, this is still a very common way for lay people and journalists to talk. For communication scholars, however, determinism is a bit of a four-letter word! Perhaps the best example is the linguistic determinism of the so called Sapir–Whorf hypothesis which, in simple terms, proposes that our language dictates the way we think. ◎ In much the same way, psychologists struggling over the famous nature–nurture debate may sometimes adopt a more biological determinist position by assuming that it's our genes alone which control our psychological make-up.

◎ To find out more about linguistic determinism, try the website of the Linguistics Society of America and an essay written by Dan Slobin, a professor at Harvard University [**www** BT3: 5].

Culture and human behavior are complex things, and technological determinism is clearly not an adequate way to explain the interplay between new communication technologies and social interaction – there are always a range of social, economic, governmental and cultural factors which also need to be considered. Having said which, technological determinism does offer a useful foil against which to evaluate our analyses and interpretations of the impact of computer mediation on communication. Each one of the underlying assumptions of technological determinism is therefore a potential line of attack – a way of criticizing claims about CMC and about the relationship between the internet and social life. Every time you come across someone making a claim about the effect of the internet on some or other aspect of social life or human communication, keep asking yourself to what extent they are falling into the trap of being too deterministic about technology.

This is precisely what cultural critic Jonathan Sterne (1999: 258) argues (see stimulus readings from Basic Theory: Unit 2). In a provocative attempt to counter many of the wildly exaggerated claims often made about the internet, he suggests that the internet is in fact a mundane, banal technology which has simply been caught up in the same old 'technophilic' and 'technophobic' wrangle. The reason it's a banal technology is that, for many people, it has become so deeply integrated into their daily lives they don't even give it a thought most of the time (also see Basic Theory: Unit 6). In the same vein as the recommendation we've just made, Sterne advises CMC scholars to revisit the simplicity of utopian and dystopian visions, to recognize that the internet is dynamic, ideological and cultural, and to respect the inseparability of social life online and social life offline.

PUTTING THINGS INTO PERSPECTIVE: 'SHAPING AND BEING SHAPED'

BOX BT3:8 WILL THEY, WON'T THEY? EVERYDAY USERS VERSUS CELLPHONE COMPANIES

There has been a lot of press coverage and political debate in Europe especially about WAP (Wireless Application Protocol) technology as cellphone companies invested huge amounts of money in the hope of being able to exploit and make even more money from the interface between mobile phones and the internet. (See 'Ideas for further discussion and investigation'.) However, people initially appeared to be uninterested – much to the frustration of the big companies! It seems that, if they can't see any benefits, most ordinary users simply aren't prepared to buy into a technology for the sake of it. By contrast, one of the success stories for cellphone companies has been the surprising popularity of text-messaging. Originally intended as a practical way for the companies to contact their customers, no one could have predicted how rapidly and how widely used it would be – but only once people on the streets recognized its potential to enhance their everyday communication.

It's the 'ordinariness' of the internet nowadays which prompted well known CMC scholar Steven Jones to propose at the 2002 National Communication Association conference that internet should be written with a lower-case 'i'.

There are several different stands people can take in relation to technological determinism, ranging from a strong (or hard) stand which agrees with all the assumptions above, to a weak (or soft) stand which instead regards technology as one of several factors *facilitating* and *influencing* cultural and social changes. There are also other more radical positions. In particular, **social constructivism** turns technological determinism on its head by arguing that technology is instead entirely subordinate to the way it is used in particular socio-historical, culturally specific contexts. Technologies certainly don't just fall out of the sky. Seldom do they just pop into inventors' heads. Nor do users always use technologies in the ways which their developers intended them to be used. In fact, there is a constant struggle between invention and appropriation, that is, what technology is *designed* to do and what people *actually* do with it (see Box BT3:8).

From this perspective, it's not so much that technology brings about social changes as the *application* of technology. This is why scholars of media communication are invariably concerned to examine what are known as 'uses and gratifications', which is to say, what people actually do with communication technologies and what they get out of them. This does not mean, however, that technology is a totally 'neutral' conductor of our communication (remember the four key assumptions of technological determinism outlined above). In fact, there are always practical and material ways in which a technology influences the nature of communication. These are what British sociologist Ian Hutchby (2001) calls **technological 'affordances'** – the advantages and disadvantages which arise from the distinctive, material properties of any particular technology. In other words, there are simply some things you can or can't do with a communication technology. It's for this reason also that Neil Postman (1993) argues that technologies are always ideologically biased in the way they are designed. For example, he points to *intellectual* biases (e.g. the fact that much of the internet and web are coded in English), *political* biases (e.g. the inequality of access to the internet because of its relatively high cost) and, most obviously, *sensory* biases (e.g. the dependence of the internet on basic physical capacities like sight).

Needless to say, the trouble with the social constructivist position is that it ends up being too socially or culturally deterministic! Like most communication scholars, Rob Kling (1996) advocates a position which he calls **social realism**. What this means is that we need to understand the relationship between technology, culture and social interaction as more of a two-way street. It's also vital that we back up our claims with evidence and that we don't forget other important influences such as economics and politics.

BOX BT3:9 SHAPING AND BEING SHAPED

A technological system can be both cause and effect; it can shape or be shaped by society. As they grow larger and more complex, systems tend to be more shaping of a society and less shaped by it . . . The social constructivists have a key to understanding the behaviour of young systems; technological determinists come into their own with the mature ones. (Kling, 1996)

In proposing that we are therefore shaped by technology but also shape it ourselves, Thomas Hughes (1994) also suggests that the relationship will itself change as the technology matures: in the early stages it seems that users have a stronger influence (e.g. WAP technology) but as the technology becomes more and more pervasive (and invisible) its influences may get stronger and more subtle. It is important therefore to think in terms not only of the impact of computers on communication but also of the impact of communication on computers. Just as the users of communication technologies are not completely passive, nor are the uses of different communication technologies totally unlimited. Technologies will enable some uses but restrict others, and will therefore predispose people to use them in certain ways. To conclude, especially as scholars of CMC, it's worth bearing in mind the following three factors when discussing the impact technologies like the internet have on people's lives: (1) what the technology is supposed to do (i.e. its design and commercial ideologies); (2) what the technology allows people to do (i.e. its practical or material affordances); and (3) what people actually do with the technology (i.e. its uses and gratifications).

REVIEW

In this unit we started by specifying CMC's concern for the impact of technology on social interaction and interpersonal communication, before sketching the main pattern of technological development towards maturity and 'invisibility'. We then outlined the myths of hype and hysteria (utopian and dystopian visions) which often accompany the emergence of new technologies. As a way of framing these popular responses, we reviewed the notion of technological determinism and the assumptions it makes about the relationship between technology, culture and social interaction. We then considered the alternative perspective of social constructivism, before concluding with the more 'social realist' idea that technology shapes and is shaped by social life.

STIMULUS READINGS AND RESOURCES

Technology and culture: bibliography and online resources [**www** BT3:6].

Berland, J. (2000). Cultural technologies and the 'evolution' of technological cultures. In A. Herman and T. Swiss (eds), *The world wide web and contemporary cultural theory* (pp. 235–58). New York: Routledge.

Burnett, R. and Marshall, P.D. (2003). Chapter 1: Web of technology. In *Web theory: An introduction* (pp. 7–22). London: Routledge.

Chandler, D. (1995). *Technological or media determinism* [**www** BT3:7].

Murphie, A. and Potts, J. (2002). Chapter 1: Theoretical frameworks. In *Culture and technology* (pp. 11–38). Basingstoke: Palgrave Macmillan.

IDEAS FOR FURTHER DISCUSSION AND INVESTIGATION

1 The CIOS McLuhan website [**www** BT3:8] is an impressive website with an online tutorial about the key ideas of Canadian scholar Marshall McLuhan, famous for his technological (or, in this case, media) determinism. Visit the website and spend a little time following the modules called 'Culture and Technology' and 'Figure and ground'. To what extent do McLuhan's ideas about the 'global village' offer a way of understanding the impact of the internet on social life?

2 Search recent issues of mainstream newspapers online for examples of the way journalists are reporting current technological changes and media developments. You could try a selection of papers from around the world to see whether there are any interesting differences, e.g. *USA Today* [**www** BT3:9], *South African Post* [**www** BT3:10], *BBC News* [**www** BT3:11], *The Australian* [**www** BT3:12], *South China Morning Post* [**www** BT3:13], *Egypt Today* [**www** BT3:14] and *The Times of India* [**www** BT3:15]. Would you say there is a tendency to hype or hysteria?

3 Check to see what the other main assumptions of technological determinism are which Daniel Chandler (1995) identifies [**www** BT3:7]. How might each of these be applied to the way people commonly talk about the internet?

4 In thinking about the influence users have over new communication technologies, following the coverage by the BBC of the debate about WAP ('wireless application protocol') in Britain and Europe from September 2000 [**www** BT3:16], January 2001 [**www** BT3:17] and December 2002 [**www** BT3:18]. To what extent do you see commercial interests also playing a part? Look for more recent news coverage to see what the situation is nowadays. Who's won this battle – users, big business or the technology itself?

UNIT 4

DESCRIBING CMC: INTERPERSONAL DYNAMICS

OVERVIEW

KEY TERMS

asociality and antisociality
deficit approaches
social information processing
communication imperative
impression management
hyperpersonal communication

MAIN OBJECTIVES

- Establish the central role of social and contextual information in CMC.
- Examine major approaches to interpersonal dynamics and technology.
- Review research which confirms CMC as relational communication.
- Identify some of the ways people manage their impressions online.

THE NATURE OF CMC: THE GOOD, THE BAD AND THE UGLY

BOX BT4:1 A SOLUBLE TISSUE OF NOTHINGNESS?

It is an unreal universe, a soluble tissue of nothingness. While the internet beckons brightly, seductively flashing an icon of knowledge-as-power, this nonplace lures us to surrender our time on earth. A poor substitute it is, this virtual reality where frustration is legion and where – in the holy names of Education and Progress – important aspects of human interactions are relentlessly devalued. (Stoll, 1995: 195)

www For weblinks and resources visit the CMC website at <www.sagepub.co.uk/resources/cmc>

As you can tell from having read Basic Theory: Unit 3, Clifford Stoll (Box BT4:1) is by no means alone in his rather bleak assessment of cyberspace and the impact of the internet on communication. This kind of technophobic reaction has accompanied many illustrious communication technologies and there's no reason why the internet should be an exception. What's more, this negativity has also been supported by scholars within the field of CMC. In Box BT4:2, we've quoted a controversial claim made by Robert Kraut and his colleagues following their survey of internet use. ◎

◎ You'll come across the work of Robert Kraut and his colleague Sara Kiesler again in Basic Theory: Unit 5 and in Central Issues: Unit 7.

BOX BT4:2 SAD, LONELY AND DEPRESSING?

Greater use of the internet is associated with declines in participants' communication with family members in the household, declines in the size of their social circle, and increases in their depression and loneliness. (Kraut *et al.*, 1998: 1017)

Between them, these quotes point to the two major allegations commonly levelled against CMC (Box BT4:3).

BOX BT4:3 CMC STANDS ACCUSED: POOR QUALITY, NEGATIVE IMPACT

- **Allegation of asociality.** CMC is bad communication because the *quality* of communication is reduced as a result of the technological restraints of the internet.
- **Allegation of antisociality.** CMC is bad communication because it has a negative *impact* on offline communication and offline relationships.

Underpinning these two allegations is the belief that the internet is necessarily an inadequate mode of communication and one which can actually harm people because they cut themselves off from 'real' relationships. In other words, CMC is accused of being both *asocial* (i.e. it's cold and unfriendly) and *antisocial* (i.e. it diminishes 'face-to-face' interaction). Both these claims stand in stark contrast with the opposing belief that the internet can actually lead to new, and even better, social relationships, with people communicating across geographical and social boundaries and creating new friendships and communities based on their shared interests and concerns. What's more, in Basic Theory: Unit 6, we'll also start examining the potential CMC has for enhancing social life offline.

Of course, for many years the same kinds of argument have also been made about the negative impacts of television and video games on society. Too often, however, scholars and lay people forget that, as we showed with technological determinism, the picture is a complex one and there are many different ways of using technology. There are also many different users, each with their own particular priorities and needs.

BOX BT4:4 DID YOU WATCH THAT PROGRAM LAST NIGHT?

People often criticize television for turning us all into couch-potatoes and having us all glued to the screen instead of actually talking with each other. Even though there may be some truth in this, the television can make us social in different ways. In fact, there are ways of being social *about* technology, if not actually in front of it – or through it. An example which springs to mind is the so called 'water-cooler effect' whereby people will often get together (e.g. around the office water cooler) to gossip and chat about their favorite TV shows or an exciting program on TV the night before. In this sense, therefore, TV-viewing comes to be valued not so much for itself, but rather as a source of shared cultural knowledge and an opportunity for social bonding.

FIGURE 7

Around the water cooler

In this unit and the next, we want to explore the tension between the two conflicting perspectives that online communication is either all good or it's all bad. We'll do this by examining some basic theory about the nature of relational communication in CMC – first from an interpersonal perspective (Unit 4) and then from a group perspective (Unit 5). In this sense, therefore, we start by focusing on the allegation of **asociality** and will deal later with the allegation of **antisociality** in Central Issues: Unit 7, where we consider compulsive behavior online and so-called 'internet addiction'.

The complaint that CMC is bad communication because it's poor-quality communication was one often made by early scholars of CMC, and it's still a really popular argument today – especially among lay people and journalists. In a nutshell, the argument goes something like this. Compared with face-to-face (or FtF) communication, CMC is impoverished, impersonal, ineffectual and emotionally cold. Clearly, not a very positive assessment! It gets worse, however. Because of all these things, CMC is also seen to be generally more uninhibited, more anti-normative and, even, more aggressive. Already you may be thinking that this is not how you've experienced CMC yourself. It's true that, to some extent, we're setting up a bit of a 'straw man' argument – in other words, setting up an argument just so that we can knock it down again. However, really negative perspectives like these are useful because they raise a number of important questions which we think should always be asked whenever people start making allegations about the nature of CMC:

- Is CMC really cold and impoverished? Is it always like this?
- Is CMC really uninhibited and aggressive? Is it always like this?
- Is CMC really different from FtF communication? Is it always like this?

As you can see, a recurring theme in this line of questioning is whether or not it's possible to say *conclusively* what CMC is like, and whether it's *always* this way. In other words, what we want to know is just how possible it actually is to generalize about CMC. Furthermore, how far can online communication be explained in terms of the technology itself or are there other social and contextual factors which help us better understand the way people communicate online. For example, like all communication, how do factors such as experience, motivation, relationship history, goals, age, sex, and so on affect CMC? Indeed, it's also worth asking if CMC is really all that different from communication which isn't mediated on the internet. Of course, as we suggested in Basic Theory: Unit 2, we cannot really assume that CMC is going to be the same from one genre or sub-system to the next (e.g. email, chat, webpages, newsgroups).

DEFICIT APPROACHES: PRESENCE, CUELESSNESS AND RICHNESS

Like leading CMC scholars Joseph Walther and Malcolm Parks (2002), we think one of the best ways to get to grips with the nature of CMC is to review some early studies of social interaction and technology. While some of the issues raised by early studies have since been addressed by scholars, others remain firmly locked in the popular imagination and continue to shape the way many people view online communication. In particular, we want to review three models about communication and technology which we call **Deficit Approaches** because they suggest that technologically mediated communication – and especially text-based CMC – *lacks* important qualities of FtF communication and so will always be inadequate. We'll then move on to consider an important critique of these deficit approaches known as the Social Information Processing model.

THE SOCIAL PRESENCE MODEL

BOX BT4:5 DEFINING SOCIAL PRESENCE

Social presence refers to the level of interpersonal contact and feelings of intimacy experienced in communication. In communication theory, this kind of psychological closeness is also sometimes labelled 'immediacy'. Social presence is communicated through visual cues like facial expressions, gestures and eye contact.

In the 1960s and 1970s, scholars looking at telephone communication (e.g. Short *et al.*, 1976) proposed that different modes of communication involved different degrees of 'social presence'. On this basis, different types of communication could be ranked according to whether they were (1) unsociable or sociable, (2) insensitive or sensitive, (3) cold or warm, and (4) impersonal or personal. What the Social Presence model proposes is that having fewer visual cues leads to low social presence which, in turn, leads to more task-focused and less relationship-focused communication. Because of this, scholars initially assumed that text-based CMC would rank very low because it clearly lacks the visual cues of FtF communication. Email, for example, falls somewhere between business letters and the telephone in terms of its social presence. Needless to say, FtF communication comes out pretty high on all the dimensions of social presence. In fact, one of the main criticisms of this first deficit approach is its assumption that FtF communication is an *optimal* form of communication. You just have to think about a really boring class you've attended to know that FtF, bodily presence is no guarantee of warm, personal, or sociable communication!

THE CUELESSNESS MODEL

BOX BT4:6 DEFINING CUELESSNESS

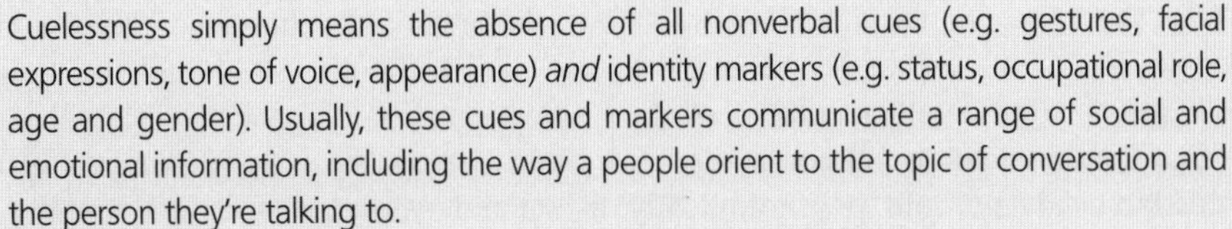

Cuelessness simply means the absence of all nonverbal cues (e.g. gestures, facial expressions, tone of voice, appearance) *and* identity markers (e.g. status, occupational role, age and gender). Usually, these cues and markers communicate a range of social and emotional information, including the way a people orient to the topic of conversation and the person they're talking to.

In a similar way to the Social Presence model, other scholars (e.g. Rutter, 1987) have proposed that the absence of visual and paralinguistic cues in technologically mediated communication means that 'psychological distance' is increased, which leads to more impersonal communication. This can be a good thing, because it means we're less prejudiced by status and physical appearance, but it can also be a bad thing, because communication is more clumsy and unspontaneous. According to Russell Spears and Martin Lea (1992), however, one of the most obvious problems with the Cuelessness model is the way it generalizes about the nature of mediated communication. What, they ask, about telephone hotlines, for example? In this case, it's precisely the *absence* of social cues that makes the telephone perfect for intimate, sexy exchanges. The same could be said of a love note scribbled on a scrap of paper and passed across a classroom. Some communication can be high in cuelessness but still be psychologically close. Surely what matters here is the *purpose* of the communication?

THE MEDIA RICHNESS MODEL

BOX BT4:7 DEFINING MEDIA RICHNESS

The media richness of a communication technology is determined by (1) its bandwidth or ability to transmit multiple cues, (2) its ability to give immediate feedback, (3) its ability to support the use of natural or conversational language, and (4) its personal focus.

The third deficit model considered here is the Media Richness model whereby scholars (e.g. Daft and Lengel, 1984) proposed that people prefer to use the 'richest' communication medium to enable the most efficient means of understanding each other. The more complex the communication task, the richer the medium that is needed. In these terms, a personal or intimate message will always require a 'rich' medium like the telephone – or, better still, FtF communication. By contrast, it was assumed that poor (or 'lean') media like text-based CMC genres like email cannot facilitate such emotionally complex interactions. Once again, face-to-face, *spoken* communication necessarily ends up being privileged over technologically mediated, *text-based* communication. What's more, as CMC scholar Patrick O'Sullivan (2000) has shown, there may also be very good reasons why we actually *want* a 'poorer' medium for communicating something complex. For example, students can avoid showing their nervousness better if they use a quick, businesslike email to request an extension from their course leader. 'Lean' media can also be a way of avoiding the discomfort of breaking bad news to people; for example, young people report sometimes breaking up with boyfriends or girlfriends by using instant-messaging (Pew Report, 2001) or even text-messaging (Thurlow and Brown, 2003).

What these three deficit models show is how scholars initially theorized interpersonal processes or dynamics when people communicate using technology. Although the studies mostly pre-dated research on computers, the assumption initially made by CMC scholars was that communication via computers and, by extension, the internet, was therefore destined to be always cold, psychologically distant and overly task-focused. Nothing, it was feared, could really compare with the detail, fluidity, warmth, intimacy and sociability of FtF communication.

SOCIAL INFORMATION: PUTTING THE PERSONAL BACK INTO INTERPERSONAL

One of the biggest problems for CMC is this tendency for people to idealize offline, FtF communication. In fact, it's not just a problem with CMC. Some time ago, communication scholar Nikolas Coupland and his colleagues (1991) suggested that people often make the mistake of assuming that successful communication can be taken for granted. Instead, they argued, *all* communication is potentially miscommunication. ◎ This really puts FtF communication in its place: no communication, whether mediated or not, is perfect. Nonetheless, the problems with the deficit models don't just end there. Between them, the three models also raise many other questions, most important of which are:

◎ We recognize this most easily when we have those frustrating 'but that's not what I meant' kinds of arguments. Or the kind of disagreement which runs 'I can't believe you took me seriously, I was only joking.' Meaning is *always* a matter of negotiation.

- Does the absence of visual and social cues *necessarily* mean a loss of sociability?
- Does task-oriented communication *necessarily* preclude relational communication?

THE SOCIAL INFORMATION PROCESSING MODEL

Well, in a classic paper Joseph Walther (1992) answered these questions by proposing the **Social Information Processing** (SIP) model of CMC. To start with, Walther noted the inability of experimental studies like most of those used in the Deficit Approach studies to make generalizations about what happens in everyday life. It's one thing for scholars to *model* CMC in theory, but it's another to know if this is really how people behave or feel when actually *doing* CMC. Walther also went further, stating that:

> Given sufficient time and message exchanges for interpersonal impression formation and relational development to accrue, and all other things being equal, relational [quality] in later periods of CMC and FtF communication will be the same. (1992: 69)

What he meant by this was that our basic need for social bonding is the same in CMC as it is in FtF communication. We still want people to like us and we usually strive to connect with people. With text-based CMC exactly the same thing is true, only it all just takes a little longer. Given sufficient time, however, people get used to CMC and develop ways of compensating for the loss of non-verbal cues – in Walther's own terms, they learn new ways of 'verbalizing relational content'.

BOX BT4:8 THE COMMUNICATION IMPERATIVE

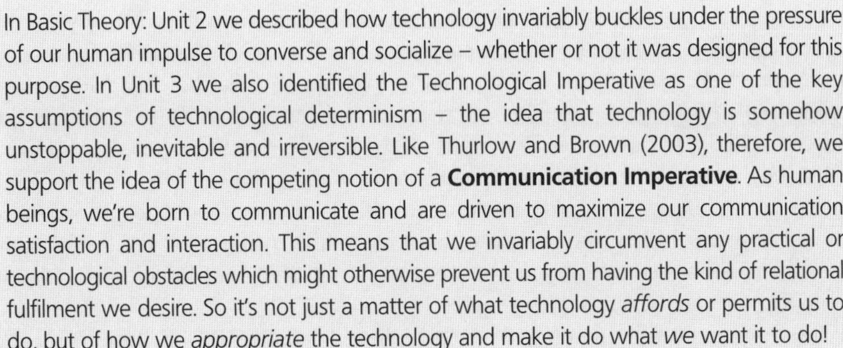

In Basic Theory: Unit 2 we described how technology invariably buckles under the pressure of our human impulse to converse and socialize – whether or not it was designed for this purpose. In Unit 3 we also identified the Technological Imperative as one of the key assumptions of technological determinism – the idea that technology is somehow unstoppable, inevitable and irreversible. Like Thurlow and Brown (2003), therefore, we support the idea of the competing notion of a **Communication Imperative**. As human beings, we're born to communicate and are driven to maximize our communication satisfaction and interaction. This means that we invariably circumvent any practical or technological obstacles which might otherwise prevent us from having the kind of relational fulfilment we desire. So it's not just a matter of what technology *affords* or permits us to do, but of how we *appropriate* the technology and make it do what *we* want it to do!

The fact of the matter is that, as you may already know from your own experience, people make and maintain good relationships online all the time. Indeed, over the last ten or so years Joseph Walther and other CMC scholars have been pretty busy doing more research along these lines. Their research findings reveal how relational and contextual factors can enhance the interpersonal nature of CMC in spite of any technological constraints (see Box BT4:9). In each case, the traditional concerns of the Deficit Approach models become more and more difficult to support.

BOX BT4:9 UNCOVERING THE INTERPERSONAL NATURE OF CMC

- **Time spent online.** Confirming the SIP proposal, CMC gets more personal the longer people spend interacting each other (Walther and Burgoon, 1992).
- **Previous interaction.** Having a relationship history increases people's feelings of interpersonal connection in CMC (Walther *et al.*, 2001).
- **Anticipation of future interaction.** Knowing that there'll be chances to interact again increases people's relational commitment in CMC (Walther, 1994).

- **Expectations and motivation.** Having a high expectation of, and motivation towards, online interaction improves the relational dimension of CMC (Utz, 2000).
- **Chronemics.** Reading time-related messages (e.g. the automatic time-stamps in emails) can increase feelings of intimacy and attraction (Walther and Tidwell, 1995). ◎
- **Emoticons.** Using graphical markers (or 'smileys') can make people feel more expressive and thus interpersonally connected in CMC (Walther and D'Addario, 2001).

◎ 'Our notions of time, how we use it, the timing of events, our emotional responses to time, even the length of our pauses all contribute to the communicative effect of time' (Burgoon, 1994: 133).

GOING HYPERPERSONAL: ONLINE IMPRESSION MANAGEMENT

It's not just in CMC that we scramble to piece together as much information as we can about people and struggle to make sure they get the right idea about us. Many years ago, the internationally renowned communication scholar Erving Goffman (1959) observed that we spend the greater part of our waking lives doing what he called **impression management**: forming impressions of others and trying constantly to influence their impressions of us. In fact, we're doing this all the time – even those people who like to say that they're not bothered by what people think of them. This is why communication ends up like an 'information game' as we strive to find out things about people and decide what and how much they should know about us. While it may look like 'information management', however, the only reason we really want all this information is so that we can support our relationships with people.

If the Communication Imperative is to be believed (see Box BT4:8), communication mediated by technology is just as susceptible to the demands of impression management as any other kind of communication. In fact, two good examples of this can be seen in Box BT4:9 where CMC participants have been found by researchers to capitalize on time tags and emoticons in order to create the right impression or to get a favorable impression of other people. It's all about making the most of what's available to foster a warm, friendly atmosphere. This is what Walther and Parks (2002) call the 'cues filtered in' approach to CMC, or what Patricia Wallace (1999) humorously calls the 'socio-emotional thaw'. In other words, in spite of the apparent coldness of CMC because of its lack of non-verbal and social cues, users eventually start to 'warm up' CMC by substituting other cues and reading existing cues more carefully. Some of the ways this can be done are shown in Box BT4:10.

BOX BT4:10 REINSTATING SOCIO-EMOTIONAL CONTENT IN CMC

- **Creative keyboard use.** Discussed in more detail in Central Issues Unit 4, and in addition to emoticons, other typographic forms like capitalization and acronyms (e.g. LOL, ROTFL) are used with creative effect to convey paralinguistic cues. Also, in MUDs and IRC, participants may use *actions* or *emotes* – short, sometimes pre-programed, phrases to express various sentiments or behaviors (e.g. **Del24 hugs Jules and feels all fuzzy inside**).

- **New identity markers.** People pay attention not only to the time-stamps in emails, but also to clues revealed about someone from their email address (e.g. if it ends in <.gov>, <.com> or <.ac> or <.edu>) and their chatroom nicknames because, as research shows, people often use a 'nick' which conveys information about them (e.g. <shydude>, <welsh4ever> or <pilotJim>).
- **Bending language rules.** Even with nothing but text, we can still tell a great deal about people from the language they use – their vocabulary, their grammar, their style. Besides, if we can't actually see social cues like age, sex and looks, we can always just ask. In CMC this is known as 'MORFing' (i.e. 'are you Male OR Female?') and often appears in the form of A/S/L? ('age, sex, location'). This kind of direct request would seem pretty rude in FtF communication but it's considered acceptable in CMC.
- **Going multimodal.** Finally, it's also common that people supplement traditional, text-based CMC with other channels of communication, so that online chatters often 'fill in the gaps' with email, snail-mail, telephone calls, personal homepages and even FtF meetings. Besides, much of the time people use online communication to maintain pre-existing offline relationships. ◎

◎ This is actually an important point also made by Walther and Parks (2002), who go on to discuss the way online relationships often come offline and how offline relationships come online. In practice, the divide between the two is much less clear.

It's partly because of all these options that are available to CMC that, a few years after proposing the Social Information Processing model, Walther (1996) went even further by putting forward the idea of **Hyperpersonal Communication** in CMC. What he meant by this was that CMC can actually be *more* friendly, social and intimate than face-to-face communication – in his own words, it 'surpasses normal interpersonal levels'. He identifies three very good reasons why someone might find CMC more enjoyable, more socially fulfilling, than FtF communication. What's interesting is that these factors often rely on what the Deficit Approach would have us believe are obstacles to intimacy.

BOX BT4:11 HOW COME HYPERPERSONAL?

- **Birds of a feather.** Online participants often have a shared group membership (e.g. an online support group) and so can end up thinking that they are more similar than they may in fact be. We always like people who are like us! (See also Central Issues: Unit 6.)
- **Looking good!** The visual anonymity which is often part of CMC means that participants can also optimize their self-presentation and maybe also stop worrying about they way they look. Both these things usually make us feel more relaxed and happy within ourselves.
- **You're all mine.** Especially with asynchronous CMC (e.g. email), CMC can slow things down a little, giving participants time to compose their messages more thoughtfully and perhaps be less distracted by other things going on. It's always nice when we think someone's paying special attention to us.

LOOKING TO THE REAL WORLD: PUTTING THINGS INTO PERSPECTIVE

BOX BT4:12 THE SYNTOPIA PROJECT: LIFE ONLINE IN THE UNITED STATES

Arising out of their extensive research on US internet use between 1995 and 2000, James Katz and Ron Rice (2002) have found a *synergy* between people's online activities and their 'real-world' lives. As one of many communication technologies, the internet is used as an extension and enhancement of people's daily routines. Katz and Rice therefore conclude the following: 'Contrary to media sensationalism, the internet is neither a utopia, liberating people to form a global egalitarian community, nor a dystopia producing armies of disembodied, lonely individuals. Like any form of communication, it is as helpful or harmful as those who use it.' [**www** BT4:1]

◎ MOOs are like MUDs – both are traditional, text-based CMC environments where people use text to describe and create an imaginary environment (see Basic Theory: Unit 2). In many ways, they are a hybrid of role-playing games and online chat.

When scholars step away from lab-based experiments, and step into the real world to conduct studies of what ordinary people are doing in CMC, then allegations about CMC being necessarily impersonal and cold are easily put to rest. In fact, whatever your intuitions may tell you, and despite what you already know, it's always important to *observe* what people do and to find out how people *feel* about what they're doing. In fact, while Walther and his colleagues have been carefully mapping the interpersonal dynamics of CMC, other researchers like Malcolm Parks and his colleagues have been doing just this: observing the kinds of relationships people form across different domains of CMC.

BOX BT4:13 MAKING FRIENDS IN CYBERSPACE

- **Relationships in newsgroups.** In a survey of 176 relatively long-term newsgroup users, Parks and Kory Floyd (1996) found that personal relationships were indeed common and sometimes even romantic. Friends communicated with each other on a weekly basis and, perhaps not surprisingly, the more frequently people interacted online the deeper their relationship was.
- **Relationships in MOOs.** In a survey of 235 regular users of MOOs, Parks and Lynne Roberts (1998) found that nearly all respondents had formed ongoing personal relationships: friends, close friends or romantic partners. Levels of relational development were typically moderate to high and marked by depth, interdependence and commitment. Most relationships had moved to other CMC genres, and a third had resulted in FtF meetings. ◎

Clearly, people do make friends in cyberspace. And they don't just leave it there, either. Sometimes these relationships become quite intimate; sometimes they also come offline. In fact, as large-scale, longitudinal surveys like James Katz and Ron Rice's Syntopia Project show, the line between online relationships and offline relationships is invariably blurred. Nowadays, far from being a cold, impersonal mode of communication, CMC is just one of many ways people have of forming and sustaining relationships.

BOX BT4:14 THE INTERNET: A 'TOGETHER PLACE'

Katz and Rice conclude that people are very busy doing social things online by building networks of contacts and participation. These are just a few of the ways it's being done:

- illness support groups
- educational mentoring/tutoring
- family-related activities
- making charitable contributions
- game playing and hobbies
- connecting ethnic minorities
- planning friendship reunions
- organizing political gatherings

As Russell Spears and his colleagues (2001) note, the main mistake made by early approaches to CMC was that they assumed *social* efficiency was the same as *technical* efficiency. In other words, the smaller the technical bandwidth (i.e. the amount of information capable of being transmitted), the smaller the socio-emotional bandwidth. As it's been proved, it doesn't have to be a problem if technology limits the information, we can still communicate a lot to each other. It's always a risky business making simplistic explanations of, or generalizations about, complex social phenomena like communication – especially those which neglect the significance of human relationships.

REVIEW

In this unit we started by sketching the allegations that CMC is necessarily asocial and antisocial, before reviewing three deficit approaches to communication and technology: the Social Presence, Cuelessness and Media Richness models. As a way of critiquing and contextualising these early ideas, we introduced the Social Information Processing model as well as the notions of a Communication Imperative and of Hyperpersonal Communication. Examples were given of studies which demonstrate the interpersonal and relational nature of CMC. Examples of strategies for online impression management were also identified.

STIMULUS READINGS AND RESOURCES

Note. Written by key scholars in the field, the first two readings offer more detailed overviews of the major approaches to computer-mediated interpersonal communication. We recommend you read just pp. 529–43 of the Joseph Walther and Malcolm Parks reading (to start with, anyway).

Baym, N. (2002). Interpersonal life online. In L. Lievrouw and S. Livingstone (eds), *The handbook of new media* (pp. 62–76). London: Sage.

Walther, J.B., and Parks, M.R. (2002). Cues filtered out, cues filtered in: Computer-mediated communication and relationships. In M.L. Knapp and J.A. Daly (eds), *Handbook of interpersonal communication* (3rd edn) (pp. 529–63). Thousand Oaks, CA: Sage.

Note. In these next readings we offer just two examples of surveys (one from the United States and one from Britain) which show how different groups of people are developing relationships and making friends online.

Katz, J.E. and Rice, R.E. (2002). Chapter 9: Involvement examples: evidence for an 'invisible mouse'? In *Social consequences of internet use: Access, involvement, and interaction* (pp. 161–200). Cambridge, MA: MIT Press.

Holloway, S.L. and Valentine, G. (2003). Chapter 6: Cybergeographies: children's online worlds. In *Cyberkids: Children in the information age* (pp. 127–52). London: Routledge Falmer.

IDEAS FOR FURTHER DISCUSSION AND INVESTIGATION

1 Do people actually use emoticons and acronyms? Some researchers suggest that nowadays they've become pretty unfashionable. What do you think? Survey your colleagues to see what the general opinion is. You could also review recent emails you've received or your instant messaging in the space of a week. How many instances of emoticons did you find? What were they being used for? You may like to draw on the following sources: Witmer and Katzman (1997) or Walther and D'Addario (2001), as well as online listings of emoticons [**www** BT4: 2] and acronyms [**www** BT4: 3].

2 The fact of the matter is that many people turn to the internet for emotional and psychological support. This usually involves a lot of trust, intimacy and self-disclosure. Have a look at the support networks listed by Steve Harris [**www** BT4: 4] or SupportPath.com [**www** BT4: 5]. You may not be able to access the newsgroups/listservs, but visit some of the websites. What kinds of issues and concerns are addressed? Thinking about the nature of CMC, why do you think people turn to the internet for support?

3 The Pew Internet and American Life Project [**www** BT4: 6] runs major surveys to see how Americans, as some of the most online people in the world, are using the internet. (As other countries become more and more 'wired', it's also possible that they'll follow similar patterns.) Go online and review the latest Pew reports to

see how people are actually making use of the internet and incorporating it into their everyday lives. Specifically, look to see how CMC is being used for developing and maintaining relationships.

4 Find a recent journal article which discusses Joseph Walther's (1996) notion of Hyperpersonal Communication. First, give the full academic reference for the article. Second, write one or two sentences to explain what the article is about. Third, with reference to what you've read in this unit, describe how the author (or authors) of the article uses, extends or applies the notion of hyperpersonal communication. If you're desperate, you could always try one of these from our main reference list: Hancock and Dunham (2001), Turner *et al.* (2001) or Caplan (2001).

UNIT 5

EXPLAINING CMC: GROUP DYNAMICS

OVERVIEW

KEY TERMS

reduced social cues
disinhibition and deindividuation
polarization
anonymity and conformity
cohesion and interactivity
social identity/SIDE model

MAIN OBJECTIVES

- Examine how groups and group identities are established in CMC.
- Introduce the Reduced Social Cues approach to CMC.
- Discuss the main dynamics which underpin group interaction.
- Consider the SIDE model of group communication in CMC.

STARTING WHERE WE LEFT OFF: GETTING TOGETHER ONLINE

We've shown how there was initially a lot of scepticism about the potential for genuine and satisfying communication in CMC based on assumptions about the lack of social and nonverbal cues and the supposedly transitory nature of interactions via computers. However, academic research and, no doubt, your own experience of the internet show that people do get together online and that many of the early claims about the nature of CMC are greatly exaggerated.

www For weblinks and resources visit the CMC website at <www.sagepub.co.uk/resources/cmc>

BOX BT 5:1 WHY DO PEOPLE USE CMC?

Swedish computer scientist Jacob Palme (2000) lists a number of reasons why he thinks people enjoy CMC genres like internet forums:

- *Status and self-esteem*, e.g. being able to communicate with experts.
- *Confidence*, e.g. being able to keep up with your area of expertise.
- *Comradeship*, e.g. being able to counter loneliness through interaction with people sharing your interests.
- *Inspiration*, e.g. being able to exchange ideas.
- *Generosity*, e.g. being able to get and give advice and support.

The fact that people find CMC a satisfying means of communicating has been clear for a long time. Back in 1996, for example, scholars Joan Korenman and Nancy Wyatt (1996) considered the activities and attitudes of mailing list members; they found that people really valued having access to information, the sense of community and being able to discuss their personal experiences. In fact, we know also from the dyadic (or one-to-one) interpersonal communication research reviewed in Basic Theory: Unit 4 that people get together online in a big way – not just in terms of numbers, but also in terms of the intimacy of the relationships they sometimes form. As an indication of just how deep some people's feeling go, have a look at this well known quote from a member of the online WELL community shortly before he died:

BOX BT5:2 FAREWELL TO THE WELL

I could start off by thanking you all, individually and collectively, for a remarkable experience, this past decade here on the WELL. For better and for worse – there were a lot of both – it has been the time of my life and especially a great comfort during these difficult past six months. I'm sad, terribly sad, I cannot tell you how sad and grief-stricken I am that I cannot stay to play and argue with you much longer. It seems almost as if I am the one who will be left behind to grieve for all of you dying . . . (*Wired* magazine, May 1997 [**www** BT5:2] ◎)

◎ Also mentioned in Central Issues: Unit 3, the WELL is one of the earliest and most major online communities [**www** BT5:1].

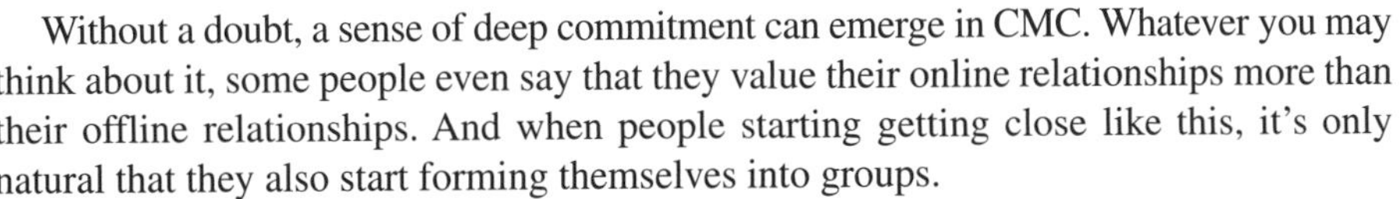

Without a doubt, a sense of deep commitment can emerge in CMC. Whatever you may think about it, some people even say that they value their online relationships more than their offline relationships. And when people starting getting close like this, it's only natural that they also start forming themselves into groups.

WHAT IS A GROUP? WHEN IS A GROUP?

The notion of a 'group' is actually a very slippery concept for social psychologists and sociologists – something they've always found quite difficult to define. For example, there's always a huge amount of variation in terms of size. In other words, how many is a group? Can two people constitute a group? Three people? What about 100 or 1,000? At what point does a group become a crowd or a community? (See Central Issues: Unit 3 for a similar discussion about 'community'.)

BOX BT5:3 DEFINITIONS OF 'GROUP'

Social groups are collectivities of individuals who interact and form social relationships. Primary groups are small and [often] defined by face-to-face interaction; secondary groups are larger and each member does not directly interact with every other (e.g. associations). (Penguin Dictionary of Sociology, *p. 97)*

A social group is where members are all persons who are classified together on the basis of some social/psychological factor(s). There is some degree of interrelatedness or interdependence among group members. (Penguin Dictionary of Psychology, *p. 310)*

What also makes things difficult is figuring out who gets to decide when a group is a group. Is it enough for the people in the group to say that they feel like they're in a group? Or do we need someone outside the group to judge if they look like a group? The first is what we call a phenomenological (or subjective) account, the second is an observational (or objective) account. The fact of the matter is that both ways are useful in helping to define a group.

Whatever confusion there might be about the definition of a group, for most everyday purposes it's sufficient to think of groups as being three or more people who interact fairly regularly and who feel that they're part of a collective. ◉ What then interests scholars of group communication more than anything are the patterns of social influence and processes of decision making in group interactions. In the context of CMC, scholars are especially interested to know how this all happens when people aren't necessarily face-to-face or co-present, and when much of what goes on is still text-based.

◉ A term often used to describe this feeling is *salience*. A group is salient to someone when it seems real or important to them.

STILL IN DEFICIT: THE REDUCED SOCIAL CUES MODEL

The deficit approaches discussed in Basic Theory: Unit 4 were mostly developed at a time when CMC hadn't really begun to take off yet – either in terms of popularity or academic research. However, the work of Lee Sproull and Sara Kiesler (e.g. Sproull and Kiesler, 1986; Kiesler and Sproull, 1992) was directly concerned with CMC. In particular, their **Reduced Social Cues** (or RSC) model, as it's come to be known, is concerned with the negative impact of computer mediation on group processes. Although the RSC model was more cautious than the Cuelessness model, it was also centred around the loss of social cues in text-based interactions. As such, it too is a deficit approach to CMC – or what Joseph Walther and Malcolm Parks (2002) refer to as a 'cues filtered out' approach.

BOX BT5:4 DEFINING SOCIAL CUES

Social cues are either static (e.g. clothing and hairstyles) or dynamic (e.g. facial expressions and gestures) and communicate a sense of status, power and leadership. They also include back channels ('feedback noises') like *uh-huh* and *yeah* which help to show that you are listening or that you want to have a turn in the conversation.

The main argument put forward by the RSC model is that the reduction in social cues makes interactions between people much more difficult to manage and, as a result, conversation becomes less fluid, less easily regulated and altogether more effortful. CMC also ends up being more task-focused, more self-absorbed and uninhibited. It's this lack of inhibition which, Sproull and Kiesler argue, means that CMC tends to undermine social norms and influences. In other words, there's less pressure on people to play by the rules and to behave appropriately. Group decisions are therefore often more extreme than in FtF interactions, and people are more likely to become aggressive with each other.

Nonverbal cues like gestures, posture and facial expressions are certainly very important in managing interactions with people by, for example, showing that you're listening, and helping to facilitate turn taking. Any communication encounter where these are not possible will certainly be more tricky. However, the main problem with the RSC model is that, even though CMC may well be less information-rich or efficient than FtF communication, it can't account for the fact that much more impoverished forms of communication such as letter-writing don't evoke extreme, aggressive or otherwise inappropriate behavior. ◎ Basically, holding computers responsible for a lack of inhibition and any subsequent aggressive or transgressive behavior is too technologically deterministic (see Basic Theory: Unit 3) and there must be other factors at play.

◎ As we discuss in Basic Theory: Unit 6, what constitutes appropriate behavior is inevitably determined by the situation and by people's social standards. The question is always, *whose* social standards?

THE UPSIDE AND DOWNSIDE OF GROUP DYNAMICS

There are in fact a number of dynamics at play in any offline group communication but which can also help understand what's sometimes going on in CMC. These are all social-psychological processes which underpin the ways people construct their identities, make relationships and build communities together. For convenience, we've chosen to highlight a handful of these group dynamics, characterizing them in terms of whether they represent the 'upside' or the 'downside' of group interaction. In other words, some of the communication dynamics emphasize the more negative, disruptive effects of group interaction, while others show a more positive, unifying influence. Together, they serve as conceptual 'tools' with which to describe, and perhaps explain, the nature of CMC.

BOX BT5:5 THE UPS AND DOWNS OF GROUPS DYNAMICS

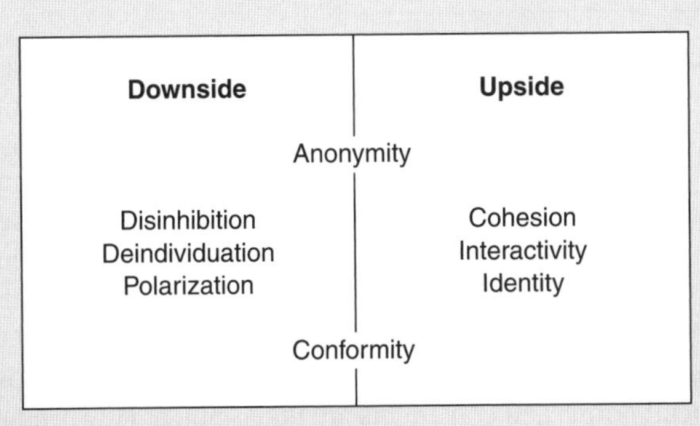

FIGURE 8

Group communication dynamics

THE DIFFERENT FACES OF ANONYMITY

On of the major 'issues' in CMC is the role of **anonymity**. Although we all have a common-knowledge sense of what this word means, it's quite important to be clear about what it means for academic purposes. To start with, as psychologist Adam Joinson (1998) points out, people usually think of anonymity as meaning that they're not *identifiable*. However, while there may often be visual anonymity in CMC because you literally can't see people, this doesn't mean that people are necessarily unidentifiable. It all depends. For example, in a chatroom someone may use a pseudonym (or 'nick') but in an email they'll probably know the other person's name. The point is that anonymity is not an either-or phenomenon, and there are always different *degrees* of anonymity which will vary from situation to situation.

Being or feeling anonymous can make people feel less inhibited by social conventions and norms, but there are different ways of looking at the effect this has on CMC. On the one hand, there's a more positive *freedom from constraints*, while on the other hand there's a more negative *freedom from responsibility*. What we mean by this is that CMC can sometimes enhance communication because people feel less afraid to speak their mind, less worried about their looks and less embarrassed to disclose things about themselves. For example, Australian researcher Lynne Roberts and her colleagues (2000) have found that shy people are much more comfortable opening up in online environments. ◎ However, anonymity in CMC can also be an opportunity for people to let their hair down, go wild and be really offensive to other people. This has been a fairly popular idea about CMC for quite a long time. For example, Rosalind Dyer and her colleagues (1995) previously maintained that verbal aggression occurred four times as much in CMC as in FtF communication. (More about this in Basic Theory: Unit 6.) What's more, the physical distance between people in CMC may also make it easier to rip into someone because you're simply less vulnerable to physical counter-attack! When all is said and done, however, it's usually impossible to know which way people are going to respond to anonymity – it's all about the situation, the relationship, the topic and so on. In other words, it's all dependent on the *context* of communication (see p. 32).

◎ Lynne Roberts and her colleagues also found that CMC actually enhanced some shy people's psychological well-being *offline*.

DOWN SIDE: DISINHIBITION, DEINDIVIDUATION AND POLARIZATION

BOX BT5:6 DEFINITION OF 'DISINHIBITION'

Any behaviour that is characterized by an *apparent* reduction in concern for self-presentation and the judgement of others. (Joinson, 1998: 44)

One of the central arguments of the RSC model is that the anonymity of text-based CMC causes people to become disinhibited and they simply stop worrying about what people think of them. As we've just shown, this can be a good thing or a bad thing. In the case of the RSC model, however, it's the 'freedom from responsibility' response to anonymity which is at issue. The argument is that, when people feel disinhibited, they lose their sense of identity and so social norms and constraints are undermined. However, as we've just suggested, it cannot be assumed that **disinhibtion** is inevitable in CMC.

As Adam Joinson (1998: 56) argues, disinhibition may well vary depending on what activity people are engaged in: whether an individual is conversing, browsing or publishing on the internet, for example. Joinson also suggests that disinhibtion in CMC is relative – highly contextualized – and not to be taken for granted. This brings us on to the closely related notion of deindividuation which, together with disinhibition, tries to explain why social norms and standards of appropriate behavior *may* disintegrate in groups.

BOX BT5:7 DEFINITION OF 'DEINDIVIDUATION'

Previously held to be an explanation for disinhibition, this entails the subjugation to the group and a concomitant reduction in self-focus.

Deindividuation is a pretty famous concept in sociology and social psychology. With an illustrious history dating from the end of the nineteenth century, 'deindividuation' accounts in part for the way people like soccer hooligans seem to lose self-control in crowds and get carried along to do crazy and sometimes violent things. What seems to happen is that the group activity simply becomes more important and the individual's self-awareness diminishes – it's almost as if the crowd or group takes on a mind of its own.

The trouble with deindividuation and disinhibition in terms of CMC is that it's always a mistake to assume that relational communication is automatically subsumed by instrumental or task-focused communication. Just because you're absorbed in a group activity doesn't mean that you can't always be aware of yourself and your relationships with other group members. Once again, it is all a matter of context: if you feel concerned about what others think (i.e. have invested in the management of their impression) you're much less likely to run amok or to deliberately hurt people's feelings.

This is not to say that being in a group doesn't have any effect on your perceptions or behavior. On the contrary. Groups can change their members' thoughts, feelings, and behavior through various forms of social influence. In fact, social-psychological research has found some very compelling evidence to suggest that making a decision as a group rather than as an individual can lead people to do some slightly odd things. One of these effects is known as 'group polarization'.

BOX BT5:8 DEFINITION OF 'POLARIZATION'

Adjusting behaviours and opinions so that they are oriented or conform to one end of a bipolar continuum. (Reber, 1985: 556)

The notion of **polarization** is a popular one in CMC because researchers have found a tendency towards extreme views in online groups, together with an absence of contradictory or moderating voices. Even in offline groups, when people start talking about controversial issues or have to make tricky decisions, there's a strong tendency for them to swing towards being either very opposed to, or very in favour of, a particular position. Psychologist Patrica Wallace (1999: 75) explains what happens like this: 'talking it over seems to intensify the individual leanings of the group members further towards extremes'. It's thought that decisions or positions become polarized because individuals are more inclined to go even further out on a limb when they know they're not alone in their view – it's a simple matter of strength in numbers. This tendency is also believed to be exacerbated in CMC because of, for example, reduced social cues. The potential for finding and flocking with 'birds of a feather' on the internet is precisely one of its advantages, and yet this can lead to a false sense of security in one's point of view.

NEITHER ONE NOR THE OTHER: CONFORMITY

However extreme the outcome may be, part of the reason why people tend to go with the flow in group discussions is because, like most of us, they also feel the pressure to conform to the majority opinion.

BOX BT5:9 DEFINITION OF 'CONFORMITY'

The tendency to allow one's opinions, attitudes, actions and even perceptions to be affected by prevailing opinions, attitudes, actions and perceptions. (Reber, 1985: 146)

As with anonymity, it's not clear always if **conformity** is a positive or negative force in group interactions. To some extent at least, it's necessary to have conformity if social order and democratic processes are to work. Most of the time people try to strike a balance between sticking blindly with the group and being fiercely independent. Nonetheless, the pressure to conform can still be very strong, especially because we're always comparing ourselves with other people. Sometimes we go as far as *converting* to the majority opinion (i.e. come to accept it as true), but most of the time we just choose to *comply* with it even if we don't believe it. Sadly, it's often easier just to give in to group pressure and go with the flow.

In fact, classic experiments by social psychologists from the 1950s showed how people will sometimes even deny the evidence before their very eyes rather than sound like the odd one out in a group. Interestingly, however, when these experiments have been replicated online, the pressure to conform actually appears to be less strong sometimes. It's thought that this may have something to do with people feeling anonymous and not too influenced by markers of status and the awkwardness of disapproving looks or raised eyebrows, for example. Of course, this doesn't mean that anything goes in CMC or that people feel at liberty to be totally independent and free-speaking. Needless to say, when it comes to group dynamics, the picture is a complex, and often contradictory, one. Much of the time there are other dynamics which mean that we're willingly pulled into groups.

UP SIDE: COHESION, INTERACTIVITY AND IDENTITY

Most of the time it's not that we feel *forced* into conforming but rather that we *want* to fit in and want to help group members stick together. For groups to work at all there has to be some **cohesion**, and it's having a sense of cohesion which makes us feel good about being in a group.

BOX BT5:10 DEFINITION OF 'COHESION'

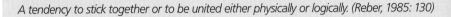

A tendency to stick together or to be united either physically or logically. (Reber, 1985: 130)

Just as with offline life, customs and conventions of communication and behavior emerge in CMC regardless of any efforts on the part of people to instigate them. One of the most obvious examples of this is the format and register of emails. It's not so long ago that relatively few people used emails. Even now, no one ever really tells us how to write an email, and yet most of us seem to follow unwritten rules about what an email should look like, how long it should be, what topics are best suited to emails, and so on. In fact, there are numerous ways in which online groups can exert social influence or control over members without having to get too heavy-handed and without the usual physical and non-verbal markers of power and persuasion.

BOX BT5:11 SOCIAL-CONTROL STRATEGIES ONLINE

There are some obvious ways in which group cohesion and solidarity are maintained online, many of which would be either completely unnecessary or even inappropriate in FtF communication:

- *Netiquette.* Often unspoken rules about what's regarded as polite, respectful, sociable behavior online [e.g. **www** BT5: 2].
- *Signs.* In virtual reality environments like MUDs and visual chat there are usually clearly indicated directions and explanations for what things are and what participants are expected to do. (See the example copied on p. 114 of Central Issues: Unit 3.)
- *FAQs.* A very common feature of many environments in cyberspace – including the web – are listings of Frequently Asked Questions to guide people to useful information but also to maintain a sense of gentle social control over participants' activities [e.g. **www** BT5: 4–5].

Margaret McLaughlin and her colleagues (1995) note how, in CMC, it's not uncommon for individual disapproval to be expressed quite blatantly if participants disturb the cohesion of a group – however unwittingly. For example, people in newsgroups or mailing lists will often reproach anyone who breaks the local rules of a group such as when a newcomer (or 'newbie') uses crude language, forwards a message without permission, has an excessively long signature, or replies to the whole group instead of the individual concerned. In most public-access CMC systems there are also moderators, sysops (system operators), or wizards – appointed facilitators, organizers and supervisors of the particular newsgroup, bulletin board, mailing list or chatroom. Moderators of online chat spaces like IRC (Internet Relay Chat – see Fieldwork Task 4) can, for example, kick people out for a while if they've been misbehaving, or even ban them indefinitely for repeatedly going against the group's code of practice. Individual users too always have the capacity to filter emails or block unwanted messages in chat spaces.

Much of what happens in group CMC is therefore no different from the dynamics of any offline group interaction, although admittedly with the added effects of *relative* anonymity and physical distance. There are, however, other special features of CMC which may facilitate group communication. One case in point is what Sheizaf Rafaeli and Fay Sudweeks (1997) call 'networked interactivity'.

BOX BT5:12 DEFINITION OF 'INTERACTIVTY'

The extent to which messages in sequence relate to each other, and especially the extent to which later messages recount details of earlier messages. (Rafaeli and Sudweeks, 1997)

According to Rafaeli and Sudweeks, **interactivity** can help explain how groups – and especially CMC groups – stick together because it's an important means of facilitating engagement and helping to sustain the stability of group membership. Interactivity is obviously a desirable aspect of all communication and is certainly not unique to CMC. However, it's the technological capacity of the internet to support interactivity which is a tremendous advantage in CMC – whether it's synchronous or not.

In a study of some 4,000 messages in public discussion groups on the internet, Rafaeli and Sudweeks looked to demonstrate how interactivity plays out in CMC. They found that a substantial number of messages were either *interactive* (i.e. commenting on connections between previous messages) or at least *reactive* (i.e. referring to a single message). They also found that more than 20 percent of the interactive messages contained an attempt at humour while more than 30 percent contained evidence of self-disclosure. According to Rafaeli and Sudweeks, frequent reference to past messages – sometimes cut-and-pasted into current messages – reveals processes of group participation, integration and bonding. Picking up on the kinds of allegations made by the Reduced Social Cues model, the conclusion they draw is this:

> The content on the net is less confrontational than is popularly believed: conversations are more helpful and social than competitive. Interactive messages seem to be more humorous, contain more self-disclosure, display a higher preference for agreement and contain many more first-person plural pronouns. This indicates that interactivity plays a role in the social dynamics of group CMC, and sheds a light on comparing interactive messages with conversation. The focus, we propose, should be on the glue: *that which keeps message threads and their authors together*, and what makes the groups and their interaction tick. (Emphasis theirs)

IDENTITY AND THE SIDE MODEL OF CMC

The truth of the matter is that we don't need FtF spoken communication to feel social or to feel part of a group. In fact, it can be better if people don't see each other. For example, if we can't see someone, we're not going to be so influenced by obvious differences between us or other physical markers (e.g. their funny looks, weird voice or uncool dress sense). As a result, we may well end up feeling more connected to the other person than would otherwise be the case. What's more, social psychologists have known for some time that group identity doesn't have to be based on real similarities or actual shared interests, and this is precisely the point made by the Social Identity Model of Deindividuation Effects in CMC.

It's a bit of a mouthful, but the **SIDE** model (for short) has made a very important contribution to scholarly thinking about the nature of CMC. Coinciding with Joseph Walther's critique of deficit approaches in CMC (Basic Theory: Unit 4), the SIDE model is based on work by Russell Spears and Martin Lea from the early 1990s. As is evident from the name, the SIDE model tries to explain CMC in terms of the combined effects of social identity and anonymity (or deindividuation). The model can be quite tricky to follow and so we suggest the following overview.

The SIDE model is based on the idea that a person's identity is comprized of their individual or *personal identity* and their group or **social identity**. ◎ Sometimes our personal identity is important to us; at other times, however, we prefer to think of ourselves as being like other people and so we prioritize our social identity. We do this all the time, irrespective of whether we're offline or online. What's interesting about social identity is that we don't really need to know very much about other people to feel connected to them – to perceive themselves as all being part of the same social group. In fact, the decision to switch from personal to social identity is based on what's been called the *minimal group phenomenon*. What this means is that our social identity is activated by a *perception* of group membership, and it's not so much a question of whether you're behaving in a group, as much as it is about the fact that you *feel* like you're in a group. We usually need only minimal information – just one or two points of comparison – about another group to think of ourselves as being part of a distinct and special group. In doing so, anyone like us becomes a member of the 'ingroup' while everyone else is automatically relegated to 'outgroup' status.

◎ The SIDE model is based on Social Identity Theory (or SIT) which has been around since the early 1980s and continues to be a hugely influential in social psychology.

According to the SIDE model, group interactions can be very strong in CMC and, as a consequence, the negative effects of group dynamics don't often happen in the way that the Reduced Social Cues model would have us believe. In fact, rather like Joseph Walther's ideas about hypersonal communication in CMC, Spears and his colleagues (2002) conclude that CMC represents a *more* intrinsically social medium of communication than the apparently 'richer' face-to-face communication. What they mean by this is that anonymity and deindividuation don't actually lead to the loss of identity, but instead they can motivate people to switch from their personal identity to their social identity. With fewer social and nonverbal cues, we're more likely to give people the benefit of the doubt. And the more salient social identity is for participants the greater group cohesion will be.

REVIEW

In this unit we started by outlining the sometimes problematic notion of 'group' before introducing the fourth 'deficit approach' to CMC: the Reduced Social Cues approach. We then went on to look at some major group dynamics: anonymity, disinhibition, deindividuation polarization, conformity, cohesion, interactity and identity. In particular, we examined the SIDE model of social identity in CMC.

STIMULUS READINGS AND RESOURCES

Castellá, V.O., Zornoza, A.M.Z., Alonso, F.P and Silla. J.M.P. (2000). The influence of familiarity among group members, group atmosphere and assertiveness on uninhibited behavior through three different communication media. *Computers in Human Behavior*, 16 (2), 141–59.

Joinson, A. (2003). Negative aspects of intra- and interpersonal internet behaviour. In *Understanding the psychology of internet behaviour* (pp. 53–84). Basingstoke: Palgrave Macmillan.

Spears, R., Lea, M. and Postmes, T. (2001). Social psychological theories of computer-mediated communication: social pain or social gain? In W. P. Robinson and H. Giles (eds), *The handbook of language and social psychology* (pp. 601–23). Chichester: Wiley.

Spears, R., Postmes, T., Lea, M. and Wolbert, A. (2002). When are net effects gross products? The power of influence and the influence of power in computer-mediated communication. *Journal of Social Issues*, 58 (1), 91–107.

IDEAS FOR FURTHER DISCUSSION AND INVESTIGATION

1 Organize yourself into a group of about four or five people from your class – preferably people you wouldn't normally hang out with. Set up a simple email distribution list or some other online chat space (see Fieldwork: Task 2). Try and get a short, one-off debate going about a mutually agreed, but fairly contentious, topic such as animal rights or immigration. Make notes about the following. Who controls the conversation? How is turn taking decided and shared? Do some people emerge as discussion leaders? If so, why and how?

2 Find a recent study by the SIDE research team (e.g. Russell Spears, Martin Lea or Tom Postmes) which examines some aspect of group/intergroup dynamics in CMC. Giving the full academic reference, write one or two sentences explaining what the study is about. Then describe how the researchers have extended or applied the SIDE model. If you're not sure, you could always try one of the following studies from our main reference list: Postmes *et al.* (2000), Lea *et al.* (2001), Spears *et al.* (2002).

3 Businesses are often keen to take advantage of new communication technologies such as mailing lists, intranets and teleconferencing. Sometimes they also rely on what's called computer-supported co-operative work (CSCW) and group decision support systems (GDSS) – usually just known as *groupware* for short. Starting with Tom Brinck's brief overview [**www** BT5:6], find out what you can about groupware and the ways it's used to facilitate communication in large organizations. (This is something you may also like to pursue in more detail in Focus Areas: Topic 3.)

4 Track down examples of groups which exist only online – these could be primary or secondary groups (see Box BT5:3, p. 60). How do they seem to be managing group relations? How stable does membership appear to be? One fairly well known example we can suggest is the way that people around the world are organizing themselves into protest groups around issues like global capitalism, the environment and international trade barriers/tariffs [e.g. **www** BT5:7–9]. Arguably, this type of grass-roots organization is where a truly global community may be seen to be emerging. What do you think?

UNIT 6

CONTEXTUALIZING CMC: 'FLAMING' AND EMBEDDED MEDIA

OVERVIEW

KEY TERMS

flames and flaming	embedded media
interactional-normative framework	social capital

MAIN OBJECTIVES

- Consider 'flaming' as a case-study example for basic CMC theory.
- Outline the 'normative-interactional framework' for online aggression.
- Reiterate the inadequacy of decontextualized explanations of CMC.
- Discuss the embeddedness of the internet and everyday CMC.

This unit is slightly different from the other Basic Theory units. What we want to do here is pull together, and recap, some of the main ideas covered so far. The way we'd like to do this is by discussing *flaming* (i.e. aggressive interactions online) as a kind of case-study example of concerns about the deficiency of CMC, and also the persistence of technologically deterministic explanations for online communication. The focus of this case study will be the work of CMC scholars Patrick O'Sullivan and Andrew Flanagin, whose framework for understanding 'problematic behavior' in CMC reiterates the need always to *contextualize* online communication and to avoid simplistic explanations for what are otherwise complex social interactions. Following on from this, and as a way of wrapping up, we end the unit by discussing the notion of 'embedded media' and the importance of considering not just the principles and theory of CMC, but also the daily 'realities' of CMC. In other words, we recommend always keeping an eye on how ordinary people are actually making use of the internet and incorporating (or embedding) it into their everyday communication.

www For weblinks and resources visit the CMC website at <www.sagepub.co.uk/resources/cmc>

CMC: A LICENCE TO THRILL, SPILL AND KILL?

The kinds of allegations made against CMC by deficit approaches like the Reduced Social Cues model are actually quite persistent – often the favorite position of many journalists and other lay people. As you may know from your own experience, there is still a popular idea that online communication cannot really be social and certainly not as social as 'proper' or 'normal' communication – which usually means FtF communication. In these instances, there's a tendency to portray the internet as a problematic communication environment where people feel free to, or even compelled to, behave in extreme and inappropriate ways. This is what we nickname the 'thrill-spill-and-kill' myth of CMC, by which we mean the exaggerated idea that online communication is all about people:

- indulging themselves in abandoned cybersex, gambling and other thrill-seeking activities;
- divulging any number of intimate details about themselves and spilling their guts to total strangers; and/or
- bombarding everyone else online with an endless stream of rude, insulting, aggressive and inflammatory remarks – in effect, killing all sense of online harmony.

We'll come back to the 'thrill-seeking' side of things later in Central Issues: Units 6 and 7 on cybersex and 'addiction'. We've also already looked at the second of these issues in Basic Theory: Unit 4 when we considered the ways people build relationships online which are not all that different from the kinds of relationships they build offline. For now, however, what we want to do is tackle the last of the three issues by addressing the idea of online aggression and the notorious idea of 'flames' or 'flaming' in CMC.

BOX BT6:1 WHAT IS A FLAME?

Flames (or **flaming**) are often understood to be hostile and aggressive interactions in CMC such as:

- incendiary messages
- inflammatory remarks
- rude or insulting messages
- vicious verbal attacks
- nasty and often profane diatribe
- derogatory, obscene or inappropriate language
- overheated prose
- derisive commentary

BOX BT6:2 WHEN IS A FLAME A FLAME?

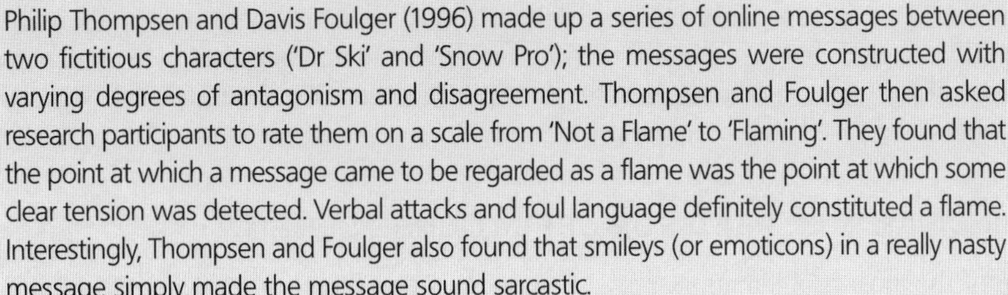

Philip Thompsen and Davis Foulger (1996) made up a series of online messages between two fictitious characters ('Dr Ski' and 'Snow Pro'); the messages were constructed with varying degrees of antagonism and disagreement. Thompsen and Foulger then asked research participants to rate them on a scale from 'Not a Flame' to 'Flaming'. They found that the point at which a message came to be regarded as a flame was the point at which some clear tension was detected. Verbal attacks and foul language definitely constituted a flame. Interestingly, Thompsen and Foulger also found that smileys (or emoticons) in a really nasty message simply made the message sound sarcastic.

According to the Reduced Social Cues approach discussed in Basic Theory: Unit 5, CMC is especially prone to aggression because interaction is less easily regulated and is more uninhibited. Indeed, traditional laboratory studies of CMC (e.g. Siegal *et al*., 1986) routinely found higher percentages of remarks containing swearing, insults, name calling and hostile comments in CMC than in FtF communication. As we've already seen, however, challengers of this research (e.g. Walther, 1992; Spears *et al*., 1992) did not find such high levels of flaming unless participants were under a time pressure. Besides, more naturalistic studies have also found that, while so-called 'flame wars' do occur, they're more common on some sub-systems than on others – for example, in group forums rather than in emails. Different CMC niches clearly have in place different ways of mitigating or controlling aggression.

Although it's been some time since scholars talked about online aggression in such exaggerated terms as 'flame wars' (see 'Ideas for further discussion and investigation' at the end of this unit), there's still at lot of indecision and uncertainty about just how susceptible CMC is to aggression. For example, at the University of Valencia in Spain, Virginia Orengo Castellá and her colleagues compared the levels of flaming in group discussions using emails, video-conferencing and FtF communication. They found that flaming was rare but nonetheless more likely to occur in CMC (i.e. emails) than elsewhere. It is precisely because of this kind of conflicting information about online aggression that we want to present the framework proposed by CMC scholars Patrick O'Sullivan and Andrew Flanagin for analyzing online aggression. We also think this kind of approach offers a number of useful ideas for analysing CMC more generally.

INTERACTIONAL-NORMATIVE FRAMEWORK: CONTEXTUALIZING FLAMES

BOX BT6:3 DEFINITION OF INTERACTIONAL-NORMATIVE FRAMEWORK

An interactional-normative framework focuses on interpretations of messages from multiple perspectives in the situated and evolving context of appropriateness norms. (O'Sullivan and Flanagin, 2003: 67)

In trying to make sense of all the different scholarly ideas about flaming, O'Sullivan and Flanagin recommend using what they call an **Interactional-Normative Framework**. They argue that, like all social behavior, online aggression is extremely complex. This is especially because cultural, local and relational norms about what constitutes aggression usually differ from one person to another; they also change over time, and from one medium (or sub-system) to another. The Interactional-Normative Framework is based on four main principles.

PRINCIPLE ONE: NEED FOR DEFINITIONAL CLARITY

One of the most problematic aspects of flaming is that there's a tremendous amount of definitional ambiguity; in other words, there's simply not enough agreement amongst lay people or scholars about what the term actually means. (Box 1 above shows the range of different ideas people have.) For O'Sullivan and Flanagin, the crux of the problem is this: 'one person's "hostile language" is another person's polite reminder, an attempt at humour, or a poorly worded but well-intended message.'

PRINCIPLE TWO: DIRECT CONSIDERATION OF SOCIAL AND RELATIONAL CONTEXTS

It is precisely because of this definitional ambiguity that the relational nature of communication must be taken into consideration – an outsider cannot really know what's going on between two people in conversation with each other. Something which might sound rude to an outsider may or may not be intended as such by the person who said it. There are many obvious examples of the way we say 'impolite' things to our friends (e.g. 'Don't be such a jerk!' or 'Come on, you old bastard!') but without meaning to be unkind or rude.

Closely related to this idea is the need to examine the interactional norms which guide behavior and help us to understand it. Different groups have different norms for behavior and so also different rules about when people consider a norm to have been violated or broken. Obviously, when chatting among your friends a whole different set of rules about appropriate interaction apply than when you're in a classroom discussion or talking with your parents and so on.

PRINCIPLE THREE: INVESTIGATION OF FUNCTIONS RATHER THAN RELIANCE ON VALUE JUDGEMENTS

Too often people make judgements about the appropriateness of messages based only on message content – on the evidence of the words themselves. But a message cannot be a flame until someone considers it a flame. In other words, it's all about context and function, not simply form and content. A good example of which is swearing in an email or chat message. Who decides whether this is flaming? The person who says it? The person who it is said to? Or what about the person who 'overhears' it (i.e. a third party)?

Most discussions about flaming and online aggression are based on underlying value judgements such that this kind of behavior is always presented as negative, antisocial and undesirable. However, sometimes, a little bit of aggression or tension can be a good thing – the sign of healthy, robust conversation or debate, for example. Odd as it may seem, one of the main functions of name-calling (like the examples we just gave) is to express affection and to bond with people. Rather than assuming that flaming is always bad, and instead of focusing on what it looks like, it's more relevant to examine *why* it occurs and what function it serves.

PRINCIPLE FOUR: PRIORITIZATION OF COMMUNICATION OVER TECHNOLOGY

Finally, the assumption that flaming is in any way unique to CMC, or even necessarily caused by the technology, is nonsense. Such claims can only be technologically deterministic. There are certainly features of CMC (e.g. relative anonymity and the loss of some nonverbal cues) that will shape the way interactions happen, but these factors cannot dictate CMC. It's not helpful to blame the technology when social and relational factors are a better indication of how and when someone's likely to be aggressive or impolite. After all, we've all probably had experiences of aggressive interactions in FtF communication – not to mention on the telephone, in letters, and so on.

As we suggested in Basic Theory: Unit 4, scholars recognize that no communication is perfect. The only way we can really make sense of each other is to rely on interactional norms and relationship histories to help us construct and interpret messages. Taken out of context, words may look impolite, cold or aggressive even if that's not how they were meant. According to O'Sullivan and Flanagin, it's all a question of intention and interpretation: what was intended by the sender of the message and how the message was interpreted by a recipient. And we can make judgements about people's intentions and interpretations only on the basis of the norms of the group they're in and the relationship between them. O'Sullivan and Flanagin demonstrate how this works by presenting various hypothetical scenarios whereby a potential flame is analysed in terms of how it is regarded by the sender, the recipient or an onlooker. We've chosen just four of these scenarios to show you here.

BOX BT6:4 MULTIPLE PERSPECTIVES ON FLAMES

Sender's perspective	Recipient's perspective	Onlooker's perspective	Conclusion
Doesn't intend message to be aggressive	Interprets message as aggressive	Interprets message as aggressive	**A newbie flame** Even though recipient and onlooker judge the message to be inappropriate, the sender doesn't. Perhaps the sender is insensitive to existing norms – or simply ignorant of them because they're new to the group
Intends message to be aggressive	Doesn't interpret message as aggressive	Doesn't interpret message as aggressive	**A failed flame** Even though the sender meant the message to be aggressive or rude, no one saw it that way. Once again, maybe the sender's just new or incompetent
Intends message to be aggressive	Doesn't interpret message as aggressive	Interprets message as aggressive	**A missed flame** In this case the only person who doesn't see the message as a flame is the intended recipient. This could be because the recipient's new to the group and doesn't know when someone's being rude to them!
Intends message to be aggressive	Interprets message as aggressive	Interprets message as aggressive	**A true flame** In this last case everyone's in agreement. The sender intended the message to be aggressive and both the recipient and onlooker interpret it as such. The norms of the group have been deliberately broken and everyone feels offended

FIGURE 9 Multiple perspectives on flames. *Source* Based on O'Sullivan and Flanagin (2003: 78 f.)

In this way, each one of the main principles in O'Sullivan and Flanagin's framework can, we think, be usefully employed in just about any area of CMC. Whatever the topic, the issues are pretty much the same. By tackling the so-called 'dark side' of the internet,

O'Sullivan and Flanagin address many of the erroneous claims typically made about the nature of CMC. Their approach to flaming also sets an excellent example by situating CMC in the broader context of human communication. Like the SIDE model, the Interactional-Normative Framework shows how social factors like group norms and relationship histories will usually be what explain the nature of CMC best of all. It's always problematic when outsiders alone make judgements about what is appropriate or good in a particular communication situation; the perspective of all parties involved always needs to be taken into account.

EMBEDDED MEDIA AND THE DAY-TO-DAY REALITY OF CMC

Based at the University of Haifa in Israel, Sheizaf Rafaeli is one of the editors of the *Journal of Computer-Mediated Communication* [**www** BT6:1]. In 1996 he and his colleague, John Newhagen, published in the first issue of the journal a discussion 'Why communication scholars should study the internet' [**www** BT6:2]. In doing so, they noted what they saw as the five major technical qualities of the internet which distinguish CMC from 'ordinary' communication. The idea is that each individual factor alone doesn't necessarily make CMC special, but rather it's the combination of all five qualities which does.

- *Packet switching:* makes CMC an uncontrolled kind of communication.
- *Sensory appeal:* makes CMC an increasingly multimodal communication.
- *Interactivity:* makes CMC very responsive/reflexive communication.
- *Synchronicity:* means CMC is flexible, high-speed and 'time-warping'.
- *Hypertextuality:* means CMC is non-linear communication.

One of the biggest problems with so much lay (and sometimes also scholarly) thinking about the internet and CMC is the assumption that communication mediated by computing technology is necessarily going to be all that different from FtF communication. In fact, one of the biggest challenges for scholars and students of CMC is trying to distinguish between the *unique* features, the *special* features and the *ordinary* features of online communication. From what we know of things, it's our impression that there's actually not a lot about CMC which is truly unique, although there is much which is very special and certainly very interesting. There's no questioning the fact that communicating via the internet does bring with it a novel mix of advantages and disadvantages. Most of the time, however, what goes on in CMC is pretty ordinary and just like any other kind of communication – just by different means.

When we say that CMC and the internet are 'ordinary' what we mean is that, for many people, they are everyday and not all that unusual – they're a regular, customary part of many people's lives. According to internet scholar Philip Howard (2003) this is what makes the internet an '**embedded media**', which means the way that people are increasingly reliant on the internet to achieve a whole range of daily activities – whether it's shopping, staying in touch with family, advertising professional services, socializing with friends or just taking time out to play games or listen to music. Here's how Howard puts it himself: 'Understanding society online requires that we study media embeddedness – how new communication tools are embedded in our lives and how our lives are embedded in new media.' ◎

◎ Howard wonders how long it'll be before we have to stop calling the internet a 'new' medium. Besides, the boundaries between 'new' and 'old' media are becoming increasingly blurred and so the terms are themselves not altogether useful.

In some respects, the internet is by its very nature more embedded than traditional media like the television, radio and newspapers because it's interactive – not just in terms of people talking to people, but also because, unlike with old media such as television programs, people don't just *consume* internet content but they also *provide* it (e.g. personal homepages and weblogs). All of this means that our engagement with new media is much more active than used to be the case.

BOX BT6:5 HOW EMBEDDED IS THE INTERNET?

The 'embedded media' perspective examines both the *capacities* and the *constraints* of a technology like the internet. In other words, how does it hinder social interaction and how does it facilitate social interaction? According to Philip Howard (2003), this can be assessed in terms of *fit, position* and *link* by asking the following questions:

- Does the internet fit or suit our daily routines? Has it become entrenched into everyday, social lives?
- Does the internet improve people's social position or status? Does it enhance the quality of their lives by increasing information and understanding?
- Does the internet link or connect different spheres of people's lives? Does it do this more efficiently than traditional media?

Judging from many people's lives – especially in the countries of North America, Western Europe and East Asia – it's possible to answer yes to all the questions in Box BT6:5. More often than not, people go online to increase what Robert Putnam (2000) calls their **social capital** which is all about the breadth and depth of their social worlds. This is usually achieved using CMC as a means of reinforcing and enhancing people's existing social networks. Sometimes also, as we've seen in Basic Theory: Unit 4, people use CMC to extend their social networks and make new friends.

However, this doesn't all happen in exactly the same way, and it's not always easy to make assumptions about what people are actually doing in CMC. Not only do different people have different levels of access to the internet (see Central Issues: Unit 1), but different people also use the internet in different ways. In fact, we discussed in Basic Theory: Unit 3 how people don't always use technology in the ways it was intended to be used. According to the embedded media perspective, all these differences in patterns of usership make it vital that scholars undertake local and 'immediate' analyses of CMC – in other words, looking at how specific groups of people use communication technologies in their immediate social contexts.

BOX BT6:6 WHAT BUSINESS WANTS VERSUS WHAT PEOPLE WANT

One concern these days among supporters of cyberspace is the impact of commercialization on the internet, which commentators worry will make it less of a user-driven media and more of a mass medium. Indeed, when it comes to the internet, big business would far rather we were all shoppers than surfers. However, commercial interests can't always control online behavior. David Silver and Philip Garland (2003) have shown nicely how young women quite happily ignore online advertisers' desperate attempts to turn the internet into just another shopping experience. What young women really want the internet for is instant messaging and the chance to chat with friends. In this way we're reminded not to make assumptions about the ways people use the internet – social life online is far from predictable.

In his report *The Internet Goes to College* Steven Jones (2002) reveals how useful it is to investigate local uses of CMC and the internet. In this report Jones presents the findings of his research team's large-scale survey of internet use among several thousand university and college students across the United States. ◎ According to Jones, students are especially heavy users of the internet compared with the general population but, as a group, they are also pioneers of the internet. In this sense, therefore, it wouldn't make much sense generalizing about the role of CMC in the general population based on a survey of students – although there may be some similarities.

◎ It's because it's such a 'networked' country that so much internet research is being done in the United States. The kinds of social patterns portrayed may or may not be applicable to other countries, however.

BOX BT6:7 STUDENTS ARE CMC PIONEERS!

The main conclusions drawn from the *Internet Goes to College* report were as follows:

- Use of the internet is part of college students' daily routine. It is integrated into their daily communication habits and has become a technology as ordinary as the telephone or television.
- For most college students the internet is a functional tool, one that has greatly changed the way they interact with others and with information as they go about their studies.
- College students use the internet nearly as much for social communication as they do for their education. But just as they use the internet to supplement the formal parts of their education, they go online to enhance their social lives.

WRAPPING UP BEFORE MOVING ON

In their review of the literature about online relationships and interpersonal communication (see Basic Theory: Unit 4), Joseph Walther and Malcolm Parks pinpoint one of the most frustrating tensions in studying and researching CMC. Although we are oversimplifying things a little here, Walther and Parks describe two different ways of researching CMC and internet behavior (Box BT6:8) both of which have their strengths and weaknesses.

BOX BT6:8 TWO APPROACHES TO CMC RESEARCH

Approach 1

Strength. There are studies which rely on controlled, lab-based experiments, where researchers try to identify the specific variables and processes which help explain why CMC works like it does (or doesn't). This approach is one usually preferred in mainstream Psychology and Computer Science.

Weakness. The trouble with this type of research is that it tends to single out individual genres of CMC (e.g. email, chat, MUDs) for the purposes of investigation and doesn't really get to see how people actually use these genres in everyday circumstances.

Approach 2

Strength. There are other studies which are more ethnographic, where researchers try to observe and describe what ordinary people do (or don't do) in their everyday CMC practice. This approach is one usually preferred in Sociology, Anthropology and Cultural Studies.

Weakness. The trouble with this type of research is that it isn't really able to explain the variables and processes which explain why CMC works the way it does (or doesn't).

Do you see the problem? The weaknesses of one approach are the strengths of the other – and vice versa. As such, it seems pretty impossible to reconcile the differences between them. Ideally what's needed is a combination of the two, capitalizing on the strengths of both. In effect, this is the same old difference between qualitative and quantitative research; where the one approach looks for ethnographic detail and individual differences, the other looks for experimental control and broad social patterns. What makes things even more complicated in CMC is that, just as scholars begin to pin something down, like the emergence of text-based relationships, the playing field shifts again, with webcams and multimodal interactions which are no longer exclusively text-based anyway.

On this basis, we leave you with one thought as you head off into deeper study of CMC:

> If social worlds were merely relative, that would be easy. If they were merely regular that would be easy. I find myself torn between a desire to savour humanity's myriad ways of being and to uncover how they are all the same. This makes my work difficult. (Glassner, 1979: 1)

This quote is from well known scholar of social interaction Barry Glassner. We think what he's saying here sums up nicely the dilemma we all face when trying to research and study human behavior. The trouble, according to Glassner, is that social life is never unique but neither is it all the same. This means we have always to try and describe the patterns in everybody's ways of doing things and at the same time consider how every one of us is different, attaching different meanings and values to the world around us. In other words, we can certainly make some generalizations about CMC and social life on the internet, but we can never assume that it's true for everyone and all the time. Once again, we are reminded of the paradox represented by our recurring fractal image: a kind of patterned chaos. Everything is different but it's also all the same!

BOX BT6:9 STOP PRESS! SOCIAL RESPONSIBILITY OR CYNICAL PROFITEERING?

Just about the time we were getting this book ready to go to print, Microsoft announced that it had taken the controversial decision to close all of its MSN chatrooms in Britain [see **www** BT6:3]. The reason, said Microsoft, was to protect children from adult abusers. The real reason, say others, had more to do with profit. In other words, chatrooms weren't making any money for MSN.

Have a look also at the Guardian newspaper article titled *The myth of Satan's web* [**www** BT6:4]. This incident has special relevance for Basic Theory: Unit 3, Central Issues: Unit 6 and Fieldwork: Task 4. However, ask yourself, what are the implications of Microsoft's decision – not just for chatrooms but for CMC generally and for the future of social interaction on the internet? What does it tell you about the relationship between technology and society, the struggle between capitalist and democratic values in cyberspace, and about the ways ordinary people choose to interact online?

REVIEW

In this unit we started by considering what flames are, before turning to examine the interactional-normative framework as a way of contextualizing online aggression. This perspective was also presented as a useful means of analysing CMC more generally. We then turned to discuss the notion of 'media embeddedness' and the everyday uses made of CMC and the internet by people to gain social capital. We concluded with a brief look at the two main approaches to studying CMC and the need to combine qualitative and quantitative research methods in order to understand CMC better.

STIMULUS READINGS AND RESOURCES

Baker, P. (2001). Moral panic and alternative identity construction in Usenet. *Journal of Computer Mediated Communication*, 7 (1). Available (4 April 2003) online: <http: //www.ascusc.org/jcmc/vol7/issue1/baker.html>.

Howard, P.H. (2003). Embedded media: who we know, what we know, and society online. In P.H. Howard and S. Jones (eds), *Society online*: *The internet in context* (pp. 1–27). Thousand Oaks, CA: Sage.

Jones, S. (2002). *The internet goes to college*: *How students are living in the future with today's technology*. Pew Internet and American Life Project. Available (2 April 2003) online: <http: //www.pewinternet.org/reports/pdfs/PIP_College_Report.pdf>.

O'Sullivan, P.B. and Flanagin, A. (2003). Reconceptualizing 'flaming' and other problematic communication. *New Media and Society*, 5 (1), 67–93.

IDEAS FOR FURTHER DISCUSSION AND INVESTIGATION

1 Have a look at the account of 'flame wars' given by Wikipedia [**www** BT6:5]. In the light of what you now know about online aggression, what do you make of this 'definition'? What do you make of the notion of 'flame war' itself? In addition to the practical frustration of time lags mentioned here, what other practical or technical sources of frustration can you think of? You might like also to look at the introduction to Mark Dery's (1995) book *Flame wars: The discourse of cyberculture* [**www** BT6:6].

2 One way that people look to be aggressive online is via more frivolous sites like The Dick List [**www** BT6:7]. However, there are numerous examples of hate speech online such as neo-Nazi and other sites like that of the Imperial Klans of America [**www** BT6:8]. What do you make of the difference between these two examples? In what ways do they both reveal something about CMC? To look for more information about hate speech online, you may like to visit the US-based Human Rights Information Network [**www** BT6:9].

3 Thinking about the 'embeddedness' of CMC and the internet, conduct a straw poll of students from elsewhere on campus and find out how they are making use of internet technologies and CMC. How familiar are they with the different technologies (e.g. chat, email, webcams, etc.)? What opinions do they have about the way the internet is developing and changing? You may like to compare your findings with the Pew report by Steve Jones (see stimulus reading on previous page).

STRAND 2

CRITIQUE: CENTRAL ISSUES

'THE CRITIQUE OF RECEIVED IDEAS'

The most important pillar of intellectual life we come to now is what Pierre Bourdieu calls 'the critique of received ideas' (see p. 4). What this means is that, as scholars, we must always question ideas and assumptions which are taken for granted – even if these ideas have been regarded as 'normal' and 'acceptable' by the majority of people for a long time.

Having learned some basic theory, you are now in a strong position to extend your critical awareness and understanding of CMC. In this Central Issues strand, we introduce you to a selection of key issues and current concerns in the field of CMC. Because it offers an overview of important ethical and international issues in CMC, we do recommend that you start with Central Issues: Unit 1. However, the rest of the units in this strand can be read in any order

Remember, what always interests us in CMC is social interaction, and this is all about identity, relationship, and community. Because of this, the issues and concerns raised in each of the units in this strand are central not only to CMC, but also to communication more generally. In fact, as we suggested in Basic Theory units, one very good reason for studying CMC is that we can learn more about the nature of human communication when we look to see how it is affected by technology.

UNIT 1

ONLINE ETHICS AND INTERNATIONAL INEQUITIES

OVERVIEW

KEY TERMS

autonomy
ethics/online ethics
digital divide
globalization
privilege
public sphere

MAIN OBJECTIVES

- Discuss the privilege of internet access and CMC participation.
- Examine a series of related ethical issues which underpin online communication.
- Consider international and other demographic inequities regarding the internet.
- Identify a range of organizations promoting online rights and equalities.

PRIVILEGE AND POLITICS

It's easy to take our privileges for granted. Many people reading this book will live in countries where people are free to say and write pretty much what they want, and to do so without threat of punishments such as imprisonment, torture and even murder.

www For weblinks and resources visit the CMC website at
<www.sagepub.co.uk/resources/cmc>

BOX CI1:1 RIGHTS AND PRIVILEGES

We need to keep in mind that a **privilege** is a special advantage or benefit associated with particular people. Privileges are not 'rights' in the traditional sense that are associated with legal protection, but abilities and benefits that are not earned, but come with assumed social, economic and political power.

Rights	**Privileges**
Legal and political associations	Cultural and social associations
Center on personal freedoms	Center on access to information and power
Deal with issues of security and personal freedom	Deal with issues of socially constructed abilities
Protect against slavery and tyranny	Protect those in power by reaffirming hierarchies
'Human rights should be protected by the rule of law.' (UN Declaration of Human Rights, 1998)	'The real goal of democracy is to embrace differences . . . and expand access to privilege and power.' (Henry Giroux, 1998)

Most of us are surrounded by communication channels and tools that keep us constantly connected to sources of information and to people in our communities: a technological infrastructure. This infrastructure is centered in particular cultures, and we are privileged because as part of those cultures we are able to participate in the technological infrastructure. Email, telephones, mobile telephones, faxes, text-messaging – at any given moment we can be reached through numerous technologies. But think about what's necessary to make all those technologies function. To send email, we need not only an email address, but an internet service provider (which costs some money) and a computer (which costs a lot of money). Think again – what else do you need to be connected? What if you had sporadic electricity? What if you had no telephone lines or mobile network connections?

For a billion people around the world, this is daily reality. Consider the cost of infrastructural basics which people in poor countries do not have (see Box CI1:2).

BOX CI1:2 THE COST OF GETTING ONLINE

- The national average monthly wage of farm workers in South Africa is less than R400 (approximately US$50). Most workers on that wage can't afford transportation into the village to buy groceries, let alone afford to use technology at current prices.
- Students in the Bulgarian capital Sofia have spent as much on monthly housing as they would on their internet service provider connection (Lengel, 2000).
- Citizens in the United States pay 1.2 percent of their average monthly income for internet access.
- That 1.2 percent in the United States is the same as the percentage of a worker's annual income in the following countries: 614 percent in Madagascar, 278 percent in Nepal, 191 percent in Bangladesh, 60 percent in Sri Lanka.

(Bridges.org, 2001; UNDP, 2001)

These figures illustrate what's known as the **digital divide**. This is a popular term that suggests there is a division between nations or communities who have access to communication technology and those who don't. People in those nations or communities who don't enjoy access to technology are often called the 'information have-nots', versus the 'information haves'. More often than not, the 'information have-nots' live in poor nations. Sometimes the 'have-nots' are in disadvantaged groups in the rich nations in North America and Europe. The term also addresses international inequities, which we use to mean not only inequality of access to communication technology, but that this unequal access is also an injustice.

Take a look at the map in Box CI1:3 which illustrates the digital divide. Notice the dark areas where internet participation is most active. Conversely, the lighter the colors are, the fewer people online. United Nations research reports that nearly 90 percent of internet use occurs in richer, usually more industrialized countries which accounts for only 15 percent of the global population (UNDP, 2001).

BOX CI1:3 INTERNET USERS WORLDWIDE

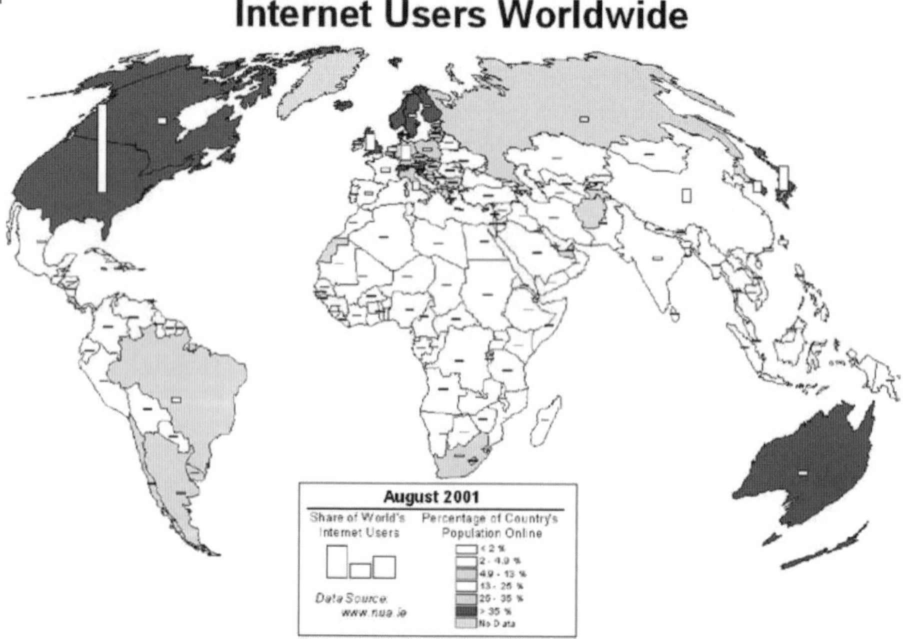

FIGURE 10 Internet users worldwide [WWW CI1:1]. *Source* copyright 2002 Matthew Zook http://zooknic.com

FREEDOM TO COMMUNICATE?

Looking at the map in Box CI1:3, we can't help but wonder who therefore has the privilege to communicate online? Who is left off the map? For what reasons are certain geographical regions hindered in their efforts to get online? The freedom to communicate is often politically and economically charged. While many of those in the privileged debate talk about the freedoms that the internet affords, fewer voices share the challenges of those who are politically and economically disenfranchised. And there are many. There are 1.5 billion members of the world community who live on less than a dollar a day, those who renowned economist Jeffrey Sachs for example (2003) calls 'the bottom billion'. ◉

◉ At present, less than 1 percent of the world's population is part of the so-called 'knowledge economy'.

This bottom billion is part of what is often known as the information- or media-poor. On the other end of the spectrum are the information- or media-rich, those who have easy access to technology and who are able to participate in online communication. The 'information-poor' are left behind as the 'information-rich' progress economically, politically, socially and intellectually. As internet researcher Manuel Castells (2000: 7) claims: 'The ability or inability of societies to master [information] technology, largely shapes their destiny.'

A United Nations report on the digital divide estimates that 4 billion people around the world will probably never get online (UN News Center, 2001). Over half the world's population has never made a telephone call, so certainly well over half have never engaged in CMC. One factor which either can hinder or free communication structures is **globalization**. This concept addresses the increased mobility of goods, services, labor, technology and capital throughout the world. While globalization is not new, its pace has increased with widespread access to the internet and related technologies. Critics contend that globalization promotes the spread of cultural values, norms and practices that stem from capitalist, Western nations. Others suggest that the increased mobility and information flow resulting from globalization lead to more open, free societies. The internet, these scholars suggest, plays a part in that freedom. Nevertheless, despite increasing access to the internet in the poor and newly industrializing nations, the freedom to communicate is still a concern for most citizens in it, because they feel left behind by those in rich nations who have benefited from widespread access to communication technology for many years.

ONLINE ETHICS

You can see from the map in Box CI1:3 that getting online is a privilege not enjoyed by all. Then, once online, there are other important privileges often taken for granted, like privacy, safety and security. Being treated fairly and sensitively online is also a privilege. What do you do if you are treated unfairly online because of the language you speak, or your gender, or other facets of your cultural identity? What if you are marginalized because of who you are in 'real life'? Would you consider changing your identity or becoming anonymous online as a result?

One way to explore these questions is through the study of **ethics** and, in particular, **online ethics**. The study of ethics, also known as moral philosophy, examines how we systematize, defend and recommend ideas about what is right and wrong, given the particular cultural context. Online ethics is a form of ethics specifically pertaining to how we communicate online.

BOX CI1:4 THE BIRTH OF COMPUTER ETHICS

Online ethics stems from computer ethics, which was first developed in the early 1940s by technology developer Norbert Wiener. Wiener and colleagues were commissioned to develop information feedback systems used during World War II. Through this work, 'cybernetics', or the science of information feedback systems, was born. Along with the new scientific field, Wiener also came up with groundbreaking ideas about the ethical implications of technology. (Bynum, 2000)

One way to understand online ethics is to look at the Association for Computing Machinery (ACM) code of conduct [**www** CI1:2]. Founded in 1947, the ACM is the world's oldest and largest educational and scientific computing society. Its membership of 75,000 computing professionals, living and working in more than 100 nations, draws upon the ACM as a forum for exchanging ideas and information about computing.

The ACM is the premier computing organization in the world. Thus you'd expect that the ACM code of conduct would be one of the most important systems of ethical considerations for computing and online activity. While there are numerous other normative codes in computing, such as the Computer Ethics Institute's 'Ten Commandments of Computer Ethics' [**www** CI1:3], the ACM arguably best outlines fundamental ethical considerations pertaining to online communication:

BOX CI1:5 ACM CODE OF ETHICS AND PROFESSIONAL CONDUCT

The AMC code, adapted here, provides a practical look at online ethics.

General moral imperatives

ACM members will . . .

Contribute to society and human well-being.
Avoid harm to others.
Be honest and trustworthy.
Be fair and take action not to discriminate.
Honor property rights including copyrights and patent.
Give proper credit for intellectual property.
Respect the privacy of others.
Honor confidentiality.

More specific professional responsibilities

ACM computing professionals will . . .

Improve public understanding of computing and its consequences.
Access computing and communication resources only when authorized to do so.

Organizational leadership imperatives

ACM members and organizational leaders will . . .

Articulate and support policies that protect the dignity of users and others affected by a computing system.

(Source: ACM [**www** CI1:2])

In thinking about the imperatives in Box CI1:5, what seems to be a central concern is the need to be fair and not to discriminate. Of course, lots of people don't follow this standard. There are many types of discrimination that occur online. For example, you'll read about how women have reported being discriminated against online in Central Issues: Unit 5. Another way we can look at ethics, however, is by examining another type of discrimination – the discrimination that occurs because of international inequality between rich and poor nations that hinders some communities from getting online in the first place.

ADDRESSING ALL KINDS OF INEQUALITY ONLINE

The problems surrounding access and marginalization through communication technology occur not only in poor nations and communities. Other forms of inequality, such as being disenfranchized by differences in language, gender, age, physical ability, race and ethnicity, are evident in CMC throughout the world. Women and girls tend to be treated unequally as they build their skills in computing. Urban dwellers are more likely to engage in CMC than those in rural areas. University graduates are far more likely to have internet access at home than those who never finished high school (NTIA, 2002).

In Central Issues: Unit 4, for example, we discuss how so much web content continues to be in English even though only about 36.5 percent of internet users around the world are actually native English-speakers [**www** CI1:4]. Other cultural difference within countries and continents are also important. For example, researchers argue that there is a digital divide between northern and southern European nations, where 44 percent of the Finnish population is online, compared with only 23 percent of Italians (Darlington, 2002).

Racial and ethnic inequalities are also evident in online communication. Only 5 percent of US internet users are African-American (Nua, 2002). Latino households in the United States are less likely than African-American, and far less likely than Caucasian, US households to own a PC (Statistical Research, 2002). Meanwhile the demographic data on Black British people online is only recently emerging. In 'The truth of multicultural Britain', Sunder Katwala (2001) critiques the British government for not collecting information on ethnicity and internet access, despite its efforts at increasing the number of British people coming online. Similarly the Institute for African-American e-culture notes that all communities, particularly those who are underrepresented, must be involved in technology at all levels, from engaging in CMC to owning the firms that allows them to do CMC. 'Nothing less than such full participation in IT is acceptable in a society which aspires to democracy and freedom' [**www** CI1:5].

For online equity, clearly the most critical factor is economic power. For example, as one of the wealthiest, most heavily 'internetted' countries in the world, the United States too has tremendous inequalities. Consider these demographic details: two-thirds of the population of the United States are online. For those who are economically privileged, the figures rise: nearly 90 percent of all US households with an income of $75,000 are online. By contrast, only a small minority of the poorest segment of the United States (those with an average annual household income under $15,000) are online. Also, White people are more likely than Latinas and Latinos in the United States to benefit from interpersonal communication using the internet (Hacker and Steiner, 2002).

Economic power usually impacts another concern that is often overlooked in equity debates: the speed of access. Researchers say speed and bandwidth are ethical considerations. The majority of users around the world access the Internet over a Public Switched Telephone Network (PSTN), or 'dial-up', far slower than an Integrated Services Digital Network (ISDN) line or Asymmetric Digital Subscriber Line (ADSL) link (Darlington, 2002). Consider conflicts in places like Kosovo. Often the only communication out of such regions is through CMC. With inconsistent telephone connection, however, dial-up access frequently fails, halting the distribution of vital information. Many citizens use CMC to let their families outside conflict regions know they are alive. When the content of CMC communicates life-or-death situations, speed and consistent line access are crucial.

DEMOCRACY: THE PUBLIC SPHERE AND CMC

The idea of democratic discourse and the promotion of civil society through CMC draws on the ideas of German philosopher Jürgen Habermas. Habermas conceptualized the notion of the **public sphere**, a space where informed citizens could reach consensus through open debate. While Habermas analyzed the public sphere in spaces such as seventeenth- and eighteenth-century coffee houses in Europe, CMC scholars have situated Habermas's ideas for the internet as a 'virtual' space where citizens could articulate issue-based politics that were in opposition to dominant ideological and political voices (Mided, 2000). There are numerous online spaces where oppositional CMC is articulated. In 1991 ZaMir Transnational Net [**www** CI1:6], became one of the first spaces of democratic CMC, was created. Named after the Serbo-Croatian word for 'peace', ZaMir was an electronic mail network which allowed people to discuss the complex civil and ethnic conflicts which led to the Balkan wars in the Yugoslav successor states. ZaMir was one of the most valuable communication channels for the anti-war and human rights organizations throughout Southeastern Europe (Herron and Bachman, 2000). Active primarily during the mid to late 1990s, a series of message boards allowed users in Serbia and elsewhere the opportunity to communicate, create alliances and encourage peace (Box CI1:6).

BOX CI1:6 'SARAJEVO ALIVE, SARAJEVO ON LINE'

Our network around the world is linking the people of the besieged city of Sarajevo to the Internet Community. One of the greatest restrictions felt by the citizens of this city is the inability to communicate with the outside world: there is no paper to print newspapers on, there are no telephone lines linked twenty-four hours a day with the outside world.

One respondent on the site wrote:

Every day when I wake up in the morning, I am so happy because I am alive. Many of my friends are dead and so you can see why I am so happy, because in Sarajevo to be alive is a luxury that many people cannot afford. Right now, I am not afraid but if the shellings start again, I would go out of my mind. Those things are the worst experiences in my whole life—besides seeing my best friend's brain blown away.

(Alma Duran [**www** *CI1:7])*

'Voices from Sarajevo', a similar project to ZaMir, provided an online space for teens to develop friendships and communicate daily crises to those on the outside (Box CI1:8).

BOX CI1:7 VOICES FROM SARAJEVO

I want to invite medical students from all around the world to make contact with us. I will be glad if someone brave or courageous enough is going to accept this and be my guest in Sarajevo. Send us all some magazines and let us know what is happening behind 'The wall'. (Medical student Jasmin Ceranic)

These 900 days of the siege have made us learn a lot about life and death, and how you have to do things you never thought of. I live my life like today is my last day on Earth. (Zarko Karamusic)

The outside world . . . is becoming for me as an uncertain rumor. (Marko Vesovic)

GET US OUT OF HERE!!!!!!!!!!
—Sanja, Lejla, Emir, Goran, Edin, Ismar, Lela, Nino, Soopy, . . . and others, seniors in high school, on the 'Sarajevo Online' Internet project

[**www** CI1:7]

The democratic possibilities of the online public sphere are useful only if citizens have access to the internet. Think of the teens in the Voice of Sarajevo online project. How many more teens did not have the privilege of participating in that project? Those who could benefit the most from engaging in the public sphere, those who are most disenfranchised by dominant political and social power structures, are those who more likely than not are unable to engage in CMC.

BOX CI1:8 ATTEMPTS AT COMMUNITY BUILDING

Some efforts to help increase community interaction online involve getting technology into communities. In the case of helping economically disadvantaged persons get online, some initiatives tend to fall flat, while others are built on hype rather than measurable change or action. The British government developed a strategy to increase online access in depressed regions of Britain by donating 100,000 recycled PCs to the nation's poorest families. A year after the launch of the plan, only 6,000 PCs had been distributed. Further, it was estimated that some families would have to wait until 2009 to receive theirs. (Wakefield, 2001)

More successful efforts often center around community technology centers (CTCs), which are neighborhood centers offering free or low-cost internet access and technical training located in libraries, church centers and other community meeting places [**www** CI1:9]. CTCs not only create opportunities for communities to come together in the physical world, but they also support CMC and community network building across communities, cities and nations. Community networks have a long history, with the bulletin board services (BBSs) of the 1980s and FreeNets, or networks that are accessible to community members at no cost, run by volunteers, and emphasizing community involvement, activism and participation in civil society.

While such community services are fairly plentiful in rich nations, they are few and far between in poor ones. Internet Service Providers (ISPs) in poorer countries often charge exorbitant rates, rates that are high even for visitors used to the prices in the rich countries of the North. Often it is not the fault of the ISPs, but rather that of the governments in countries like Morocco which tend to impose high tariffs on imported hardware and software and who maintain telephone monopolies (Lengel and Fedak, 2004).

Examining these conditions in their article 'Africa Goes Online', Daniel Akst and Mike Jensen (2001) suggest that one of the best ways of combatting some of these issues is by encouraging even greater sharing of resources, information and access to CMC. They put it like this:

> Large-scale sharing of information resources is a dominant feature of the African media landscape. A given copy of any newspaper might be read by more than ten people, there are usually perhaps three users per dial-up internet account, and it is not uncommon to find most of a small village crowded around the only TV set, often powered by a car battery or small generator. Why not shared public internet terminals?

JUSTICE: FREE SPEECH ONLINE?

Once people are online, are they treated justly? There are numerous sites distributing unjust and extremist CMC. Owing to free speech legislation, however, it is often difficult to do anything about it. Nevertheless, governments, organizations and communities are trying to block racism and hate online. For example, the Council of Europe's Convention on Cybercrime [**www** CI1:10] encourages European countries to address hacking, virus attacks and the online hate speech found in websites, newsgroups, listservs and IRC (Internet Relay Chat) which distribute racist and xenophobic materials and ideas. IRC channels such as #nazi, #skinheads, #Aryan, #kkk, and #racial-identity, attract users to participate in hate speech online (Glassman, 2000). Certain regions with a history of ethnic strife and increasing nationalism seem to be particularly susceptible to online hate, as evidenced above in the Sarajevo and ZaMir online networks.

Another concern regarding justice is the ability to speak your mind freely. Think what it must be like to live in an authoritarian or semi-authoritarian regime. What you say can and likely will be used against you. Many people living under such a regime will often self-censor their communication (either online or offline) in order to keep safe from government crackdowns (Box CT1:9).

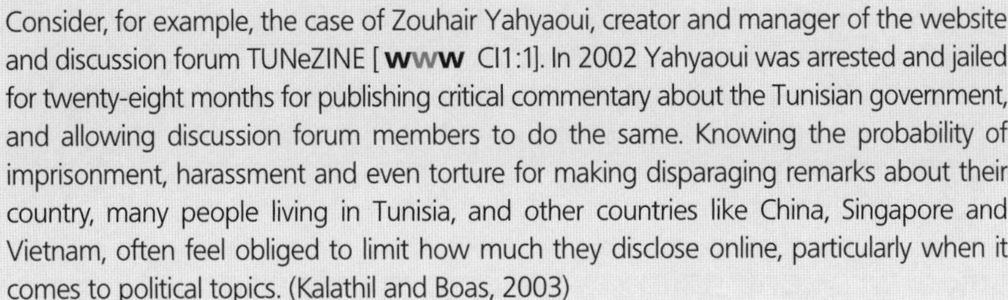

BOX CI1:9 SELF-CENSORSHIP AND CMC

Consider, for example, the case of Zouhair Yahyaoui, creator and manager of the website and discussion forum TUNeZINE [**www** CI1:1]. In 2002 Yahyaoui was arrested and jailed for twenty-eight months for publishing critical commentary about the Tunisian government, and allowing discussion forum members to do the same. Knowing the probability of imprisonment, harassment and even torture for making disparaging remarks about their country, many people living in Tunisia, and other countries like China, Singapore and Vietnam, often feel obliged to limit how much they disclose online, particularly when it comes to political topics. (Kalathil and Boas, 2003)

PRIVACY, CORPORATE COLONIZATION AND OTHER CONCERNS

In an article on the internet and the public sphere, New Zealand-based researcher Lincoln Dahlberg (2001) contends that the increasing state and corporate 'colonization of cyberspace threatens the **autonomy**' of public interaction online:

> State censorship of the Internet and online surveillance continues to threaten free speech and public interaction online, whether it be in the form of official blocks to access or hidden monitoring of messages. An even greater threat to public discursive spaces online may be coming from the increasing privatization and commercialization of cyberspace.

What exactly does he mean by autonomy? The term is derived from two Greek words: *auto*, meaning self, and *nomos*, meaning law or rule. Autonomy suggests independence, free will or action. It means being able to speak or care for oneself, rather than being spoken for by others. Autonomy also means the right to self-govern, as in the way online communities are self-governed, rather than to be regulated or manipulated by an outside body. There are many ways to examine online autonomy, such as how online anonymity can increase autonomy, how students can be more autonomous in their learning through CMC, and how health and medical CMC can increase patient autonomy.

One of the biggest concerns for online autonomy is the right to privacy. For example, Richard Spinello (2001:140), an expert on cyber-ethics, morality and law, notes, 'Privacy is under siege as never before thanks to the power of digital technology.' In much the same way, researchers Seamus Miller and John Weckert (2000: 255) say that 'the coming into being of new communication and computer technologies has generated a host of ethical problems, and some of the more pressing concern the moral notion of privacy.' Problems about privacy in CMC cannot be ignored. In fact, many researchers argue that privacy is *the* most important ethical concern surrounding the internet. Many users want to keep their identities private, maintain personal autonomy and control their actions while online. But that's not always easy.

Why do privacy problems exist online? While the ethics of privacy in CMC have been widely analyzed, few researchers have actually discussed the technical considerations of the lack of privacy online. Spinello (2001) says privacy problems stem from technical aspects of the programming code which undermine privacy on the web. Technology reporter David Hamilton (2000) suggests that the web's privacy vulnerabilities are attributed to the way it was developed. He argues the infrastructure of the web allows demographic and personal data collection by advertisers and marketers. Our browsing can be monitored as well, through cookies and web bugs. ◉ Internet protocol addresses are easily manipulated to divulge information about us (Hamilton, 2000). This issue is a consideration for our discussion about online identity and anonymity in Central Issues: Unit 2. Are we really able to be anonymous if our addresses create an inescapable identifying mark on us?

BOX CI1:10 CMC STICKS AROUND CYBERSPACE

As well known CMC scholar Joseph Walther (2002) reminds us, our messages remain available on the internet long after we send them. Messages sent within virtual communities, Usenet newsgroups, electronic distribution and mailing lists, asynchronous discussion archives, IRC or bulletin boards can be researched and retrieved without users' knowledge. What are the ethical implications of this for CMC researchers? What are the ethical implications for anybody who engages in CMC?

◉ Companies often use 'cookies', unique identifiers to track how you move around their websites. For a discussion of how 'cookies' threaten privacy online see [**www** CI1:12].

Another privacy concern is spam, or unsolicited email messages – or electronic junk mail. In 2003, for example, Brightmail, an anti-spam company, found that 40 percent of email messages in Britain were unsolicited (silicon.com, 2003). Brightmail also reported that British spam had increased 7 percent in under two months. An IT manager of a UK firm reported to silicon.com that he had been contending with 8,500 spams per day and 500,000 spams in just two months (silicon.com, 2003). Across the Atlantic, a study by Harris Interactive in the same year found that 74 percent of internet users in the United States wanted spamming outlawed. The most annoying spam messages, according to Harris respondents, were pornographic, followed by those sent by companies promoting financial projects and real estate. Worse yet is fraudulent spam, the best-known case being the so-called 'Nigerian email scam', highlighted in Focus Areas: Topic 2.

What can be done about CMC privacy online? Organizations like the Electronic Frontier Foundation [**www** CI1:13] and Privacy International (PI) [**www** CI1:14] examine surveillance and privacy invasion. In the case of PI, members, who include ICT specialists, lawyers, judges and journalists from forty countries, raise awareness around the world about issues such as military intelligence and workplace surveillance. Privacy International also deals with encryption. Programmer Phil Zimmerman developed an application called Pretty Good Privacy (PGP) enabling users to encrypt their email with a code that even military computers could not crack. Although some experts say it is crackable, it is 'pretty good enough' for the US government to ban transporting the application across international borders.

Decreasing international (and local) inequality online, and increasing critical awareness of power, politics and privilege, are important to keep in mind as you work through the following Central Issues units. It's also helpful to understand how CMC is not a privilege enjoyed by all, nor are the ethical constructs of freedom, equality, democracy, justice and autonomy.

REVIEW

In this unit, we started by discussing the privilege of internet access and CMC participation. We examined a series of related ethical issues which underpin online communication. Examining the concept of the digital divide, we considered how poor nations and disenfranchised communities in rich nations have unequal access to the internet. For those who do have access, we looked at online spaces designed for persons in global regions in conflict which enhance community and relationships online. We examined democratic discourse and the ideas of the public sphere developed by German philosopher Jürgen Habermas. Finally, we identified some organizations promoting online rights and equalities.

STIMULUS READING AND RESOURCES

International Center for Information Ethics [**WWW** CI1:15].

Digital Divide Network [**WWW** CI1:16].

Digital divide resources, Bridges.org [**WWW** CI1:17].

Brey, P. (2000). Disclosive computer ethics. *Computers and Society*, 30 (4), 10–16.

Bridges.org (2001). Spanning the digital divide: Understanding and tackling the issues [**WWW** CI1:18].

Walther, J.B. (2002). Research ethics in internet-enabled research: human subjects issues and methodological myopia. *Ethics and Information Technology*, 4, 205–16.

Warschauer, M. (2003). Dissecting the 'digital divide': A case study in Egypt. *The Information Society*, 19(4), 297–304.

IDEAS FOR FURTHER DISCUSSION AND INVESTIGATION

1 What do you think have been the most important ethical values for CMC and internet use in the past decade? Read 'Serving the community', developed by the Computer Professionals for Social Responsibility, which was written in 1993 [**WWW** CI1:19]. What were the key ethical considerations in the early 1900s? What has changed since that time, do you think?

2 What factors might account for international inequities in CMC? What are the implications for the digital divide in the poor nations? What about in your own community? Pick a country from South America, Africa or South Asia and research how many people are online. Try to find out what types of people they might be. Think about what specifically could be done to bridge the digital divide.

3 Recall from our previous discussion, less than 1 percent of the world's population is a part of the knowledge economy. Visit Cyberatlas [**WWW** CI1:20] or Nua internet surveys [**WWW** CI1:21] to see how many people are online from various geographical regions around the world. Then look on these sites to find the latest

demographic figures on inequality within your own country. What, if anything, is surprising about these figures? What did not come as a shock?

4 Take a look at organizations like Electronic Frontier Foundation [**www** CI1:13] and the Privacy International [**www** CI1:14]. In what ways do they advocate online rights, privacy and autonomy? Search for similar organizations online and examine what other ethical issues are being addressed now. What ethical concerns do you think will emerge in the future? Why?

UNIT 2

ONLINE IDENTITY: REAL OR VIRTUAL?

OVERVIEW

KEY TERMS

symbolic marking
identity construction
identification and multiple identities
technologies of self
disembodiment and identity play
online self-presentation

MAIN OBJECTIVES

- Discuss the connection between offline and online identities.
- Consider the fluid and multiple nature of identity as a process.
- Critique the notions of disembodiment and online identity play.
- Outline aspects of the online presentation and performance of self.

A NIGHT ON THE TOWN: WHO SHALL I BE TONIGHT?

Imagine you're going out for the evening with some friends. It's more than likely you'll spend time thinking about what to wear. Whether you're conscious of these choices or not at the time, you'll probably want to fit in with everyone else by wearing the same sort of clothes. Alternatively, you may want to make a point of looking different from them. Whatever clothes you choose they'll inevitably communicate something about you. Each garment is therefore regarded as a **symbolic marker**, saying something about how you want to present yourself to other people, how you feel you fit in with the group, and how you want others to perceive you. This is often done in an even more obvious way in subcultural groups like Punk, Grunge, Goths, Hip-Hop and Garage who often follow a more clearly marked dress code.

www For weblinks and resources visit the CMC website at <www.sagepub.co.uk/resources/cmc>

Symbolic marking is one strategy available for representing ourselves on a daily basis. Another very obvious example of symbolic marking is to be found in national flags [see **www** CI2:1]. These powerful symbols can also mean a great deal to whole societies of people: one of the greatest insults people can sometimes make is to burn another country's flag. But markers don't always have such clear-cut boundaries. Consider how college sweatshirts from Harvard or Oxford University are worn by people around the world. Why wear another college's sweatshirt? In this instance, symbolic marking is used to buy into an image – both literally and figuratively; whether they're in Brisbane or Beirut, perhaps the sweatshirt offers its wearer some of the kudos or status that these institutions appear to hold.

Symbolic marking plays a role in who we want to be and how we want to be seen. In fact, what it exposes is the way that our identities are something we're doing all the time – sometimes quite consciously, other times less so; sometimes as individuals, sometimes as groups. Recall from Basic Theory: Unit 4 how we're managing people's impressions of us just about every minute of the every day. Symbolic marking is a fairly concrete, material way in which to communicate identity; often, however, it's a much more subtle and almost covert activity.

WHAT IS IDENTITY? AND WHY BOTHER?

In some respects, identity is the most obvious thing in the world. Identity is really all about addressing the simple question 'Who am I?' In answering this question, people must consider (1) what they think about who they are, and (2) what stories they tell other people about themselves. In doing so, people can piece together a sense of their *personal identity*. The fact is, however, that identity isn't only a matter of what we think about ourselves or what we tell others about ourselves. Other people too have a say in our *social identity*, which is based on (3) what others think about who we are, and (4) the stories they tell about us – either to our face or to other people! In fact, our identity is like a constant dialogue between them and us. ◎ This is what scholars refer to as the socially constructed nature of identity. In other words, our sense of 'I' is put together in relationship with other people. It's why scholars also talk about **identity construction** – identity is something we put together with the help of others. Some theorists also note how we usually also locate ourselves in relation to someone different from us – we know who we are because we also know who we are not.

◎ You may also like to refer to our brief discussion about social identity in Basic Theory: Unit 5 (see p. 67).

But why is identity important? Why bother? Well, in one sense, identity is just a way of trying to make sense of the chaos or variety in our lives. Just as stereotypes help to organize the constant flow of social information around us, identities help us organize all the different feelings, ideas, beliefs, attitudes and values we have. Cultural Studies expert Jeffrey Weeks (1995, in Bell, 2001) says that our identity is therefore a 'necessary fiction', while social theorist Anthony Giddens (1991) has famously described identities as 'projects of the self'. What they both mean by this is that identity is something which we are working on all the time and that, in doing so, we like to be able to tell a structured, coherent story about who we think we are – with a beginning, a middle and an end. This way of thinking about identity as a process hasn't always been how scholars have understood identity. In fact, many lay people still think of identity in a very different, more traditional way.

SHIFTING PARADIGM: IDENTIFICATION AND MULTIPLE IDENTITIES

> Identity is not as transparent or unproblematic as we think. Perhaps instead of thinking of identity as an already accomplished fact . . . we should think instead of identity as a 'production' which is never complete, always in process. Identity is a matter of 'becoming' as well as of 'being'. It belongs to the future as much as to the past. (Hall, 1990: 222–37)

As identity scholar Stuart Hall suggests, the notion of identity is actually a complex one and not to be taken for granted. Ever since the period in history known as the Enlightenment in the eighteenth century, scholars and lay people alike have thought about self-identity as a straightforward matter. It was thought that we each of us have an *essential* or natural identity which, usually by the time we reach adulthood, is supposed to have been formed. What this meant was that identity was also believed to be *unitary* (i.e. we each have one, 'true' identity), *fixed* (i.e. it's established during adolescence) and stable (i.e. it stays basically the same). This traditional concept of identity is still incredibly influential today, and people commonly talk about 'finding oneself' or 'finding your true identity' or 'the real me'. As a result, there's been a tendency to think of identity in very reified or objectified terms – a thing which we own or can discover.

According to Hall, however, over the last hundred years or so there have been some radical new ways of thinking about human nature. Important insights from Freudian psychology, Marxist economics and feminist politics have had a huge impact on the way we think about identity. In fact, there's been what scholars call a *paradigm shift* – a tremendous re-evaluation of a major area of scholarly knowledge which had previously been taken as truth. ◎ Current theorists now regard identity as being much more flexible, multidimensional and, as we've seen, *socially constructed*. As a result, nowadays we're encouraged to think not so much about identity as **identification** – it's a process we're working on all the time. In keeping with this idea, identity is also regarded as more open-ended and a lifelong project. Long after adolescence, people continue to worry about, and work on, their identity. Depending on the situation we're in, the people we're talking to, the stage of life we're at, the mood we're in, we choose to present (or represent) different aspects of ourselves. It's for this reason too that scholars also talk about our having **multiple identities** – people take on different identities throughout their lives and find new ways to represent themselves to the world.

◎ If you'd like to read more about these issues we recommend Kathryn Woodward's *Identity and Difference* (1999).

The difference between traditional and contemporary ideas about identity is important to CMC because many early approaches to identity in cyberspace were heavily influenced by the newer notions of identity. At the same time, however, people have often misundertood online identity because they've failed to understand the constructed, fluid and multiple nature of identity.

TECHNOLOGIES OF SELF: GOING ONLINE

> The dissolving of older communal contexts, in which signs and meanings seemed fixed and stable, thereby making one's self-identity more secure, has meant that

> individuals must now reach out through the media for information, models, norms and signs in order to get the cultural material with which to construct their lives. (Holmes, 1997: 32)

Taken from his paper on virtual identities, David Holmes makes a really interesting observation about identity nowadays. Previously, most people lived in communities more strictly defined along national, ethnic, religious and class lines. Consequently, identity didn't seem like such an issue and people just took their identities for granted on the basis of nationality, gender, religion, occupation and so on. More recently, however, most of us are lucky enough to live in much more exciting, multi-ethnic, international environments. People also move about a lot, whether by choice (e.g. tourists and business travelers) or by force (e.g. economic migrants and refugees). One upshot of all this is that we've increasingly turned to the media as a resource for constructing our identities. Television, movies, magazines, radio, music and so on all offer a million different role-models and lifestyle choices.

Just as social interaction never takes place in a vacuum, however, our identities are still affected by the time and place and the society in which we live and interact with others. As such, we have to recognize the powerful influence of dominant ideologies in controlling and sustaining people's sense of themselves. Dominant ideologies impose their own norms and rules. If you don't fit in with society's norms, the likelihood is that you'll be marginalized. So our identity is partly formed by the ideological climate into which we're born and in which we live and partly by the choices we make.

Famous twentieth-century philosopher Michel Foucault wrote about the *Technologies of power*, the means by which dominant ideologies are represented (e.g. newspapers and television), but also spoke about the **technologies of self** as the means by which individuals represent themselves – the ways they talk themselves into existence through letter-writing and diary-keeping, for example (see Martin *et al*., 1988). According to communication scholar Daniel Chandler (1998), the internet and, specifically, the web are truly powerful technologies of self, enabling opportunities for identity construction. He puts it like this: these 'technologies of the self' allow us not only to think about our identity and to transform the way we think of ourselves, but also to change ourselves to who we want to be'. In fact, the internet is unique in the history of communication technologies because it offers ordinary people the *potential* to communicate with vast numbers in a way that before was possible only for the very wealthy and very powerful.

◎ You can also read Daniel Chandler's (1998) conversation with 'Paul', who talks about the feelings of identity liberation he's experienced through CMC [**www** CI2:2].

BOX CI2:1 THE POWER OF THE PERSONAL HOMEPAGE

Daniel Chandler reports the follow comments from people talking about their personal homepages. ◎

It helps to define who I am. Before I start to look at/write about something then I'm often not sure what my feelings are, but after having done so, I can at least have more of an idea.

Somehow, publishing my feelings helped validate them for myself.

(Chandler, 1998: 10)

With specific reference to personal homepages on the web, Chandler discusses how it's not just the websites which are often 'under construction' but also the identities of the people making the pages. Through the use of what he calls *bricolage*, people piece together a mosaic of biographical details and other symbolic markers: photos, favorite links, badges, wallpapers, graphics, and so on. Personal homepages may not always be of great importance to those who come across them, but they're profound, creative opportunities for people to reflect on themselves and think about how they want to represent themselves to the world. At the same time, it's the various processes of writing, recording and presenting their chosen facts and thoughts for the webpage which construct their thoughts, feelings and their identities.

IDENTITY PLAY: NOBODY KNOWS YOU'RE A DOG IN CYBERSPACE

Early on, scholars and journalists were very excited by what they saw as the liberation offered by the relative anonymity of CMC – particularly in the interactive sub-systems like chatrooms, bulletin boards, newsgroups and MUDs. This anonymity, it was claimed, paved the way for **disembodiment** – an identity which was no longer dependent on, or constrained by, your physical appearance. Some of the most sweeping claims made for the internet were that it would give an opportunity for those whose voices had not been heard before to speak and be heard. Included among their number, so the claim went, would be the marginalized and the disenfranchized.

Internet scholar Sherry Turkle famously wrote about the immense potential for people to 're-invent' themselves via CMC:

> You can be whoever you want to be. You can completely redefine yourself if you want. You don't have to worry about the slots other people put you in as much. They don't look at your body and make assumptions. They don't hear your accent and make assumptions. All they see are your words. (Turkle, 1995: 184) ◎

◎ You may recall Turkle's notion of the 'subjective computer' from Basic Theory: Unit 3 (p. 40).

Calling the computer 'a second self,' she also described how her own online communication put her in a new relationship with her own identity. In exploring the developing symbiotic relationship between humans and computers, she described this as part of a larger cultural process, pointing out how CMC questions the stability of meanings and the lack of universal and knowable truths. In other words, as people participate in CMC, Turkle said, they become authors not only of text but also of themselves, constructing new selves through social interaction. 'You are the character and you are not the character, both at the same time. You are who you pretend to be' (1990: 289). Turkle quotes one person as saying, 'Why grant such superior status to the self that has the body when the selves that don't have bodies are able to have different kinds of experiences?'

Here's how Mark Dery (1995: 2–3) describes what disembodied, text-based communication offers:

> A technologically enabled, postmulticultural vision of identity disengaged from gender, ethnicity, and other problematic constructions. On line, users can float free of biological and sociocultural constructions, at least to the degree that their idiosyncratic language usage does not mark them as white, black, college-educated, a high-school dropout, and so on.

The question which needs to be asked, of course, is whether CMC really does offer any liberatory potential? Certainly, in FtF encounters, sexual/gender and ethnic identity are overpoweringly defining. Within seconds we make assumptions and form impressions about people based on what we see: age, dress, height, weight, sex, skin color, physical disability, and so on. Online it's surely got to be different. You can certainly manage people's impressions more easily by choosing to tell other people what you want – you can decide what to reveal and what to hide. In theory, CMC offers a special opportunity for **identity play** – pretending to be someone else or just portraying different aspects of yourself. A woman can play at being a man and vice versa. The color of your skin can be irrelevant if you want it to be. Gay people can come out online without the usual fear of prejudice and discrimination. You need never know that the person you're communicating with is deaf or is in a wheelchair.

BOX CI2:2 DOGGONE IDENTITY

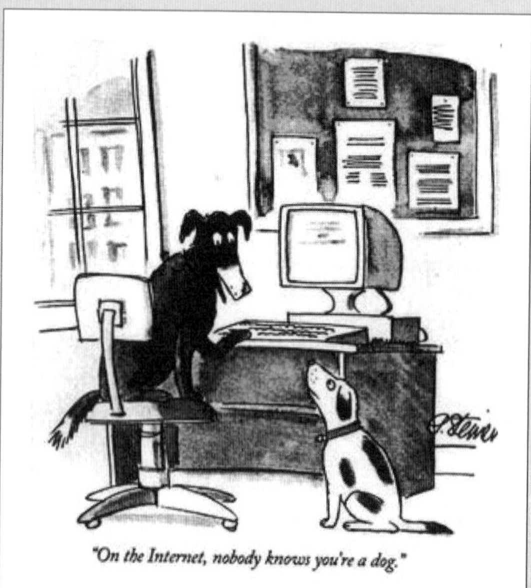

"On the Internet, nobody knows you're a dog."

FIGURE 11

From the *New Yorker* of 5 July 1993

REALITY BITES: THE PRESENTATION OF SELF ONLINE

BOX CI2:3 CYBERSPACE AND RACE: THE COLOR-BLIND WEB?

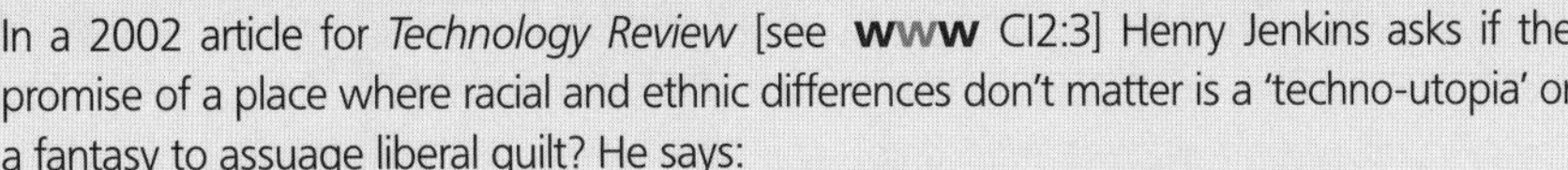

In a 2002 article for *Technology Review* [see **www** CI2:3] Henry Jenkins asks if the promise of a place where racial and ethnic differences don't matter is a 'techno-utopia' or a fantasy to assuage liberal guilt? He says:

Like many White liberals, I had viewed the absence of explicit racial markers in cyberspace with some optimism – seeing the emerging 'virtual communities' as perhaps our best hope ever of achieving a truly color-blind society.

But, following a short survey, Jenkins found that ethnic minority participants in an online forum reported that others simply assumed everyone else in the forum was White – even to the point of telling racist jokes. As a result, Jenkins feels forced to conclude:

Perhaps when early White Netizens were arguing that cyberspace was 'color-blind,' what they really meant was that they desperately wanted a place where they didn't have to think about, look at or talk about racial differences.

In their well known 1997 paper 'Hyperbole over Cyberspace', Eleanor Wynn and James Katz critiqued what they saw as exaggerated claims for identity play in CMC and the idea that cyberspace could ever really liberate identity from the body. While they agreed that homepages illustrate an effort 'to pull together a cohesive presentation of self across eclectic social contexts in which individuals participate' (pp. 26–7), they problematized Turkle's talk about an 'escape from the physical person' – the so called 'disembodied self'. Their argument was that identity processes and communication may be far more complex than Turkle suggested. Certainly there is room for play and performance, but this is also true of offline identity practices as well. The trouble with much of the early excitement about identity play in cyberspace is that it tended to exaggerate the realities of online communication in terms of what people actually do and what they actually want to do.

Indeed, as Robert Burnett and David Marshall (2003) rightly point out, much of the early writing about identity play online was based on particular CMC contexts like MUDS, where fantasy and play are their *raison d'être* – it's why people go into these sub-systems in the first place – to have fun and play around. It's a game! As we discussed in Basic Theory: Unit 4, it's always a mistake to generalize about online communication on the basis of specific subcultural experiences. Besides, as we've also seen in Basic Theory: Unit 5, often people don't want to be anonymous or they simply can't be anonymous. Sometimes, even, people will be chastized by others for being anonymous.

BOX CI2:4 THE STRANGE CASE OF THE ELECTRONIC LOVER

Back in the 1980s, Lindsy van Gelder reported the following incident which has now entered the CMC halls of fame.

As an experiment to experience what it felt like to be a woman online, Alex, a fifty-something male psychiatrist from New York did a 'gender-swop', creating an online persona called Joan. Joan was a young woman who'd been disabled after a terrible accident. For a long time, Alex created a really believable story about Joan and, in doing so, developed intimate friendships with several women. When his identity play was finally exposed, however, many of these women felt they had been seriously betrayed. Others, however, didn't condemn him, but spoke warmly about the special relationship they felt they'd had with Joan.

As Paula Roberts (1996) points out, it's not easy to know what the motives were behind Alex's identity play; whether he had a professional or scholarly interest in exploring being a woman or if he just wanted to find a way to win women over. One mistake people often make about online identity is to exaggerate the idea of play while forgetting that offline identity itself is as much a performance. We considered in Basic Theory: Unit 4 how people manage their own and others' impressions online as well as offline. We show different aspects of ourselves – different personae – to different people all the time without thinking it odd at all. This is what identity is all about – a constant activity – whether online or offline – of choosing how to represent ourselves to people.

We started this unit by imagining that you were getting ready to go out. If you like, you were being invited to choose how to represent yourself, how to 'perform' on a particular occasion – an evening out with friends. This idea of human interaction as 'performance', and the creativity and freedom of choice associated with forming identities, was something explored by renowned communication scholar Erving Goffman. In his famous book *The presentation of self in everyday life* (1959), Goffman used theatrical performance as an extended metaphor for how we present ourselves in daily social interactions. Goffman writes about the *performer* and the *character* involved in the act of self-presentation in these interactions. The important thing is that the *character* which the *performer* creates is not identical to the person who creates it. On this basis, in CMC, the internet simply offers us a different sort of 'stage' on which to perform our identities and to work on our **online self-presentation**.

It's therefore important to put online identities into context: first, in the context of the fluid, multiple nature of *offline* identity, and second, in the context of what people are really up to in cyberspace. Based on research findings, Joseph Walther and Malcolm Parks (2002) comment on the degree to which people tend to play with different identities online, but usually in less exaggerated or dramatic ways than expected.

BOX CI2:5 TEEN IDENTITY PLAY

According to the Pew Internet and American Life Project, 'fully 56 percent of online teens have more than one email address or screen name and most use different screen names or email addresses to compartmentalize different parts of their life online or so that they can experiment with different personas'.While teenagers used such subterfuges as pranks or for privacy, adults tend to use subtle deceptions about age, appearance, occupation or life circumstances to achieve a wider range of goals. Such fabrications are performed in the context of games or simple curiosity, as potentially self-therapeutic investigations of aspects of the personality, to avoid online harassment or elevate social standing, or merely to impress. (Walther and Parks, 2002: 529–63)

CONSTRUCTING IDENTITIES ONLINE: HOW MUCH TO TELL? WHAT TO TELL?

In thinking about the similarities between online and offline identity construction, we've found the Johari Window to offer some helpful insights. Named after Joseph Luft and Harry Ingham (1973), the Johari Window is a convenient tool for thinking about identity and communication. Focusing on important aspects of effective interpersonal communication which include openness and perception, the Johari Window shows two main dimensions along which we organize and understand the presentation of ourselves to others: those aspects of our behavior and style that we're aware of, and those aspects of our behavior known to other people. ◎

◎ The quadrants are not necessarily equal or static. They'll vary from person to person and depending on the context of the communication taking place. The balance may also change during someone's lifetime.

BOX CI2:6 THE JOHARI WINDOW

	Known to self	Not known to self
Known to others	① Open	② Blind
Not known to others	③ Closed	④ Dark/unknown

FIGURE 12
Johari window

1. **Quadrant One (Open):** This area represents the public self, and includes information readily available to the other person in a face-to-face communication situtation.
2. **Quadrant Two (Blind):** This area might include habits or mannerisms – manifestations of shyness or arrogance, for example – of which the person is unaware.
3. **Quadrant Three (Closed):** People with large Closed areas are thought to make good listeners, while people with small Closed areas are more likely to be outspoken and frank.
4. **Quadrant Four (Dark/unknown):** Some psychologists believe that an accident or a particular (perhaps stressful or illuminating) moment can serve to give people new insights into hidden aspects of themselves.

What's the relevance of all this to CMC? Well, firstly, the Johari Window reminds us of the complex decisions we make about self-disclosure and impression management – whether online or offline. As the model shows, people communicate their identities both voluntarily and involuntarily – they don't always know what they're giving away. ◉ Secondly, the Johari Window also reminds us that, although openness is often considered an important quality in communication, it can also be inappropriate or even dysfunctional. For example, someone with an exceptionally large Open area may not always be sensitive to the complexity of a situation; inappropriate sharing doesn't always contribute to effective communication and can, indeed, sometimes lead to discomfort and misunderstanding. The Johari Window also shows how important feedback is. Perceptiveness and openness are not an end in themselves but only part of a complex entity, as much online as in face-to-face communication.

◉ Wynn and Katz point out how status can be unwittingly revealed in CMC by, for example, people's email addresses. They quote one person as saying, 'Having an AOL address is akin to living on the wrong side of the tracks!'

One major difference between online and offline identity work needs to be recognized. Since there's not always a clearly defined, standard 'audience' in CMC, it's sometimes harder than in FtF communication to decide what's appropriate in terms of self-disclosure and self-presentation. In fact, Chandler, notes the unusual blurring in CMC of the boundary between what's public and what's private. Some personal homepage creators often appear not to have thought about this, to have considered who may, or rather may not, be visiting their website. This has led some people to joke that, if homepages are about individuals responding to the question 'Who am I?' a reasonable response may be 'Who cares!' As DiGiovanni (1995, in Chandler, 1998) remarks, for all their careful identity construction, the personal homepage often simply ends up being a fanclub of one!

VIRTUAL OR REAL? ONLINE IDENTITY AND IDENTITY ONLINE

As the boundaries erode between the real and the virtual, the animate and inanimate, the unitary and the multiple self, the question becomes: Are we living life on the screen or in the screen? (Turkle, 1995: 10)

Following up on Turkle's much quoted question, we turn now to the question that preoccupies many people: which is more 'real', one's offline identity or one's online identity? As we've seen before, there's nothing sacrosanct about FtF communication in terms of being more 'real'. It's seldom a question of one or the other. People in fact move freely between their offline identity and virtual identity. As Walther (2002) has shown, 'in cyberspace the connection between the self and the self-presentation becomes mutable'. This, he points out, is in stark contrast to what happens in the physical world, where society often demands each person to have a stable and physically *identifiable* identity – for the purposes of tax collection, for example!

All identity, however, is performance; all identity is multiple and dynamic. We shift our identities from moment to moment throughout any day, depending on what it is we're doing and who it is we're doing it with. As such, the distinction between 'real' and 'virtual' is problematic for at least two reasons. The idea that we have a 'real identity' falls into old ways of thinking that our identity can ever be fixed, stable and essential. It also implies that online identities are somehow not real in spite of their being both meaningful and important to people. The kind of identities which people have online and those they have offline are all part of an ongoing process of identification. This is why we think it's more helpful to talk about *identity online* than *online identity*. Online identity implies that we have an identity which is somehow distinct or separate from an offline identity. Perhaps instead we're busy with the same identity project but can do it online or offline – we sometimes take our identify construction online and at other times we take it offline.

REVIEW

We started this unit by looking at the social construction of identity and how the meaning of the term 'identity' has shifted. Looking at early claims for identity play online, we then went on to critique assumptions about anonymity and disembodiment in CMC. With reference to the Johari Window, and Goffman's ideas about identity as performance, we then discussed the connection between online and offline self-presentation and self-disclosure. We concluded by considering whether identity offline is more 'real' than identity online.

STIMULUS READING AND RESOURCES

Note: This unit is very closely linked with Fieldwork: Task 6 titled 'Constructing identity: personal homepages and webcams'.

Bell, D. (2001). Chapter 6: Identities in cyberculture. In *An introduction to cybercultures* (pp. 113–36). London: Routledge.

Burnett, R. and Marshall, P. D. (2003). Chapter 4: Webs of identity. In *Web theory: An introduction* (pp. 61–80). London: Routledge.

Nakamura, L. (2002). Chapter 5: Menu-driven identities: making race happen online. In *Cybertypes: race, ethnicity and identity on the internet* (pp. 101–35). New York: Routledge.

Wynn, E. and Katz, J. (1997). Hyperbole over cyberspace: self-presentation and social boundaries in internet home pages and discourse. *The Information Society*, 13 (4), 297–328. Also available (15 April 2003) online: <http://www.slis.indiana.edu/TIS/articles/hyperbole.html>[**WWW** CI2:4].

IDEAS FOR FURTHER DISCUSSION AND INVESTIGATION

1. Visit the *Identity Page* [**www** CI2: 5] at www.theory.org – an award-winning website maintained by Media Studies scholar David Gauntlett at Bournemouth University in England. See what else you can find out about contemporary ideas about identity. In particular, follow all the weblinks Gauntlett offers and make notes about major theorists like Anthony Giddens, Michel Foucault and Judith Butler. Look out for his well known trading cards, too [**www** CI2:6].
2. Visit Yahoo!'s directory of Cultures and Groups [**www** CI2:7]. Many of the groups displayed rely on recognizable identity labels: sexual orientation and gender, race and ethnicity, religion, age and generation, location and occupation, and so on. Spend some time visiting some of the webpages and websites of groups and organizations which you've not heard of before. What other kinds of identities are there? What symbolic markers are people using to communicate their different identities? To what extent, do you think, does the internet afford an identity liberation for them?
3. Find the personal homepage of someone you know (maybe the person teaching you, or a fellow student). What kinds of particular aspects of their identity are they trying to communicate? Compare how that person presents him or herself online with how s/he presents his/her identity offline. What differences are there? Why might their identity online might be different from their identity offline? Which *seems* the more 'real' to you and why?
4. Working with either Fieldwork: Task 4 or Fieldwork: Task 5, join an online group or community and try adopting a different persona from your offline identity. How does this make you feel? What sort of person do you choose to be? Why? How long do you find you can sustain this impersonation? Do you have a sense that anyone suspected you were not really who you were representing yourself to be? How 'real' did the new identity seem to you?

UNIT 3

ONLINE COMMUNITIES: REAL OR IMAGINED?

OVERVIEW

KEY TERMS

community
Gemeinschaft and Gesellschaft
sociability and locality
imagined communities
social networks
hybridity

MAIN OBJECTIVES

- Critique the notion that online communities are either good or bad.
- Distinguish between descriptive and normative definitions of community.
- Consider theories of 'community' and social network theory.
- Highlight the hybrid forms of on- and offline community networking.

ONLINE COMMUNITY: ALL GOOD OR ALL BAD?

In Basic Theory: Unit 3, we looked at the major discourses of hype and hysteria that have surrounded all new technologies of communication, and, most recently, new media like the internet and web. One excellent example of the way in which these competing discourses play out with regards to CMC can be found in people's ideas about online communities and the impact of new communication technologies on offline communities. These are ideas which can be heard from CMC scholars and lay people alike – have a look at these two quotes:

> Computer networks isolate us from one another, rather than bring us together. . . . Computers teach us to withdraw, to retreat into the warm comfort of their false

WWW For weblinks and resources visit the CMC website at <www.sagepub.co.uk/resources/cmc>

> reality. . . . only the illusion of community can be created in cyberspace. (Stoll, 1995: 58, 137)
>
> The internet has opened a whole new frontier that has brought every person in the world together in one place. The internet is a world within itself; it is a virtual community of hundreds of millions of citizens from every corner of the planet . . . No longer do personal differences separate the seven billion citizens of the world's 244 nations; we are now one people united together. (www.intergov.org)

As with these quotes, commentators – be they academics, journalists or the people next door – try to persuade us into taking one of two extreme points of view about the connection between new technology and community. These positions are sketched in Box CI3:1.

BOX CI3:1 GOOD TECHNOLOGY, BAD TECHNOLOGY

- **Negative position**: Communication technologies like the internet are to blame for the loss of *real*, offline communities and so-called online communities are not *proper* communities anyway.
- **Positive position**: New communication technologies, and especially the internet, make possible exciting, *new* communities and help reinvigorate or enhance existing offline communities.

We've chosen to italicize what we see as some problematic words in these two positions. As we discussed in Central Issues: Unit 2, it's worth while being a little wary when people make assumptions about something being 'real', 'proper' or 'new', and especially when they opt for emotive language like 'false reality' and 'one people united', as in the quotes from Stoll and InterGov. ◎ Just as we saw with the notions of 'group' and of 'flaming' in Basic Theory: Units 5–6, it's also always useful to start by establishing some kind of definitional clarity about terms which people otherwise take for granted. So, before we start looking at *online* communities, one of the first things we need to ask ourselves is 'What exactly is it people mean when they talk about **community**?'

◎ Remember also that the dichotomy between 'real' and 'virtual' often implies that anything 'virtual' isn't real or proper.

WHAT IS [OR WAS] A COMMUNITY?

One important way of starting to address this question is to follow the ideas of sociologists Colin Bell and Howard Newby (1971), who distinguished between what they called *empirical descriptions* and *normative prescriptions*. In other words, it's important to separate the ways people try to describe what a particular community is actually like (e.g. where it is and who belongs to it) from the ways people promote or prescribe their own particular idea of what they think community *should be* like. The fact of the matter is that community doesn't mean the same thing to everyone, and discussions about the nature of online communities, and their relative strengths and weaknesses, invariably get caught up between what they are and what they should be – or, alternatively, what they are not and what they shouldn't be.

Think about it for a moment. Think about all the ways we hear the word 'community' being used around us on a daily basis: 'the African-American community', 'the international community', 'the village community', 'the gay community', 'the local community', 'the European Community', 'the Irish community', 'the farming community'. It's really hard to imagine how this word can possibly mean the same thing in the context of 'international community' as it does, say, in 'farming community'. The fact is that 'community' is a bit of a buzz-word. We hear people talking about community in all sorts of different ways and for various purposes. Most of the time it's a convenient label for a whole range of feelings and ideas about people in tight-knit, clearly identified, politically coherent collectives. In fact 'community' is often used as a rhetorical device for communicating a sense of comforting or reassuring togetherness. This is what CMC scholar Lynne Cherny (1999: 255) says is the *symbolic* use of 'community': 'In both academic literature and more popular media reports, the word "community" is often invoked in a symbolic way, with a utopian subtext.'

Such is the complexity and significance of the term for people that there's been a fairly long tradition of scholarship known as Community Studies, and much of this work comes from sociologists. In trying to define community, most sociologists look to identify the main characteristics of community. In this regard, one idea proposed many years ago by the German sociologist Ferdinand Tönnies was the distinction between what he called **Gemeinschaft** (pronounced 'guh-mine-shaft'), which are small, rural, intimate communities, and **Gesellschaft** (pronounced 'guh-zel-shaft'), which, by contrast, are large, urban, impersonal societies. For our purposes, it's the first of these which describes what are often seen as traditional or 'real' forms of community: a village where everybody more or less knows everybody else, and where people encounter each other almost daily.

Nowadays so few people live in small rural communities like these that the notion of community has obviously had to change. The question is whether locality or territoriality is a defining feature of community. Can we describe a collection of people as a community only if they're in close physical or geographical proximity to one another? For most people the answer is clearly no. You don't have to be living next door to someone – or even in the same country – to feel close to them, to share an interest with them or a sense of belonging. It's for this reason that a more useful distinction to be drawn is that between **sociability** and **locality**. This refers to the way that communities may be defined either in terms of the shared social interactions of its members or in terms of a shared geographical location. Some communities, like the old-fashioned country village, will obviously be characterized by both, but it's not necessarily true of all communities.

Technical labels like these become useful conceptual tools for scholars, who need to be able to be more specific about what they mean when talking about something as apparently vague as 'community'. To proceed critically, therefore, it's important to be clear about what type or form of community is being spoken about (e.g. village community, urban community, international community, virtual community). Wherever possible, it's also best to avoid evaluative terms like 'real', 'authentic', 'proper' and 'genuine' when describing a community. After all, one person's idea of a 'real community' is quite possibly someone else's idea of a shallow, loosely affiliated gathering.

DOES CMC DESTROY [TRADITIONAL] COMMUNITY?

BOX C13:2 AND STILL THE WORLD'S GETTING WORSE . . .

I can watch thirty-four channels of TV, I can get on the fax and communicate with people anywhere, I can be everywhere at once, I can fly across the country, I've got call waiting, so I can take two calls at once. I live everywhere and nowhere. But I don't know who lives next door to me. Who's in the next flat? Who's in 14B? . . . Community to me means simply the actual little system in which you are situated, sometimes in your office, sometimes at home with your furniture and your food and your cat, sometimes talking in the hall with the people in 14B . . . I think it's absolutely necessary for our spiritual life today to have community where we actually live. (Hillman and Ventura, 1992: 40–3)

The prescriptive take on community in Box C13:2 is clearly one which is premised on community being based on locality. What's more, psychoanalyst John Hillman and journalist Michael Ventura are evidently concerned about what they see as the negativity of technologies of communication on their sense of community. All this technology, they say, and still the world's getting worse. This is a common anxiety about online communication. Within the field of CMC, writers such as Jon Stratton (1997) and Joseph Lockard (1997) pass strong judgement on what they see as the 'moral distraction' and 'myth' of virtual communities. Both Stratton and Lockard feel that online communities inevitably lead to people evading offline or 'real life' difficulties, problems and social issues. It's something like this: while you sit chatting with your cyber-buddies, the people next door may be being robbed and a house a block away is burning down!

Well known CMC scholar Nancy Baym (1998, 2000) has spent many years studying and writing about online communities, and she examines a range of criticisms which people level at online communities: the lack of commitment between members, the lack of moral cohesion, the lack of global access, and so on. However, she also points to the lack of empirical evidence to confirm the effects of online participation on offline community. For Baym, the accusation that online communication is somehow responsible for the 'loss' of offline community is problematic for several reasons, but one in particular:

> It is fundamentally reductionist to conceptualize all 'virtual communities' as a single phenomenon and hence to assess them with a single judgement . . . [there are] countless thousands of online groups that vary tremendously. Some groups are surely bad for offline life, but there's certainly no reason to believe that most are. (1997: 63)

In Central Issues: Unit 7 we look again at how the internet sometimes stands accused of impacting negatively on offline life and so we'll leave this issue for the time being.

DOES CMC ENABLE [PROPER] COMMUNITY?

> *The question of whether or not one can find community online is asked largely by those who do not experience it. Committed participants in email, bulletin boards, chat lines [and] MUDs . . . have no problem in accepting that communities exist online, and that they belong to them. (Haythornthwaite* et al.*, 1998: 212)*

What then of the argument that, far from breaking down traditional communities, communication technologies and CMC are in fact restoring and creating them? Well, there have been many conflicting points of view. Most famously, Howard Rheingold (1993) claimed the following: 'CMC liberates interpersonal relations from the confines of physical locality and thus creates opportunities for new, but genuine . . . communities.' ◎ Many commentators, like Stoll at the start of this unit, are sceptical about claims made for online communities. Is it really possible, they ask, to have 'proper' communities in cyberspace? Writers like Joseph Lockard (1997: 225) feel that online community is a poor substitute for the 'real' thing; he concludes: 'To accept only communication in place of a community's manifold functions is to sell our common faith in community vastly short.'

◎ Howard Rheingold is most famous for his early writings about 'virtual communities'. He maintains his own website dedicated to this issue and more recent phenomena like Smart Mobs [**www** C13:1].

Is, then, the online community nothing more than a virtual substitute for the 'real' community of yesteryear? In Basic Theory: Units 4–6 we've already seen a great deal of research evidence which refutes earlier accusations that CMC is necessarily asocial, cold, task-focused, and so on. We've also seen how large numbers of people have in fact begun to establish complex arrangements of long-standing, meaningful social relationships online. It's precisely with this in mind that Rheingold feels the case for online communities is clear:

> Online communities are social aggregations that emerge from the net when enough people carry on those public discussions long enough, with sufficient human feeling, to form webs of personal relationships. (1993: 5)

So, according to Rheingold, communities are almost inevitable and are constituted on the basis of social interaction, the length of people's involvement and the strength of their feelings. Basically, people are in community with each other wherever they do things together for long enough and when they *feel* like they're a community.

At this point, it's worth turning again to Baym (1997) to see what she has to say as a scholar who, like Rheingold, has actually spent so long studying and participating in online communities herself. She argues that, however important, common interest alone is unlikely to be sufficient to build and sustain a strong sense of community. Baym draws on the key ideas of Benedict Anderson, who proposes that the thing we ought to be looking at is the style in which communities are imagined. In his now famous treatise, Anderson (1983: 15) states that 'all communities larger than primordial villages of face-to-face contact are imagined' – hence **imagined communities**. This doesn't mean that communities are not 'real' in the sense that they're not meaningful to people and can't act as powerful influences in people's lives – they are indeed both meaningful and powerful. What Anderson does mean, however, is that 'community' is not about numbers or places, it's about activities and feelings. Baym identifies four ways in which she sees community emerging through social processes: forms of expression (e.g. our talking about our communities), identity (e.g. our sense of shared group identity), relationship (e.g. our connections and interactions with others in the community) and norms (e.g. the rules and conventions we agree to live by together).

What's the conclusion of all this? Well, all we can suggest is that, while society *may* be losing one type of community, this is not to say that it's losing community altogether. In other words, online communities may not be 'traditional' communities but it seems to us that they're communities nonetheless – communities not of common location, sure, but of common interest and feeling. Like offline communities, they're also communities of practice and memory – people feel a part of online communities, they talk about their online friendship networks as communities, and they share a history of interacting together (Cherny, 1999).

RELATIONAL WEBS: SOCIAL NETWORKS ON THE NET

As we hope you can see, it's really important to disentangle from the ideology of community exactly what it is that people feel is lacking or being threatened when they bemoan the loss of 'real life' or 'traditional' community. Similarly, what is it that other people are experiencing when they describe their CMC as 'communal'? Perhaps the best way of doing this is simply to be more specific and use a more operationalized notion of community; that is, to define community in more concrete ways. So, for example, in talking about community we might be thinking of some, or all, of the following variables:

- Being in face-to-face contact and/or having regular contact.
- Having shared goals and/or producing and using shared commodities.
- Having the opportunity for dialogue and social interaction.
- Having a common cultural heritage or history.
- Enjoying unique communal features and/or developing 'organic' social formations (e.g. people often like to be able to say, 'This is the way we do things round here.').

Along these lines, one alternative approach to thinking about online communities in more practical terms is to think of them as **social networks**. In this sense, CMC scholars like Barry Wellman and Caroline Haythornthwaite (e.g. 2002) have sought to *describe* community structures rather than rely on more subjective or discursive accounts. For them, 'community' is a term best used to characterize the strength of relationships between people in an extensive network. ◎

◎ Networks are regarded as being larger than groups which have clearly defined boundaries; networks tend to be more extensive and dispersed.

> Social network analysis examines patterns of resource exchange among actors to determine how and what resources flow from one actor to another. Regular patterns of relations – i.e. specific types of resource exchange – reveal themselves as social networks, with actors as nodes and relations between actors as connectors between nodes. Social network analysis strives to derive social structure empirically, based on *observed* exchanges among actors. (Haythornthwaite *et al.*, 1998: 214, emphasis ours)

According to social network scholars, CMC is more than capable of supporting strong, multiple ties between people. Just as roads are the material infrastructure which supports the flow of commercial exchanges offline, the internet is the material infrastructure which supports social exchanges online. What's more, the internet can also increase the range of social networks by enabling people to connect with even more people than before.

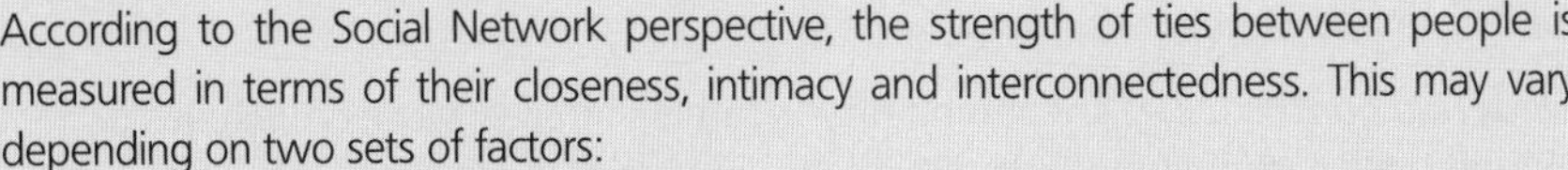

BOX CI3:3 THE TIES THAT BIND . . .

According to the Social Network perspective, the strength of ties between people is measured in terms of their closeness, intimacy and interconnectedness. This may vary depending on two sets of factors:

- What kind of tie it is, e.g. work or leisure.
- What kind of people are tied, e.g. adults or teens.
- What social positions they have, e.g. teacher or student.
- Where they are located, e.g. close or far apart.
- What mode of communication is being used, e.g. online or offline.
- The frequency of contact between people.
- The amount and diversity of information exchanged.
- The number of different communication modes used.

Research by Haythornthwaite and Wellman has shown how stronger ties are those where participants communicate more frequently, about a range of different topics and using several different modes of communication (e.g. FtF, online and telephone).

Just like offline, online participants may be bound together by strong, intermediate, or weak ties. Furthermore, social networks may be either specialized or multiplex; that is, with participants bonded through a single shared interest and a primary focus of discussion, or free to wander off-topic and discuss all sorts of other issues and concerns. Studies of computer-assisted social networks have shown that the stronger the ties and the more multiplex the activities, the more like a community a network will be.

HYBRIDITY: GRAFTING THE NEW ON TO THE OLD

In their discussion of community networking, Haythornthwaite and her colleagues (1998: 213) also make the following very astute observation:

> Just as modern neighborhood ties do not fulfill all of a person's community needs, membership in a single online community rarely meets all of a person's needs for information, support, companionship, and a sense of belonging. Virtual communities are only part of a person's multiple communities of interest, kinship, friendship, work, and locality. (1998: 213)

In social network terms, what they are saying is that online communities don't just have people wandering off-topic, but also offline. In fact, most well established online communities show participants often meeting FtF as well. Whether they are 'virtual' or 'real', no communities exist in splendid isolation. As Baym (1998: 63) concludes:

> Online groups are woven into the fabric of offline life rather than set in opposition to it. The evidence includes the pervasiveness of offline contexts in online interaction and the movement of online relationships offline. ◎

◎ What Baym says here is clearly related to Howard's notion, of 'embedded media' (see p. 75).

Baym also notes that online communities are in fact heavily influenced by pre-existing structures which enable, and encourage, people to feel (or imagine) themselves part of a community. Some of the factors which therefore need to be taken into consideration when evaluating online communities are:

- *External contexts*, e.g. are community members already work colleagues or individuals participating from home and who've never met?
- *Temporal structure*, e.g. is the CMC synchronous or asynchronous?
- *System infrastructure*, e.g. are members completely anonymous?
- *Group purposes*, e.g. what are the aims of the group? how closely are they having to, or wanting to, work together towards some goal or other?
- *Participant characteristics*, e.g. are members all men or all women or a mixture of both?

Not only does this mean that online communities are shaped by the extent of their *embeddedness* in the 'real world', it also means that online communities are often simply offline communities which have come online. In other words, these are supposedly 'traditional' communities which are exploring new ways for their members to be in community with each other. The distinction between online and offline communities is not so neat after all and you are more likely to find **hybrid** examples than anything else.

PUTTING COMMUNITY IN PERSPECTIVE

BOX CI3:4 OPENING WELCOME FROM LAMBDAMOO

* Welcome to LambdaMOO! *
****

Running Version 1.8.1r0 of LambdaMOO

PLEASE NOTE:
LambdaMOO is a new kind of society, where thousands of people voluntarily come together from all over the world. What these people say or do may not always be to your liking; as when visiting any international city, it is wise to be careful who you associate with and what you say. The operators of LambdaMOO have provided the materials for the buildings of this community, but are not responsible for what is said or done in them. In particular, you must assume responsibility if you permit minors or others to access LambdaMOO through your facilities. The statements and viewpoints expressed here are not necessarily those of the wizards, Pavel Curtis, Stanford University, or PlaceWare Inc., and those parties disclaim any responsibility for them.

[**www** CI3.2]

Thomas Bender (in Jones, 1995) is highly critical of what he sees as value-laden attempts to recapture traditional communities regardless of the quality of human relationships that may or may not have characterized them. What he means by this is that people who bemoan the loss of 'real' community and who ridicule the notion of online communities are often appealing to a romantic ideal of what traditional communities were really like.

In fact, long before Bender, Jackson (in Bell and Newby, 1971: 48) noted how the notion of *Gemeinschaft* is inevitably based on fallacious assumptions about the nature of traditional societies – their homogeneity, for example – and end up 'harking back to some pre-existing, rural utopia'. In other words, just because people live within a few blocks of each other doesn't mean they all get along. In fact, even small communities can suffer from conflict and divisions. Jon Stratton (1997: 267) is a little bit more hard-hitting. Commenting on claims made about how wonderful virtual communities are, he notes that, in the Global North, 'community' always carries a nostalgic connotation of pre-modern (or traditional or rural) communities.

> [Community] refers to a mythic understanding of the essential 'sharedness' of a way of life before the fragmentation of interpersonal interaction and the loss of taken-for-granted moral order brought about by the founding modern changes – secularization, urbanization, capitalism, industrialization, and, of course, the nation-state . . . We can begin to see that, far from being innocent, the American mythologization of the internet as a community represents a nostalgic dream for a mythical early modern community which reasserts the dominance of the white middle-class male and his cultural assumptions.

In this sense, it all very much depends on what people understand by the term 'community' (i.e. meanings and feelings) and what they hope to achieve when talking about community (i.e. motives and ideologies). It also makes a difference who's talking about community. Is it the marketing director of AOL pitching to new customers with the promise of online friendship, love and support? Or is it your local politician trying to persuade you to pay more tax for amenities and care facilities in your neighbourhood? What, for example, are InterGov (see p. 108) and LambdaMOO (see Box CI3:4) hoping to achieve in their descriptions, do you think?

> A critical awareness of the social transformations that have occurred and continue to occur with or without technology will be our best ally as we incorporate CMC into contemporary social life. (Jones, 1995: 33)

As we've said before, and as Steven Jones reminds us here, debates about the social impact of the internet invariably dovetail with what scholars elsewhere are saying about the post-industrial, information societies in which many of us live nowadays. It's usually the broader economic, social and cultural changes which make people feel uneasy and unsettled. It's perhaps not surprising, therefore, that people are often found to be searching for the kind of stability and security which they think being a part of a community will bring. Where for some people this means fighting for exclusive, traditional forms of offline community, for others it means turning to the internet to sustain and perhaps extend their existing social networks.

REVIEW

In this unit, we started by looking at the two most extreme positions sometimes taken in relation to online communities. We then considered different approaches to the notion of 'community', distinguishing between descriptive and normative perspectives, and the definitions of sociality and locality. Next we returned to discuss the ideas that CMC is responsible for the loss of traditional, offline communities, and that online communities are not 'real' communities. We then looked at the social network approach to community, which led us to consider hybrid forms of offline-online community. We concluded by putting the notion of community into perspective with reference to broader social transformations.

STIMULUS READINGS AND RESOURCES

Centre for the Study of Online Communities [**www** CI3:3].

Research Center for Virtual Environments and Behavior [**www** CI3:4].

Baym, N.K. (2000). Chapter 4 – 'I think of them as friends': Interpersonal relationships in the online community. In *Tune in, log on: Soaps, fandom, and online community*. Thousand Oaks, CA: Sage.

Brown, J. (2001). Three case studies. In C. Werry and M. Mowbray (eds), *Online Communities: Commerce, community action and the virtual university* (pp. 33–46). Upper Saddle River, NJ: Prentice Hall.

Driskell, R.B. and Lyon, L. (2002). Are virtual communities true communities? Examining the environments and elements of community. *City and Community*, 1 (4): 373–90.

Haythornthwaite, C. (2002). Strong, weak and latent ties and the impact of new media. *The Information Society*, 18 (5), 1–17.

IDEAS FOR FURTHER DISCUSSION AND INVESTIGATION

Note: The ideas covered in this unit are closely linked with Fieldwork: Unit 5, where we focus on community building in metaworlds and visual chat.

1 In thinking about both the idea of hybrid forms of community and issues of identity online, have a look at Trinidad Online (**www** CI3:5). Have a look also at the extracts (**www** CI3:6) from an ethnographic study of this site conducted by British scholars Daniel Miller and Don Slater. How do they discuss the integration between the online and offline versions of the Trinidadian community? How does the website look to communicate, support and promote their national identity?

(2) Webrings [see **www** CI3:7] are basically a way of people grouping together by linking all their websites. One of the major listings of web rings is at Webring.com [**www** CI3:8], which, in February 2003, boasted, 'We bring the internet together!' with 3.05 million unique visitors, 24 million hits, 60,500 rings, 975,800 active sites, 500,000+ registered users and 3,800+ contributing members. Have a look at some web rings. Would you describe them as networks or communities?

3 According to its own publicity, the Seattle Community Network (SCN) is a service for community empowerment, a free public access computer network for exchanging and accessing information. Visit SCN [**www** CI3:9] and see what you make of it. What kind of information is being made available? What opportunities are there for one-to-one interaction? How well does SCN appear to manage the balance between offline and online community? Is the internet being used in this way in your own local community?

4 Visit (and maybe even join) a well established online community such as the WELL [**www** CI3:10] or Echo [**www** CI3:11]. How does it seem to you? In what ways does it look to present itself as a 'traditional' community? What sorts of shared interests do its members appear to have? How do this online community compare with other types of online communities like FreeNets, special interest groups (SIGs) or fanclubs?

UNIT 4

LANGUAGE AND THE INTERNET

OVERVIEW

KEY TERMS

language and discourse
speech community
multilingualism
netlingo and netspeak
linguistic diffusion
folk linguistics

MAIN OBJECTIVES

- Critique popular, folk linguistic concerns about 'netlingo' and 'netspeak'.
- Establish the relative status of English and other languages on the internet.
- Examine the ways language and discourse are changing on the internet.
- Consider how internet jargon and styles are spreading into mainstream use.

LANGUAGE, DISCOURSE AND 'WAYS OF SPEAKING'

Weblish, netlingo, e-talk, tech-speak, wired-style, geek-speak and *netspeak*. These are all common terms which people have used to describe language in cyberspace. Although labels like these seem fairly amusing and harmless, they make potentially problematic assumptions about language generally, and about how language is changing on the internet. In particular, they assume that internet language is so different from other kinds of language that it warrants a new, special label. In fact, the popular belief often promoted by the media is that new technologies have also been radically affecting language and, in some cases, destroying 'proper' language. Have a look at this example of a newspaper headline from the British press which also makes up yet another label:

WWW For weblinks and resources visit the CMC website at <www.sagepub.co.uk/resources/cmc>

Hell is other people talking webspeak on mobile phones.

(*Sunday Times* newspaper, 27 August 2000)

Of course, what this headline also does is confuse different technologies, which is typical of the way journalists usually oversimplify the complexities of, and subtle differences in, language. To be fair, however, part of the problem is that there hasn't been a lot of expert knowledge to help explain things better. In fact, relative to other areas of CMC, there has been very little research which has tried to examine the truth behind popular, media representations about language and new communication technologies. Having said which, a small group of scholars within CMC do try to focus specifically on language, working in a sub-field of CMC known as *Computer Mediated Discourse* or CMD (see Herring, 2001).

Although the terms 'netlingo' and 'netspeak' can oversimplify things, we'll stick with them in this unit because they are convenient and recognizable, and also because they help draw attention to an important distinction made by linguists between language and discourse**.** Just as in Basic Theory: Unit 1 where we considered some of the core concepts of communication, in this unit it's important to start by establishing what we mean by 'language' before going on to discuss its place on the internet. Of course, from an everyday point of view, language seems like such an obvious thing; if we're to maintain our critical position, however, we need to have a more scholarly understanding of language.

LANGUAGE

As you might imagine, **language** is a symbolic system for creating meaning and is made up of sounds (or *phonemes*), letters (or *graphemes*) and words (or *morphemes*). These are in turn combined to form grammatical structures like sentences according to the rules (or *syntax*) agreed by any particular community of speakers. This is a marvellous thing in itself. Linguistic forms like sounds, letters, words and grammatical rules don't tell the whole story, however. Nor is meaning simply 'put together' this way. Understanding what someone means when they say something requires more than recognizing the sounds and words they use, and even if you know the correct rules of grammar, there's no guarantee that you'll be understood. Instead, meaning is *negotiated* between speakers, and we have to make careful judgements about context in order to decide what someone means – for example, the situation you are in, who the other person is in relation to you, how their voice sounded when they spoke, etc. What's more, language isn't just about giving labels to things in the world around us, nor is it solely about the transfer and exchange of information. These representational and informational functions are undeniably an important part of language, but language is actually multifunctional and can do many different things for us.

DISCOURSE

This is why scholars are more interested in what people actually *do* with language in their everyday encounters, the ways they use language to form relationships and to communicate their identities. This is why scholars talk about *language-in-use* or **discourse**. The term 'discourse' is used by many different scholars in many different ways. Although it's used here in the particular sense of 'language-in-use', in actual fact 'discourse' and 'communication' mean pretty much the same thing: both terms are concerned with social interaction and everyday encounters. However, while the notion of 'communication' always indicates a very broad, nonverbal perspective, 'discourse' tends to be more specifically directed at linguistic issues (see Schiffrin, 1994).

In this unit, therefore, while 'netlingo' is a useful term for describing the different linguistic *forms* used on the internet (e.g. the lettering, words and grammatical rules), what's also interesting is to examine people's linguistic *practices* online – the ways they are actually interacting and conversing with each other. For us this is described better by the term 'netspeak'. ◎ We don't only want to know what language on the internet looks like but also how people are using language in different ways. This is of course much more in keeping with the general focus of this book on computer mediated *communication*, and it's why those scholars interested in language and new technologies choose to refer to their sub-field as Computer Mediated Discourse.

◎ Net*speak* is itself slightly misleading because most of what happens isn't actually spoken – maybe net*write* would be better! At least 'netspeak' does convey the sense of people actually *using* language, however.

LANGUAGE VARIETIES AND SPEECH COMMUNITIES

Without wanting to get too bogged down with theory, there are just two other specialist concepts – or analytical tools, if you like – which you may find useful in thinking about language on the internet. Scholars who study the relationship between language and society (usually called sociolinguists) know that the boundaries between different languages are not always clear-cut. They also know that it's a matter of history, politics and power that some people's ways of speaking come to be considered acceptable and prestigious and a 'proper' language. In everyday talk, for example, we like to describe French as 'the language of romance', German as 'the language of science and technology' and often hear people describe English as the ideal 'global language'. We also commonly imagine that regional dialects which people speak at home are not proper languages – they're just slang or 'patois'. Contrary to all these popular (or **folk linguistic**) beliefs, however, sociolinguists know that there is never anything inherent in a language (e.g. its grammar or vocabulary) which makes it better or worse than any other language.

So, as scholars, it's important to recognize that different people have different *ways of speaking* and that it's a matter of social convention that some ways are regarded as more or less superior. This is why sociolinguists prefer to talk about different *varieties* of language to acknowledge that different groups – or communities – simply have different ways of speaking. Sometimes these varieties come to be used as the national language, at other times they continue to be 'just' dialects which people use at home or in their local communities. In fact, people usually organize themselves into communities around the way they speak – what are called **speech communities**. What's more, having a shared way of speaking also helps create a greater sense of being in a community together. Communities of people blend into one another, and we usually belong to several different communities (see Central Issues: Unit 3); in the same way, languages don't have perfect boundaries and are never 'pure' – in spite of whatever grammar books might have us believe. These same sociolinguistic principles apply also to the way language is used on the internet.

MULTILINGUALISM: LANGUAGES ON THE NET

Although this is a common mistake, it's wrong to think of netlingo (or netspeak) as necessarily being a version of English. Given the 'digital divide' discussed in Central Issues: Unit 1, there are, of course, many different speech communities whose ways of speaking seldom get a look in on the internet. It's not just people from the poorest parts of the world, however, whose voices are not heard on the internet; there are many other languages besides English spoken in otherwise media-rich countries. This raises two important questions about languages in cyberspace: (1) what is the status of different languages and (2) to what extent is English the dominant language?

BOX C14:1 WORLD LANGUAGE STATISTICS

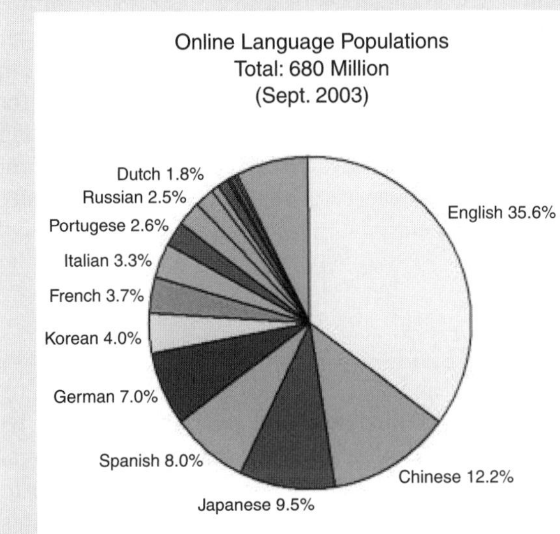

FIGURE 13

Online language populations, September 2003, total 680 million. *Source* Global Reach [**www** C14:1]

There are several different ways of assessing the demographic realities of the 'global internet village' which rely on both linguistic and geographical indicators. One of the most obvious ways to get an overview of the linguistic landscape of cyberspace is to examine the different languages spoken by internet users. In 1996 it was estimated that 80 percent of the people using the internet were English-speaking. In 2000 the figure had fallen to 54 percent, with 7.1 percent Japanese-speaking, 5.4 percent Chinese-speaking, 5 percent German-speaking, 4.7 percent Spanish-speaking and 3.9 percent French-speaking. At the time of writing this book, however, the demographics were even more different, with the number of non-English-speakers (63.5 percent) accessing the internet somewhat greater than native English-speakers (36.5 percent). (See Figure 13.) In fact, other estimates suggest that, by 2005, internet users speaking English as a first language or 'mother tongue' will be, at most, a third of all users. While European languages continue to account for one of the greatest shares of the world's internet users, most commentators agree that the future of the internet belongs increasingly to the languages of East Asia, such as Japanese, Korean and, especially, Chinese.

Another way of judging the relative spread of languages on the internet is to look at how much the actual content of webpages appears in different languages; for example, the Internet Society (with Alis Technologies) [**www** CI4:2] ran a well known survey in June 1997 as part of its Babel Project and found that about 84 percent of all webpage content was in English – followed by German (about 5 percent), Japanese (about 3 percent) and French (about 2 percent). It's highly unlikely that this is still the case today. In more geographic terms, the demographics of cyberspace are also revealed by looking at where users live. Of course, with different home languages spoken in any single country, this is a less accurate indicator of the relative status of different languages. Nonetheless, what these figures do show is the same noticeable swing away from the early dominance of the United States and, by extension, English. For example, in 1995 some 70 percent of internet users were based in North America, compared with only 50 percent in 1999 and 33 percent in 2002. While the number of Europe-based internet users has remained fairly consistent, the largest growth in internet usership has, once again, been in the East Asia/Pacific region.

Finally, domain name registration (i.e. web addresses) is also a reasonable indicator of the relative position of different languages on the internet. For example, in 2000 over 75 percent of websites had domain names registered in North America, 10 percent in mainland Europe and Britain and 7.5 percent in Asia/Pacific. In April 2001, however, for the very first time one registration company, VeriSign [**www** CI4:3], started accepting domain names using non-Roman alphabets such as Arabic, Hebrew, Hindi, Thai and Urdu [see also **www** CI4:4]. Although this hardly seems earth-shattering news, it's a really important step towards a more **multilingual** net.

LANGUAGE WARS ON THE NET?

Although people often take language for granted (and especially their own language), be under no illusion, language is always a powerful political issue. As the *Montreal Gazette* article attests (see Box CI4:2), different countries often take quite practical measures to help 'protect' their languages from the influence of other languages. On the internet, this usually means languages resisting the popularity and dominance of English, but there are also many examples from around the world where speakers of lesser-used languages are facing similar struggles (e.g. Catalan in Spain and Welsh in Britain). It's in this way too that the prevalence of English online becomes easily caught up with more widely expressed issues about language and national identity, as well as even wider issues like the globalization, 'Americanization' or 'Englishization' of world cultures.

BOX CI4:2 LANGUAGE POLICE PATROLLING INTERNET SITES

The Office de la Langue Française (OLF) has put the bite on Micro-Bytes, and other Quebec businesses with websites on the internet could be next. Micro-Bytes, a computer store, has removed most of its homepage from the net after receiving notice from the OLF last month that the company is in violation of the French Language Charter. 'Quebec enterprises that have their certificate of francization (firms with fifty employees or more) will be asked to have French on their Internet sites', an OLF spokesman said yesterday. (*Montreal Gazette*, 14 June 1997)

As usual, the picture is a complex one. Just as many speech communities are concerned about the impact of a powerful language like English, many others regard the internet as an excellent opportunity for promoting and protecting their minority language. In fact, in as much as the internet (and its Englishness) is seen as a powerful new threat, it also offers a powerful new means of challenging the spread of English. One example of this may be seen in Wales (UK) where the Bwrdd yr Iaith Gymraeg (Welsh Language Board) has a strong presence on the web [**www** CI4:5]. The website of the European Bureau for Lesser Used Languages [**www** CI4:6] is another good example of the way that smaller language communities are using new technologies to organize themselves in order to promote their ways of speaking.

Of course, there are also any number of web resources where majority languages are also promoted and taught – see for example the Foreign Language Resources page at the University of South Florida [**www** CI4:7]. Linguistic resources on the internet in fact range from the really useful, like this listing, to the truly ridiculous, such as The Dialectizer [**www** CI4:8] which offers to 'translate' standard English text into 'dialects' such as Redneck, Cockney, Pig Latin and even Hacker! On a more serious note, the translation service offered by AltaVista's Babel Fish [**www** CI4:9] attempts translations between some of the major world languages like Spanish, German, Korean, Japanese and Russian. Needless to say, given the subtlety of language, even this more sophisticated technology seems fairly crude. Here, for example, is how the last sentence looks translated into Japanese and then back again into English: ◎

> The subtlty of language being given, saying, the technology which is refined seems that considerably is vulgar from unnecessary this.

◎ This is quite a standard way of checking the accuracy of a translation. Ideally, if the translation is good, the final version should resemble the original. Go to Babelfish and try it for yourself.

It seems that, as far as languages are concerned, the internet has both its drawbacks and its opportunities. Although it's certainly another site of struggle between language varieties, it would be exaggerating the conflict to refer to out-and-out 'language wars' as Zazie Todd and Stephanie Walker (2000) do in their small study of people's attitudes to the use of different languages in online chat spaces. In fact, much of the time, internet language tells a story of people being brought together through shared linguistic practices and other interests.

LANGUAGE STYLE AND LANGUAGE CHANGE ON THE INTERNET

> Netspeak is a development of millennial significance. A new medium of linguistic communication does not arrive very often, in the history of the race.
> (Crystal, 2001: 238–9)

This quote from David Crystal, a very well known British writer about language, is fairly typical of the kinds of grand claims being made about the way language is changing on the internet, and, supposedly, *because of* the internet. In fact, Crystal suggests that internet language is a 'fourth medium' (after writing, speaking and signing) and how the rate of change has been tremendous. Not everyone shares this perspective, however, and most scholars tend to be a little more cautious. In particular, what experts of CMD are always interested to know is whether language in cyberspace is so different that it deserves to be seen as a completely new variety of language. Does it, for example, deserve special labels like netlingo and netspeak?

NETLINGO: WRITING THAT LOOKS LIKE SPEECH?

Language is changing all the time. Everybody knows that the way English is spoken and written today is very different from the way it was used four hundred years ago by William Shakespeare. Even though people don't always like the changes, language change is unavoidable and natural. And it is happening everywhere. What's more, even though Standard English may be the agreed norm for writing a college essay or a business letter, it's by no means the norm when speaking on the street – no one really speaks like they write! Nowadays, there are also more people who speak English as a second language than there are people who speak it as a first language. This is why one commentator, John Simmons, says that most English spoken these days is a kind of 'fusion English', whereby English is mixed up with other languages. **Netlingo** is no exception. The internet is just one of many factors influencing the way language is changing.

The linguistic forms of internet language are obviously influenced a lot by the physical constraints of the technology itself – most notably the fact that it is usually typed on a standard computer keyboard. There are also important social factors which have influenced netlingo, such as the jargon of computer 'geeks' and other specialists who've been so heavily involved in developing communication technologies. In this sense, the language also reveals a speech community who enjoy playing with the possibilities of the keyboard. The emphasis in netlingo is almost always on speed (i.e. trying to type as fast as you can speak) and informality (i.e. trying to be friendly). What this tends to mean is that language relies on creative typology and many of the traditional rules of grammar and style are sometimes broken – as they always are when we're trying to be laid-back and fashionable. In a nutshell, then, the most basic 'rules' of netlingo are that it uses whatever is possible with the computer keyboard, but that it also tries to save as many keystrokes as possible.

◎ These examples and those in Box CI4:4 are used by Crispin Thurlow (2001) in his entry on internet language for the *Enclyclopedia of Sociolinguistics* (Oxford: Elsevier).

BOX CI4:3 NETLINGO?

Some of the most commonly recognized features of netlingo are these: ◎

- word compounds and blends (e.g. *weblish*, *shareware*, *netiquette*, e- and *cyber*-anything);
- abbreviations and acronyms (e.g. *THX* 'thanks', *IRL* 'in real life', *F2F* 'face-to-face', *some1* 'someone');
- minimal use of capitalization, punctuation and hyphenation – or none at all (e.g. *cooperate* and, of course, *email* and *internet*);
- generally less regard for accurate spelling and/or typing errors;
- less or no use of traditional openings and closures (e.g. use *Hi* or *Hello* instead of *Dear*. . .). Sometimes people will use nothing at all – especially in online chat and instant messaging where your user ID is given automatically.

A good example of research in this area is Milena Collot and Nancy Belmore's study (in Herring, 1996) based on a sample of nine online bulletin boards. They compared a corpus of 200,000 words from the bulletin boards with language from traditional genres of written and spoken English. They found that 'electronic language' was more friendly and immediate, although still somewhat more formal than speech. In fact, the language of the bulletin boards was rather like the language of a public interview or a letter. In a similar way, Naomi Baron (1998) has also tried to draw a linguistic profile of emails. In her study she concluded that, in terms of their format, grammar and style, emails are a 'creolizing linguistic modality' – which is to say, a hybrid form of speech and writing. (This is similar to what Crystal says in the quote above.) Baron also noted the strong tendency to break traditional conventions of written language to help create the more sociable orientation of speech.

NETSPEAK: SPEECH THAT LOOKS LIKE WRITING?

The best place to observe **netspeak** and the language of conversation (i.e. discourse) on the internet is obviously in the channels of synchronous CMC (e.g. online chat, instant messaging, MUDs). While there are also other technological restraints like transmission time lags, what we see is that people are really keen to find imaginative ways to reinstate the kinds of social cues often absent from written text. Once again, people want to type as fast as they can but also to be as informal and friendly as they can. Remember, it's all about relationship. Discourse in these niches is therefore highly interactive, dynamic and spontaneous – especially when there are multiple participants.

BOX CI4:4 NETSPEAK?

Some of the most common typographic strategies used to achieve this interactional style are:

- letter homophones (e.g. *RU* 'are you', *OIC* 'oh, I see'), acronyms (e.g. *LOL* 'laugh out loud', *WG* 'wicked grin') and a mixture of both (e.g. *CYL8R* 'see you all later');
- creative use of punctuation (e.g. multiple periods . . . exclamation marks *!!!!*);
- capitalization or other symbols for EMPHASIS and *stress*;
- onomatopoeic and/or stylized spelling (e.g. *coooool, hahahaha, vewy intewestin* 'very interesting')
- keyboard-generated *emoticons* or *smileys* (e.g. : -) 'smiling face' ,-) 'winking face', @>—;— 'a rose');
- direct requests (e.g. *A/S/L* 'age, sex, location?' and *GOS* 'gay or straight?')
- interactional indicators (e.g. *BBL* 'be back later', *IGGP* 'I gotta go pee', *WDYT* 'what do you think?')
- with more elaborate programming, colored text, *emotes* (e.g. *{Sender} *eyes you up and down**, *{Sender} *cries on your shoulder**) and other graphic symbols (e.g. images of gifts and accessories in Virtual Worlds).

In considering netspeak in IRC (Internet Relay Chat), Christopher Werry (in Herring, 1996) characterized it as 'interactive written discourse', and this was not just in terms of linguistic forms like those above. In particular, he noted that the organization of interactions was very complex; for example, different conversational strands running at the same time, short turns (usually only about six words), high degrees of 'addressivity' (i.e. the use of *nicks* to avoid ambiguity with multiple participants), and minimal back-channelling from listeners (e.g. *uh huh*, *mm hm*). If you think about the way you would typically have a conversation while sitting round a table with a group of friends, you can probably recognize the kind of discourse which Werry's describing. It sometimes seems like chaos but everything usually works really smoothly! Once again, even though it is not face-to-face, and is typed, the language of the internet invariably looks more like speech than writing.

We've already mentioned several factors which account for some of the ways language and discourse have been changing on the internet. As with communication more generally (see Basic Theory: Unit 2), the answer always lies in a wide range of contextual variables such as the type of channel being used (e.g. email or instant message), the participants (e.g. teen chatters or business colleagues) and the topic and purpose (e.g. love letter or customer complaint). In her chapter on CMD (see 'Stimulus reading'), Susan Herring (2001) outlines a number of other variables, such as physical (or 'medium') variables like granularity (i.e. how transient or durable messages are), or social variables such as whether or not the channel is moderated by someone. As we have already seen, it is the social variables which invariably shape online interaction – the same is true of netspeak.

FOLK LINGUISTICS AND THE SPREAD OF NETLINGO

Another very popular claim made about netlingo is that it is proliferating beyond the immediate context of CMC and that this poses a serious threat to standard varieties of language. For example, from time to time we hear concerned voices about how young people are losing the ability to spell and write 'correctly' because of the internet. Although it is obviously too technologically deterministic to blame the internet for such changes (see Basic Theory: Unit 3), there has certainly been a diffusion of online terminology into offline domains; for example, computer-related terms like *multi-tasking*, *windows*, *hacking* and other items of netlingo such as *spamming*, *cyberspace*, *cyberculture*, *shareware*, *hypertext*, *snail-mail* and *flame*. Sometimes these words even make it into dictionaries. ◎ This spread of netlingo is what experts would call stylistic or **linguistic diffusion** – when one way of speaking starts to seep into another. Netlingo is also having an influence on languages other than English, leading to popular reports of 'CyberSpanglish' with isolated terms like *surfeando el Web* and *estoy emailando*. This of course ties in with issues we discussed earlier, about the combined impact of English and netlingo. Which is why, in some cases, languages like French are resisting such influences by promoting their own equivalents for certain terms (e.g. *bavardage* for chat and *un pirate informatique* for a hacker).

◎ You may be interested to look at Village Online's *Glossary of internet terms* [**www** CI4:10] to see how many you recognize as having wider, everyday currency.

As we suggested at the start of this unit, there is a lot of **folk linguistics** (i.e. popular, lay talk about language) and not a lot of expert linguistics. For example, one interesting aspect of language on the internet which remains under-researched is the emergence of labels like *weblish* and *netlingo*. Where do these terms come from? Who invents them?

How do they become more widely used? Another interesting change which no one seems to document is the gradual 'evolution' of netlinguistic terms such as the way *E-mail* becomes *e-mail* becomes *email*, or *Internet* becomes *Net* and then *net*. Although they tend to be more humorous than academic, two notable attempts to record more systematically the development of language on the internet are Constance Hale's (1999) excellent (and entertaining) book *Wired Style* and the online dictionary *Netlingo* [**www** CI4:10] which claims to list thousands of words and definitions describing the technologies and communities of cyberspace.

BOX CI4:5 FIRST 'SMILEY' FOUND

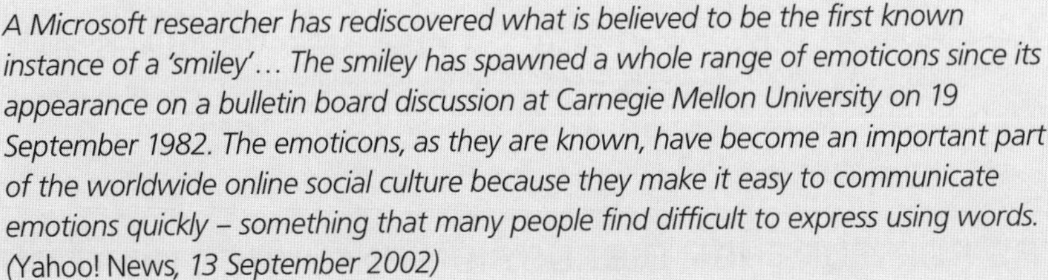

A Microsoft researcher has rediscovered what is believed to be the first known instance of a 'smiley'... The smiley has spawned a whole range of emoticons since its appearance on a bulletin board discussion at Carnegie Mellon University on 19 September 1982. The emoticons, as they are known, have become an important part of the worldwide online social culture because they make it easy to communicate emotions quickly – something that many people find difficult to express using words. (Yahoo! News, *13 September 2002)*

New ways of communicating and using language are emerging all the time as a result of technological *and* social changes. What was once new, trendy and cool, eventually becomes formal, old-fashioned and uncool. (Even the smiley seemed like a major breakthrough at one time!) This is by no means something special to the internet but is the way language has always evolved. It's a mistake ever to think of language as being something fixed or sacred. Of course, there will always be people in society who want to privilege their ways of speaking over other people's ways of speaking, just as there will be other people who don't want their way of speaking (and writing) to change. We might call these people 'linguistic puritans' – people who are very strict, have very rigid principles and who disapprove of anything *they* regard as frivolous and inappropriate. In the face of many changes these people's voices often rise up even more loudly than before. (Remember the newspaper headline from p. 119.) Our job as scholars, however, is to be critical and to resist making sweeping judgements about how language is changing and the impact this is having elsewhere.

REVIEW

In this unit, we started by defining the terms language and discourse which, for convenience, we labelled netlingo and netspeak. We also briefly considered the technical terms 'language variety' and 'speech community'. We then looked at a range of methods for assessing the status and politics of English and other languages on the internet. Turning next to examine research on language change on the internet, we also listed the most familiar forms and practices of netlingo/netspeak. We concluded by discussing folk linguistic concerns about linguistic diffusion.

STIMULUS READINGS AND RESOURCES

Global Reach [**WWW** CI4:1].

NetLingo [**WWW** CI4:11].

Baron, N. (1998). Letters by phone or speech by other means: the linguistics of email. *Language and Communication*, 18, 133–70.

Herring, S. (2001). Computer-mediated discourse. In D. Schiffrin, D. Tannen and H.E. Hamilton (eds), *The handbook of discourse analysis* (pp. 612–34). Oxford: Blackwell.

Thurlow, C. and Brown, A. (2003). Generation Txt? The sociolinguistics of young people's text messaging. *Discourse Analysis Online*. Available (22 October 2003) online at <http://www.shu.ac.uk/daol/>. [**WWW** CI4:12]

Warschauer, M., El Said, G. R. and Zohry, A. (2002). Language choice online: Globalization and identity in Egypt. *Journal of Computer-Mediated Communication*, 7 (4). [**WWW** CI:13]

IDEAS FOR FURTHER DISCUSSION AND INVESTIGATION

1 Use some of the weblinks provided to establish what some of the most recent statistics are for multilingualism on the net (e.g. try Global Reach website and the Alis Technology/Internet Society's Babel Project). How different is the demographic picture from the one we have depicted at the time of preparing this book? What noticeable changes and trends can you identify?

2 Go back through your old emails for the last month or so and note as many as possible of the features (words, expressions, presentation style, layout, spelling, etc.) which appear to be typical of emails. What about the topics of conversation? What evidence do you find to support the idea that there is a distinctive 'email genre'?

3 Over a period of about a week, keep a diary of your use of your mobile phone or instant messaging. Who phones/messages you? Who do you phone/message? How long do you speak? What sorts of things do you talk about? Transcribe some of your text messages or instant messages, making a note of any interesting examples of abbreviations, acronyms and other typographical markers.

4 Have a look at the article by Thurlow and Brown (2003, stimulus reading above) published by Discourse Analysis Online [**WWW** CI4:12]. This paper presents a small study of cellphone text messaging and addresses the media hype that young people have reinvented and/or destroyed traditional language. In terms of your own knowledge of mobile telephony and text messaging nowadays, how well does this paper represent the issues? How does the study of text messaging relate to computer-mediated discourse, do you think?

UNIT 5

WOMEN AND THE INTERNET

OVERVIEW

KEY TERMS

digital gender divide
gender
gender masquerade
online harassment/cyberstalking
diaspora

MAIN OBJECTIVES

- Discuss the nature and extent of gender differences in CMC.
- Consider women's/girls' attitudes towards, and experiences of, technology.
- Examine some of the opportunities and 'spaces' for women online.
- Evaluate the 'digital gender divide' especially in poor nations.

WORLDWIDE WOMEN

In her weblog *Notes of an Iranian Girl* Shahla Aziz writes:

> Women's struggle here, of course, is different from the West. [Women] strive to be considered a full witness in court and have the right to travel without your husband's permission . . . With more than 20 percent unemployment and lack of real opportunity for women, the only way to assure any kind of upward mobility is still a good marriage. Only now, a good marriage is considered to be one with someone who holds a Western passport – an exit to a better life.
> [**www** CI5:1]. ◎

◎ 'Weblogs' are online journals that usually contain short, frequently updated postings arranged chronologically. The activity of journalling in these documents is called 'blogging'.

www For weblinks and resources visit the CMC website at <www.sagepub.co.uk/resources/cmc>

Before widespread participation in CMC, Shahla's story would probably never have reached us. Women have historically had little access to media, communication technologies and the opportunity to build communities and share experiences with other women on a global basis. CMC offers opportunities to change this, but only if women are active participants. In its early developments, men were almost exclusively the inhabitants of cyberspace. Now, however, women online are the norm rather than the exception. Nevertheless, many researchers argue there is a digital gender divide. Recall from Central Issues: Unit 1 that the digital divide is a concept through which the inequality in computer technology use is mapped. It refers to the gap between regions or groups of people that are left behind in use of computers and the internet and those who take access for granted. The **digital gender divide** is an extension of this concept, and focuses specifically on the inequity of women's access to and use of communication technology.

BOX CI5:1 GENDER AND GENDERED SPACE

Gender refers to a socially constructed means of categorizing people, usually as masculine or feminine, and assigning particular ideals and characteristics to those categorizations. The term 'gender' should not be interchangeable with the term 'sex' which refers to biological categories of male and female. It is important to note that many scholars argue that gender is fluid rather than fixed and that there is an unlimited spectrum of possible gender identities, of which masculine and feminine are simply positions on a continuum.

The term 'gendered space' refers to physical or virtual space that is associated with a particular gender because of the activities that occur in the space. Think about 'boardroom space' and 'kitchen space' and the genders associated with each.

COMPUTER EDUCATION AND GAMES: YOUNG MALE DOMAINS?

It starts when children are young. Women and girls who try to enter the world of computing and computers often report feeling isolated and/or intimidated. Women and education researcher Pamela Haag (cited in AAUW, 2000) says:

> When it comes to today's computer culture, the bottom line is that while more girls are on the train, they aren't the ones driving. To get girls 'under the hood' of technology, they need to see that it gets them where they want to go.

How can the computer culture change to be more gender-sensitive? In an attempt to generate more participation by women and young girls, technology-oriented training programs, computer classes and entertaining websites have been created specifically for women. These websites, and training and learning programs are intentionally female-gendered in order to attract female participation (Newsom and Baker-Webster, 2002). The sites themselves and online literature associated with these female-oriented programs often use 'traditionally feminine' language and images, so that women and girls can participate more comfortably. The sites and programs also use gender stereotypes to promote a gendered style of technology participation.

The problem is that these sites and programs are creating a female-gendered space that clashes with the predominantly male field of the computer industry. Sharon Schuster, President of the American Association of University Women Educational Foundation (cited in AAUW, 2000), says:

> The same reasoning applies to computer games. Computer games don't have to be the virtual equivalent of GI Joes and Barbies. We have to think less about 'girls' games' and 'boys' games' and more about games that challenge our children's minds. When it comes to computer games and software, girls want high-skill, not high-kill.

Like Haag and Schuster, researchers like Janet Morahan-Martin (2000) argue it is not the technology itself but the 'culture' of computerization and computing that is highly gender-stereotyped and contributes to the digital gender divide. A minority of computer games are sold to girls, she notes. The majority of computer games contain exaggerated representations of gender – the spaces within the games are masculine. Music, images and actions all embody a sort of 'super macho' *hypermasculinity*. Throughout the games, submissive, sexualized women are featured.

There are notable exceptions. Lara Croft, the widely popular main character of the computer game *Tomb Raider*, has captured the public imagination and the global market like no other virtual character. ◎ Like many computer game characters, Lara Croft is hypersexualized, but unlike many, she is tough and in control, and one of the only female characters who has succeeded in navigating a traditionally male space. Box CI5:2 illustrates characteristics often shared by women and female characters in online games.

◎ If you haven't already, we reccommend you watch the movie spin-offs with Angelina Jolie!

BOX CI5:2 GENDER IN GAMING, GENDER IN CHAT

About female participants:

- Text-based gaming environments (e.g. MUDs and metaworlds) boast a more balanced female-to-male audience ratio than graphically driven games and visual chat, which have a largely male audience. Fattah *et al.* (2002) and Bodmer (2001) found that in the United States in particular women and girls now make up a small majority of online gamers.
- Earlier research by Brenda Danet (1996) and Jennifer Mulcahy (1997) suggests that women role-play for different reasons than men. Text-based games are more character and role-play-driven, rather than action-driven, as are the graphic games, which may suggest a reason for feminine interest. More recently Katelyn McKenna (2003) reported females are more likely than males to derive long-term enjoyment from gaming, and therefore more women than men play as they get older (into their late twenties and thirties).
- Women are more likely to participate in online chat and emailing than men, according to Bodmer (2001).

About female personae:

- Feminine stereotypes are often highly visible in female personas used in games and chat, most evidently in idealized female body types and levels of charisma or appeal.
- Feminist scholars argue that a majority of female stereotypes in gaming are also associated with violence – and these characters are created for men to play (Schumacher and Morahan-Martin, 2001).

- Stereotypes are also associated with women in chat rooms, according to Wolf (2000) who found that, in particular, women appear to enjoy the ability to use emoticons and other visual images to express their emotions.

BOX CI5:3 TYPES OF CYBER VIOLENCE

- **Online contact leading to offline abuse.** This usually starts with online misrepresentation then leads to abusive offline contact and crime.
- **Cyberstalking.** Tracking someone's actions online with illegitimate intent.
- **Online harassment.** Use of the internet to communicate with another party online against her or his will, including making personal threats. Like cyberstalking, online harassment is subject to prosecution by law.
- **Degrading representations.** Online representation of women through images or text that is disrespectful and/or harmful towards women generally.

(Herring, 2002)

One of the earliest reported cases of online harassment is detailed in Box CI5:4.

BOX CI5:4 AN EARLY CASE OF ONLINE HARASSMENT

In 1993 Stephanie Brail received harassing email messages from someone in her computer discussion group in retaliation for anti-sexist remarks she had made to the group. These messages, identified only by either the name 'Hemroid' or 'Mike' and with a false, untraceable email address, included announcements that her opinions were worthless, profanity-laced rape threats and reams of pornographic text. As a response to the harassment, Brail formed Systers, a community of women responding to sexual harassment online [**www** CI5:2]. Brail (1996) found that 100 of 500 respondents to a Systers survey had been sexually harassed online.

It is important to note that not just women, but members of any marginalized group, can become targets of cyberhate and cyberharassment. In the case of Brail's harassment, she explained that within the newsgroup the men willing to defend women were themselves harassed. The broad appeal that Brail made to her own newsgroup and others exhibits evidence of the power of CMC to facilitate activism quickly and efficiently. Her appeal was necessary, however, because the domain of CMC is also open to the same problems that we potentially experience communicating face-to-face.

Numerous researchers have shown men are by far the majority of perpetrators and women are the vast majority of victims of violence and harassment, in both the physical world and, Brail argues, the virtual world. Sites like Cyber-stalking.net [**www** CI5:3] report the most current cases of online harassment. Sample cases reported on Cyber-stalking.net include a woman who was stalked by someone claiming to be an FBI agent and a British man sentenced to two years in prison for carrying out a 'cyber-terror campaign' against a Canadian woman. Volunteer organizations such as Working to Halt Online Abuse (WHOA) [**www** CI5:4], help victims of abusive CMC and educate the public and law enforcement officers about online harassment.

'FEMINIZING' THE INTERNET AND CMC

Along with writing about the gender differences in CMC and the challenges to women computer users, Stephanie Brail and other early adopters created some of the first women-oriented web communities such as Webgrrls International [**www** CI5:5], Cybergrrl [**www** CI5:6], and Femina [**www** CI5:7]. Brail founded Amazon City to reach women around the world and change the way they see themselves. More recently, she created the interactive, creative 'herspace' to encourage and promote community-building for women artists and performers [**www** CI4:8]. There are also numerous mailing lists either for women or about issues concerning women.

The Institute for Women and Technology [**www** CI5:9] and the United Nations' group INSTRAW, among others, are seeking to raise awareness about the gendered nature of access to communication technologies. INSTRAW promotes the need to increase women's participation online through training resources and funding, and gender-sensitive policy development, regulation and action [**www** CI5:10]. The affiliated INSTRAW GAINS network allows user-driven online communities, whose members come from nearly 100 nations, to share knowledge related to gender equity policy development.

In another way to encourage more female participation online, some feminine gendered sites are incorporating women-oriented styles of communicating. This builds on arguments that women and men communicate differently, similar to Mary Flanagan's choices in creating the JosieTrue.com site for girls. Since women communicate narratively, journalling and blogging are ways that women are comfortable communicating.

BOX CI5:5 WOMEN, WEBLOGS AND DIASPORAS

Blogging keeps people connected with their communities, either next door or across the globe. Due to the increase of **diasporas**, or large-scale movements of communities and populations, entire cultures have become displaced from their historical and geographical roots. CMC allows these communities to expand globally while maintaining contact with others of their heritage.

Consider Shahla Aziz's blog. Hers is one of the 10,000 weblogs emerging from Iranians in just over a year's time. Most, like Shahla, live in Iran and are keen to share dialogue about Iranian cultural identity, build relationships both within and outside the country, and maintain the Iranian diasporic community worldwide. Many women like Shahla write openly about politics, culture and society. Unlike Shahla, many prefer to remain anonymous (Derakhshan, 2003).

Under authoritarian governance, speaking one's mind can result in major problems. At best, users who say anything critical against their nation or government may be silenced in subtle ways, from 'problems' with their telephone line or Internet Service Providers (ISPs) or confiscation of computer equipment. Many national governments in Africa and Asia have constituted internet-specific legislation in keeping with their controls on critical speech in other media and in the public sphere. At worst, users who are even just suspected of saying anything critical online are subjected to imprisonment and, some argue, even torture or murder.

WOMEN'S CMC IN GLOBAL CONTEXTS

Few studies discuss women users in poor or newly industrializing nations. In their study on gender and technology, Nancy Hafkin and Nancy Taggart (2001) report 22 percent of internet users in Asia and 38 percent in Latin America are women. Merely 6 percent of internet users in the Middle East are women. No definitive statistics are available for users in Africa.

Sophia Huyer (2001) of Women in Global Science and Technology (WIGSAT) argues that women can be empowered through control of communication and therefore the flow of information. CMC crosses not only national barriers, but also barriers between traditionally gendered spaces. While women may gain access to men's spaces (politics and the public sphere) through CMC, this also may allow men access to spaces generally reserved for women (home and private spaces) and lessen women's empowerment there (see Central Issues: Unit 1 and Focus Areas: Topic 3). Sarah Murison of the United Nations Development Program on Gender ranks access to technology as the third most important issue facing women, after poverty and violence. She explains that communication technologies are controlled by men, and therefore women are prohibited access in many regions.

Despite the many patriarchal, or male-dominated, systems in the Global South, women's organizations are narrowing the gender and technology gap there. Women are participating by building online communities to increase supportive dialogue, exchange information and promote activism. Building women-centered communities between the Global North and South aids how women face challenges around the world. For example, the Vrouwen ontmoeten Vrouwen (Women meeting Women) project in the Netherlands is a forum for women's organizations to distribute news online and discuss issues ranging from women and the environment to the results emerging from international forums on women's rights.

Particularly in times of crisis, citizens are silenced by traditional media, economic hardship and authoritarian governments. It is in such times that CMC is arguably the most important means for women to voice their concerns. From the Independent Women Journalists in Kosova [**www** CI5:11] to the Revolutionary Association of the Women of Afghanistan (RAWA) [**www** CI5:12], women's groups reported on the crises in their countries long before these crises made the front pages and opening stories of Western print and broadcast news. They are often challenged, however, to reach their own communities. Sharida, a RAWA member, notes: 'Unfortunately we cannot hope to use the internet to bring information to our own people. Can you use the internet to communicate with the eleventh century?' Women like Sharida are in the minority of women who enjoy access to engaging in CMC. Rosemary Brisco (2001), member of the Digital Divide Task

Force of the World Economic Forum, says: 'Three-fourths of women have not yet pressed the 'Power' button' to connect them to larger global communities'.

Those who do have access work to connect women with global communities. Women in the Global Digital Society Research and Practitioners' Group, for example, gather data on women's access to and use of IT worldwide. Comprised of women from Afghanistan, India, Israel, Morocco, the United Kingdom and the United States, the group examines access for women in the Global South. The group is also creating strategies for bridging the digital gender divide, and for facilitating the training of trainers who will work closely with civil society and non-governmental organizations (NGOs). The group has been guided by the efforts of Women's Learning Partnership for Rights, Development and Peace (WLP) [**www** CI5:13]. With partner organizations in Africa, Asia and the Middle East, WLP works to redefine women's and girls' roles in their communities, through leadership training, technical skill building and the creation of gender- and culture-specific multimedia educational materials.

These efforts make CMC more gender-balanced. Through community building and activism, women are finding new ways to raise their voices against gender imbalance and harassment. Community-building efforts through CMC foster both gender equity and, more broadly, the future growth of participatory democracy. Recall from Central Issues: Unit 3, collaborative links and community building through CMC benefit those who have been marginalized by differences in race, gender, class, ethnicity and nation. Participation in an open computer-mediated dialogue affords women a space to enhance both local and global understanding of such issues as national and ethnic differences, economic problems and communities in crisis. Women want to voice their concerns to the world, and CMC creates a space to do just that.

REVIEW

In this unit, we've examined gender difference and CMC. We have analyzed the factors that contribute to women's/girls' attitudes and use of CMC in relation to men's/boys'. We have explored why women have felt marginalized in cyberspace, and how and why men and women communicate differently online. We've also looked at cyberstalking and online harassment, which have demeaned women and girls. We've investigated issues of online gender anonymity. We have assessed the digital gender divide and the impact of CMC in poor nations and regions that have experienced political, economic, social and cultural change and, at times, crisis.

STIMULUS READINGS AND RESOURCES

AAUW (2000). *Tech-savvy: Educating girls in the new Computer Age*. Washington, DC: American Association of University Women.

Herring, S. C. (2003). Gender and power in online communication. In J. Holmes and M. Meyerhoff (eds), *The Handbook of Language and Gender* (pp. 202–28). Oxford: Blackwell.

Plymire, D.C. and Forman, P.J. (2000). Breaking the silence: lesbian fans, the internet, and the sexual politics of women's sport. *International Journal of Sexuality and Gender Studies*, 5 (2), 141–53.

Schumacher, P. and Morahan-Martin, P. (2001). Gender, internet and computer attitudes and experiences. *Computers in Human Behavior*, 17 (1), 95–110.

IDEAS FOR DISCUSSION AND INVESTIGATION

1 Take a look at several websites of interest to you that have bulletin boards. Can you tell which posters are men and which are women? How? What cues are you using? Are you basing these decisions on gender stereotypes? Based on your reading and analysis of the online and offline resources, do you think that women and men have recognizably different styles in CMC, contrary to the belief that CMC reduces the impact of gender difference?

2 Take a look at the brief notes about wikis in Focus Areas: Topic 9 and also look at the wiki sites at [**www** CI5:14] and [**www** CI5:15]. Do you think these sites are female-friendly? Are they exclusively female? Do you think that there should be female-only sites? Would that help build gender balance online? Why or why not? What other sites have you been to that illustrate some of the same characteristics as these wikis?

3 Visit a couple of online gaming sites – one MUD (text-based game) and one graphic game (visually driven). Which do you prefer? Why? What are the primary differences you see between the gaming styles? Do you agree that text-based games appeal more to women and graphic games appeal more to men? Are there particular stereotypes that affect your opinion? What other things do you think impact this gender style? What might you do to change these games so that they are more gender-balanced?

4 How do you think your 'real life' gender affects your participation in CMC? Are there online spaces you've been to that definitely don't appeal to you? Is this, in part, because of any gender stereotyping you do of yourself? Visit some specifically gendered sites, for example Colormathpink.com [**www** CI5:16]. Now go online and search for some male-gendered sites. How did you find these sites? How do you know that they are gendered? What visual and text-based cues are on the sites that gender them? Do you prefer sites aimed at your gender or sites aimed at another gender? Why?

UNIT 6

INTERPERSONAL ATTRACTION, CYBERSEX AND CYBERPORN

OVERVIEW

KEY TERMS

interpersonal attraction
cybersex
sexual health
pornography
moral panic

MAIN OBJECTIVES

- Address critically one of the more controversial aspects of cyberspace.
- Discuss how the internet can influence interpersonal attraction.
- Consider the nature of cybersex and the experience of online eroticism.
- Examine the debate about pornography on the internet and web.

ALL TALK AND NO ACTION

Why have a unit about cybersex and cyberporn? The short answer is because they're some of the most frequently talked about aspects of cyberspace. They're also some of the most popular activities in cyberspace. According to sexologist Raymond Noonan (1999), the first <alt.sex> newsgroup was set up in 1988, and there's been no stopping people since. In fact, Al Cooper and his colleagues (2000) have suggested that 20 percent of all internet users engage in some kind of online sexual activity, from seeking information or advice about sexual health and romance, to engaging in sexually-oriented chat, to viewing erotic images or buying erotic materials. In fact, if you just type 'sex' into Google or any search engine, you'll be amazed to see the volume of material returned – or maybe not.

www For weblinks and resources visit the CMC website at <www.sagepub.co.uk/resources/cmc>

Alternatively, check the real-time record of uncensored search-terms maintained by MetaSpy [**www** CI6:1], which shows how often people are looking for 'adult' material online. Either way, there's little doubt about the kind of 'saucy' CMC many people are in search of!

It's partly for this reason that sex on the net has also become a source of such intense fascination and, often, exaggeration in the press and in popular discourses about new communication technologies. In Box CI6:1 we've included just three typical examples of the way newspapers like to make sweeping statements about these issues, usually basing their reports on dramatic, but sometimes misleading, statistics. Needless to say, concerns about online sexual activities also often get caught up with broader issues about the commercialization, censorship and control of the internet, as well as general anxieties about the protection and welfare of children and young people.

BOX CI6:1 WHAT THE PAPERS SAY

One in ten web dates ends in bed

Nearly 25 percent of the 2,000 women surveyed by New Woman Online had formed a romantic relationship over the web. Most of them eventually met F2F. (*Guardian* newspaper, 28 September 2000)

Cybersex addiction widespread

In a new survey, almost one in ten respondents indicated they are addicted to sex and the internet . . . and about one in four acknowledged that their online sexual activities have felt out of control or caused problems in their lives. (MSNBC News, 18 July 2002)

One in three view online porn

Pornographic internet sites are proving a big hit with UK sufers with more than a third of users regularly visiting them. A survey by NetValue found that 3.6 million people in Britain log on to adult websites. (BBC News, 22 June 2000)

For all this talk, however, what's most surprising is just how little scholarly action there's been. Like it or not, however, sex and pornography are central issues in internet studies and the study of CMC. We still think it's important to be up-front about our own position. We've not written this book because we necessarily agree with all the issues we cover; nor do we include this unit because we want to promote cybersex or cyberporn! The only things we promote in this book are scholarship and a critical attitude. Sometimes this does mean having to deal with embarrassing and politically or morally sensitive issues. It's important to be able to discuss such issues in an academic fashion and to establish more contextualized understandings amidst all the hype and hysteria. Most important of all, we believe that any discussion about attraction and sexuality on the internet also helps clarify some major theoretical issues about the nature of CMC and the distinction too easily drawn between what's 'real' and what's 'virtual'.

ONLINE ROMANCE AND INTERPERSONAL ATTRACTION

Of course, whatever the press headlines might have us believe, it's not all just about sex on the internet. Much of what happens in the way of online **interpersonal attraction** is about love and romance. A clear manifestation of this is the proliferation of web-based dating agencies like Cyberdating International [**www** CI6:2], which teases us with the words 'because, you never know who you'll meet!' Or there's Match.com [**www** CI6:3], which just offers to help you 'meet your match'. On the other hand, there's also Adult Friend Finder [**www** CI6:4], which goes further by promising to 'put a little spice in your sex life!' Either way, the internet is seen here to facilitate romantic exchanges in more or less the same way newspapers and magazines have been for many decades. What's different, however, is that, because of the technological affordances of speed and synchronicity, CMC can also offer something much more immediate and interactive.

From the CMC research discussed in Basic Theory: Unit 4, we've already seen that, while it may take longer to make friends in cyberspace, people eventually do, and when they do these are often very intense and meaningful relationships – sometimes valued even more highly than offline relationships. Psychologist Patricia Wallace (1999) examines a range of factors which influence the establishment and maintenance of interpersonal attraction. In particular, she looks at reasons why people are usually attracted to each other and considers how this might compare with the formation of romantic relationships in CMC. We'll just pick out the four main points she makes here (Box CI6:2).

BOX CI6:2 FOUR GOOD REASONS TO FANCY SOMEONE ONLINE

- *Promise of future interaction.* One important factor in determining how likely we are to be attracted to someone is whether or not we anticipate future interaction – there's little point investing time and energy in someone if you're never going to see them again! This is why, in CMC, frequency of contact and a commitment to spending time online are such good predictors of the likelihood of an intimate relationship. So the same principle simply applies to online as well as offline attraction.
- *Birds of a feather.* Although we sometimes like to think that 'opposites attract', the fact of the matter is that research shows how it's more a case of 'birds of a feather stick together'. In other words, the law of attraction states that people with similar attitudes and ideas are more likely to be attracted to each other. Here's where the internet really comes into its own: one thing cyberspace really does afford – often more so than life offline – is the chance to associate with like-minded people. So the fact that you may know only a few things about someone online is often enough for you to make up your mind about them; as long as you both have enough in common you are likely to be attracted to each other.
- *Self-esteem and humor.* One good reason for liking someone is if they like you – we always like people who make us feel good about ourselves! In fact, this is partly how we become increasingly attracted to people, by showing an interest, paying compliments and being responsive. Once again, there's no reason why these aspects of

interpersonal attraction may not be communicated in cyberspace; in fact, what many people find so appealing about online chat and messaging is just how attentive people often are. Social attractiveness is also closely linked with the use of humor, which, though joke-telling and word-play, may also be conveyed with great effect in CMC.

- *Self-disclosure and intimacy.* Although physical appearance is usually extremely powerful in shaping our attraction to someone (or not!), there are also many advantages to the relative anonymity afforded by the various communication niches of the internet. Part of the process of getting to know and like, and maybe even love, someone is the intimate and trusting act of disclosing things about ourselves. As we have seen, in CMC people often feel much freer to drop their guard, to let their hair down and to reveal much more about themselves than they might face-to-face – hence the 'hyperpersonal model' (Walther, 1996). (Remember also Roberts *et al.*'s self-identified shy people in Basic Theory: Unit 5, p. 62.)

Basically, then, the promise of future interaction, together with similarity, humor and self-disclosure, ensure that there's little about CMC which would prevent most of us from finding someone potentially attractive in cyberspace. In fact, it may be argued that CMC makes things even easier for finding someone attractive. And where there's attraction, there's the potential for sexual attraction; and where's there's sexual attraction, there's the potential for sex.

ONLINE SEX: VSEX OR CYBERSEX?

Perhaps, we should first start by asking what sex is, even though the answer probably seems really obvious. Without getting into too much detail, the most important point to make is that sex is usually defined by dictionaries like the *Concise Oxford Dictionary* in quite loose terms like 'mutual attraction and desire' and 'the gratification of these desires'. Importantly, it's not *necessarily* defined only in terms of physical intercourse – even if this is what we usually think of in an everyday sense. Even within long-term, intimate relationships couples sometimes have different ideas about what 'proper sex' or 'good sex' should be about. Besides, if sex were such an obvious matter, people wouldn't be making big money selling guidebooks on 'how to enhance your sex life'. Nonetheless, whether or not sex must involve physical contact between two people is still a point of debate (see 'Ideas for further discussion'), and is something which rests as the heart of **cybersex** – or what Nancy Deuel (1996: 131) calls 'Vsex'.

> I feel . . . that Vsex . . . is a creative sexual outlet in the form of interactive personalized erotica, providing a mental (and no doubt physical) stimulation. Unlike RL sex, however, in the anonymity of cyberspace there is little pressure or stress of the sort imposed on an individual by another's physical presence.

What Deuel is arguing here is that online sexual experiences, however 'virtual', can be no less real or meaningful to people. It's for this very reason that we prefer not to use the term *virtual sex* (or *Vsex*) and instead favour less ambiguous terms like *computer-enabled sex* or just *cybersex*. Whatever label we choose, however, sexual encounters on the internet are some of the least understood aspects of interpersonal relationships in cyberspace. As Noonan (1999: 146) notes, the role of sex on the internet is usually just politely ignored. Even though there are no exact figures, it seems that online sex is pervasive and popular in virtual communities. For example, in one study cited by Noonan, as many as 52 percent of respondents reported having had cybersex, 36 percent of whom had reached orgasm and 25 percent said they had faked it.

In what have to be some of the most comprehensive studies to date – although by no means without their problems – Al Cooper and his colleagues conducted online surveys of just over 9,000 people in 1998 (see Cooper *et al*., 1999), and then again in 2000 with nearly 40,000 people (see Cooper *et al*., 2001). ◎ Some of the most noteworthy findings to emerge from the first survey were that:

◎ One of the biggest problems with this type of research is that it can rely too heavily on self-selected respondents. In their 2002 paper, however, Cooper *et al.* try to address this and other methodological issues.

- The vast majority (92 percent) of respondents reported spending under eleven hours a week visiting sex sites, although as many as 13 percent of them reported accessing sex sites while at work.
- Seventy-five percent of respondents said they kept their online sexual pursuits secret, something which most of them did not feel guilty about.
- Men were six times more likely to engage in online sexual activities than women, and, while men preferred to look at erotic images online, women tended to favour sexual chat rooms.
- Sixty-one percent of respondents reported sometimes lying about their age when visiting sex sites but only 5 percent of them reported switching sex.

Just how many people have cybersex is one thing, what cybersex actually is, is another. At its broadest, online sexual activity can involve a range of CMC niches such as adult chat rooms, sex-related websites, webcam sex and sexually explicit newsgroups.

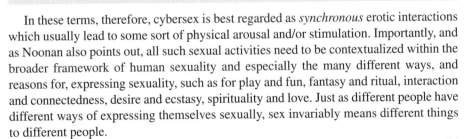

BOX CI6:3 CYBERSEX IS . . .

. . . suggestive or explicit erotic messages or sexual fantasies exchanged via the computer connected with others who are online at the same time. (Noonan, 1999: 163)

. . . a series of communications protocols and virtual actions occurring in real-time between two (or more) participants that establish explicitly sexual stimulation as the focus of the interaction. (Deuel, 1996: 130)

In these terms, therefore, cybersex is best regarded as *synchronous* erotic interactions which usually lead to some sort of physical arousal and/or stimulation. Importantly, and as Noonan also points out, all such sexual activities need to be contextualized within the broader framework of human sexuality and especially the many different ways, and reasons for, expressing sexuality, such as for play and fun, fantasy and ritual, interaction and connectedness, desire and ecstasy, spirituality and love. Just as different people have different ways of expressing themselves sexually, sex invariably means different things to different people.

So what actually happens in cybersex? Nancy Deuel (1996) offers an unusually candid discussion of what text-based, computer-enabled sex is actually like – although it's still far from explicit. Normally starting with suggestive self-descriptions (or 'nicks') with varying degrees of sexual overtone (e.g. *female-nudist*, *BigMan*, *femmefatale*), people may also use other descriptive information and orientations, depending on the CMC niche (e.g. 'emotes' and 'whispers', or 'props' such as clothing). As Deuel puts it, the range of activities is limited only by people's imagination and their typing skills. Certainly, physical activity can vary from playful sexual banter with little offline emotional engagement or physical involvement to more activity offline. More often than not, cybersex proceeds with auto-stimulation and masturbation. According to one writer cited by Deuel, cybersex therefore ends up rather like a blend of phone sex and raunchy pen-pal letters. As participants become more and more aroused, there's a greater sense of simulation in terms of the development of real-time interaction, mutual stimulation, the right tempo and the unfolding of expression (e.g. *ooooh yehhhhhhh!!!!*).

Of course, nowadays, cybersex is not just text-based, which is what Deuel was writing about back in 1996. Online romantics and lovers also supplement their text-based interactions by sending photos, directing each other to personal homepages, or connecting up by means of webcams. It's in this way that online romances often end up offline. In her research, for example, Andrea Baker (2000) examined the online relationships of couples who had met in a range of online contexts (e.g. chat, newsgroups and MUDs) and found that the relationships involved varying levels of commitment, from friendship and dating, to cohabitation or marriage. A typical pattern of relationship development for online couples was to start making telephone calls and then eventually to meet face-to-face. In point of fact, not only do many online relationships make their way offline, but much online sexual and romantic communication is done by people to supplement their offline personal relationships. For example, email and instant messaging can be useful ways for couples to stay in touch while apart. Similarly, in her discussion of teenage online romances, Lynn Clark (1998: 159) notes how young people often use chat spaces to experiment with different ways of flirting and being romantic with each other in preparation for their offline social lives. Once again, the division between online and offline is blurred. ◎

◎ Recall the discussion of 'hybridity' in Central Issues: Unit 3 (p. 113).

Cybersex is clearly an exciting and important sexual outlet for many people, although probably for most people, just one of many possible ways of expressing themselves sexually. For some people, however, cybersex is just too good. In their second, larger survey, Al Cooper and his colleagues also found that nearly 10 percent of male respondents were 'addicted' to cybersex (and cyberporn), compared with just 6 percent of females. While the issue of so-called 'internet addiction' is covered in Central Issues: Unit 7, this does raise one other useful point about online sexual activity.

SEXUAL HEALTH AND ONLINE INFORMATION AND SUPPORT SERVICES

Very briefly, and before going on to discuss cyberporn, it's also worth making the point that there's a world of sexual activity on the internet which is more educational than erotic. By this, we mean the range of websites and online resources offering useful **sexual health** information. In fact, if you run a search for 'sex' through Google, you are just as likely to find a website offering safer-sex advice as you are to find webcam porn. Especially for people who may not otherwise be able to access sensitive or potentially face-threatening information offline, internet resources like these offer a more comfortable way of finding out all sorts of information and advice. One good example we can think of is young people concerned about issues around sexually transmitted diseases or pregnancy and contraception advice. Perhaps also anyone with questions about their sexual orientation.

BOX CI6:4 A SELECTION OF ONLINE SEXUAL HEALTH, INFORMATION AND IDENTITY RESOURCES

- Safersex.org [**www** CI6:5]
- The Sexual Health infoCenter [**www** CI6:6]
- The Body (HIV/AIDS awareness) [**www** CI6:7]
- Sexual Health.com [**www** CI6:8]
- Sex, etc. (a website for teens) [**www** CI6:9]
- Body Positive (about body image) [**www** CI6:10]
- The Gay Student Center [**www** CI6:11]

By recognizing this more educational or informational function of the internet, we are better able to put into perspective all the negative assumptions about online sex – or 'sex-negative perspectives', as Raymond Noonan calls them. Of course, there are also many opportunities to find out about academic research in these areas as well, such as the Australian Research Centre in Sex, Health and Society at LaTrobe University [**www** CI6:12]. One interesting research paper made available on their website is a report titled *It's just easier* by Lynne Hillier and her colleagues which looks at the unique opportunities on the internet for young gay and lesbian people (Hillier *et al.*, 2001).

ONLINE PORNOGRAPHY: MORAL PANIC, MORAL MAZE

Any discussion about online sexual activity inevitably and eventually comes round to talking about cyberporn. Indeed, one thing that there's no shortage of is statistics about the prevalence and economics of online sex sites. At the time of preparing this book, for example, we undertook a fairly random review of some widely available figures which included the following:

- Online **pornography** revenues in the United States are expected to reach $400 million by 2006, compared with $230 million in 2001.
- Thirty-six percent of British internet users regularly log on to adult sites, a fifth of whom are students.
- Some 8.49 million Asian internet users visited adult websites in January 2001, which is equivalent to nearly 50 percent of all active Asian internet users; in Korea, which has the highest number of visitors to adult sites, 39 percent of them are women.
- In 2001, there were 74,000 adult websites accounting for 2 percent of all web content on the net and bringing in estimated profits of US$1 billion.

As Canadian scholar Michael Mehta (1998) says, it's ironic that one of the most high-tech, modern communication technologies is widely used to satisfy one of the most basic of human drives: sex. In many respects, cyberporn has also been at the forefront of communication/s in cyberspace, with the ever growing popularity and ubiquity of technologies like webcams and streaming video. In an article for the journal *CyberPsychology and Behavior*, however, Storm King (2000) makes her position very clear, describing all this as 'the psychological consequences of communication anarchy'!

Remember, if you ever need to find out what's meant by some technical term, just type a straightforward request (e.g. 'What is streaming video?') into a search engine like Ask Jeeves <www.ask.com>.

It's emotive language like this which has made it very difficult for scholars to engage properly with these issues. Indeed, one of the biggest stumbling blocks in any debate about pornography is the difficulty in deciding what's meant by charged terms like 'obscene', 'indecent', 'perverted', 'weird' or 'unnatural', and where one draws the distinction between what's 'erotic' and what's 'pornographic'. Part of the problem is that these are such subjective, culturally and historically defined terms; one country or person's idea of 'softcore' is another's idea of 'hardcore'. Often what you think is a real turn-on someone else will think is a bit kinky, while someone else will consider it a perversion. What you and your friends find perfectly acceptable in terms of sexual practice your parents might find perfectly shocking. Ultimately, any perspective on pornography is based on subjective social, political, ethical and moral judgements. In the case of online pornography, judgements also need to be informed by an understanding of the technology involved.

One of the best examples of how public discussions about pornography and the internet can be both technologically misinformed and highly emotive was *Time* magazine's famous report about cyberporn in 1995. The magazine story was based on a notorious study by Marty Rimm in which he had looked at a large amount of sexually explicit material on the internet. Foolishly for an internet researcher, however, he had chosen to overlook the crucial distinction between different communication niches in cyberspace. The claim made by Rimm, which was dramatically published in a cover story by *Time*, was that some 83 percent of hardcore pornographic pictures were widely available on the internet, posing a tremendous threat to children – hence the dramatic image on the cover (Figure 14). In fact, only 1 percent of the nearly 100,000 images Rimm looked at were on newsgroups and most of what he found was available only through subscription-based adult bulletin boards. As such, his claim also hinged on a gross generalization across online contexts.

A much more detailed discussion of this case can be found at The Cyberporn Debate, hosted by *elab* at Vanderbilt University [**www** CI6:14].

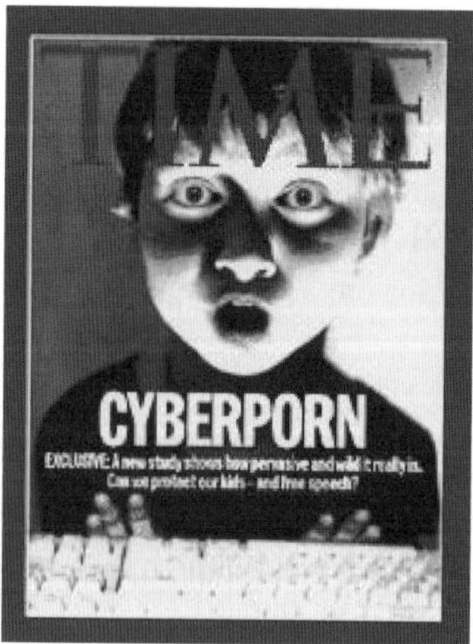

FIGURE 14

Time magazine, 3 July 1995. *Source elab* at Vanderbilt University, Nashville, TN

In many respects, the *Time* magazine fiasco is a good example of what Israeli scholars Erich Goode and Nachman Ben-Yehuda (1994) call a **moral panic** whereby, after a period of uncertainty and rumourmongering, a topical issue is suddenly taken up by the media and the public with surprisingly credulity and certainty. In short, there is a public outcry.

BOX CI6:5 WHAT IS A MORAL PANIC?

A moral panic is characterized by the feeling, held by a substantial number of the members of a given society, that evil-doers pose a threat to the society and to the moral order as a consequence of their behaviour and, therefore, 'something should be done' about them and their behaviour. (Goode and Ben-Yahuda, 1994: 31)

The rapid spread of a moral panic is explained in part by a psychological phenomenon known as the 'availability heuristic' which psychologist Patricia Wallace (1999) helps explain. It means that anything sensational will often pop into our heads much more easily or quickly, and if something comes to mind easily, people often make the mistake of assuming that it must therefore be more widespread or prevalent than it necessarily is. However, just because something springs to mind doesn't mean it's important.

The notion of a moral panic is actually a useful one to bear in mind when thinking about CMC and the internet more generally. As we showed in Basic Theory: Unit 3, popular ideas about new technologies are so often influenced by fairly ignorant (unempirical) exaggerations in the popular imagination. In terms of sex and the internet, for example, both Wallace and Noonan are quick to point out just how similar to other communication technologies these issues are. Erotic and pornographic material is produced across many media: telephones, televisions, cameras, videos, movies and, of course, books and magazines. Prior to the internet, a long-standing, popular concern was the impact of violent television programs on children, and a moral panic existed about so-called 'video nasties'. Nor are scholars clear about what the effects of pornography really are, whether online or offline – not least because the issue is so easily lost in a moral and political maze.

> On the internet, as in real life, it is left to the individual to navigate her or his own way through the dizzying array of sex information and services available. As a result, too, there are often those who seek to impose their own agendas and viewpoints on what others may view or the services to which others may have access. (Noonan, 1999: 143)

In fact, all this brings us neatly to concerns about the restriction and regulation of pornography on the internet, and especially in the context of children and young people. Related to the *Time* magazine article from 1995, you will no doubt be well aware of other panics about sexual perverts 'stalking' the internet and preying on children ◉ . There have of course been important efforts to promote filtering software and to establish methods for monitoring content and restricting access to 'adult' material. Needless to say, however, the issues are complex and often quite contradictory, as Michael Mehta (2001) explains (see 'Stimulus readings' below). It is also essential to contextualize any concerns about sex and the internet. For example, in the case of 'paedophile internet stalkers', did you

◉ Please look at box BT6:9 on p. 79 and read about how Microsoft has entered this public debate.

know that as much as half of all child sex abuse is committed by parents, and is almost always committed by people known to the child, including uncles, cousins, grandfathers and, occasionally, female relatives? ◎ These are shocking statistics and in no way excuse the crime; they are, however, just the kind of details we need in order to think more complexly about cybersex and cyberporn and to situate new communication technologies in their broader social context.

◎ If you're interested in finding out more about this, try the National Society for the Prevention of Cruelty to Children at <www.nspcc.org.uk>, although similar figures are also found in other countries too.

Make no mistake, cyberporn is also big business. Although we may like to think that where there's sex there's love, the truth of the matter is that it's more likely to be love of money! One good indication of just how much money is to be made by the online sex/porn industry is a commercial organization like the XXXMedia Group [**www** CI6:13] which offers specialist consulting services to people wanting to set up their own cyberporn websites. At the end of the day, the internet invariably reflects the sexual desires and romantic aspirations of its users and the societies to which these people belong. It is wrong (i.e. too simplistic, too technologically deterministic) to hold the internet solely responsible for the prevalence of cyberporn. Certainly, anonymity, physical distance and perceived lack of accountability will contribute to participation in these more controversial aspects of cybersociety. Nonetheless, while there are without question people for whom cybersex and cyberporn may be compelling pastimes, there are also many people who simply get bored after a while and don't bother. Either way, sex and pornography are ultimately about relationship and identity, and as such constitute important topics for discussion in CMC.

REVIEW

In this unit, we started by explaining why cybersex and cyberporn are worthwhile topics for discussion in CMC before going on to think about love and romance more generally in the context of interpersonal attraction. We then looked at sex and cybersex, acknowledging how it is not always clear what these necessarily entail. Brief mention was made of health education and information resources on the internet. We finished by discussing the prevalence of, and public debates about, cyberporn and pointed to the importance of finding more complex, contextualized ways to understand these moral rather than technological issues.

STIMULUS READINGS AND RESOURCES

MetaSpy (for popular search terms) [**www** CI6:1].

The Cyberporn Debate (Vanderbilt University, USA) [**www** CI6:14].

Cybersex and Cyberporn (University of Amsterdam, Netherlands) [**www** CI6:15].

Baker, A. (2000). Two by two in cyberspace: getting together and connecting online. *Cyberpsychology and Behavior*, 3 (2), 237–42.

Cooper, A., Scherer, C. and Marcus, I.D. (2002). Harnessing the power of the internet to improve sexual relationships. In A. Cooper (ed.), *Sex and the internet: a guidebook for clinicians* (pp. 209–230). New York: Brunner Routledge.

Mehta, M.D. (2001). Pornography in Usenet: a study of 9,800 randomly selected images. *CyberPsychology and Behavior*, 4 (6), 695–704.

Noonan, R.J. (1999). The psychology of sex: a mirror from the internet. In J. Gackenbach (ed.), *Psychology and the Internet: Intrapersonal, interpersonal and transpersonal implications* (pp. 143–68). San Diego, CA: Academic Press.

IDEAS FOR FURTHER DISCUSSION AND INVESTIGATION

1 Search the web to see some of the latest figures for the prevalence of online sex and pornography. How do these figures compare with the ones we've reported here? What appear to be the dominant issues or concerns being reported? What/who are the main sources (e.g. academic, commercial or media) providing this kind of information?

2 Is it possible to cheat on your offline partner by having sexual relations with someone online? How far do you have to go in order to be unfaithful? Where would you draw the line between surfing, flirting and infidelity? Have a look at the way this issue is discussed – sometimes in quite an emotive way – on the website Infidelity-Infidelity.com [**www** CI6: 16]. Issues such as these raise important questions about what's 'real' and what's not.

3 Print off a copy of *New to cyber liaisons* [**www** CI6: 17]. This is a personal account of an email romance/cybersexual encounter written in 1997 by a disabled woman called Sue. What is most striking to you about the way Sue tells her story? What issues does Sue and Rob's romantic relationship raise? What does their encounter reveal about the opportunities and difficulties of CMC?

4 Thinking specifically about attempts to monitor and control cyberporn, have a look at some of the issues about censorship on the internet by visiting the website of the Australian organization Libertus [**www** CI6: 18]. Its page titled 'The debate: government control or individual responsibility?' looks at examples of attempts to censor 'problematic' content. In particular, consider the case of Yahoo!'s struggle in the French courts following an order to block French users from buying Nazi memorabilia auctioned on its US site see also [**www** CI6: 19]. In this regard, what do you think the best solutions should be for pornography?

UNIT 7

ANTISOCIAL BEHAVIOR, ONLINE COMPULSION AND 'ADDICTION'

OVERVIEW

KEY TERMS

addiction and compulsion
Internet Addiction Disorder
Problematic/Pathological Internet Use
antisocial behavior
online gambling

MAIN OBJECTIVES

- Examine the allegation that CMC is necessarily compulsive and antisocial.
- Review the history of, and debates about, so-called Internet Addiction Disorder.
- Consider online gambling as a case-study example of compulsive behavior online.
- Critique generalizations about CMC, with particular regard to problematic behavior.

ANTISOCIAL, ADDICTIVE CMC: SETTING THE SCENE

The year is 1989. The key player is 'superhacker' Kevin Mitnick, known as the most wanted computer hacker in the world. Mitnick pleads guilty to stealing security programs and illegal possession of long-distance telephone codes. Instead of being imprisoned (although he would spend nearly five years behind bars for subsequent allegations), Mitnick is sentenced to six months' rehabilitation to treat his 'computer addiction'. The director of the rehabilitation center is reported as saying Mitnick needs treatment because, in her own words, his 'hacking gives a sense of self-esteem he doesn't get in the real world . . . This is a new and growing addiction.'

www For weblinks and resources visit the CMC website at
<www.sagepub.co.uk/resources/cmc>

Now cut to 1991 and the beginning of Britain's 'hacking trial of the decade'. At Southwark Crown Court in London the first major case is being heard under the new Computer Misuse Law which introduced strict penalties for unauthorized access to computer systems. Three defendants are charged under the Act. However, while two of them have pleaded guilty, nineteen-year-old Paul Bedworth is claiming extenuating circumstances due to computer addiction. Expert witness Professor Griffith-Edwards of the Maudsley Hospital declares Bedworth is 'an obsessive person, totally besotted with computers . . . he's hooked on computing . . . The child, whose best friend is a computer rather than a person, is not going to function normally in society.' Bedworth is duly acquitted.

These are both real stories retold by Carla Surratt (1999) and they add to the colorful history of computer or internet addiction, with its hackers, cybersex addicts and so-called 'cyber-widows'. Popular interest in 'internet addiction' took off in the 1980s with the rise of hackers like Mitkin and Loyd Blankenship (a.k.a. 'The Mentor'). In his online narrative *Hacker's Manifesto*, Blankenship describes how at school he was smarter than other students, but teachers and family regarded him as an under-achiever. His identity changes, however, when he's online. This is how he describes the feeling he gets when he hacks into a system:

> A door opened to a world . . . rushing through the phone line *like heroin through an addict's veins*, an electronic pulse is sent out, a refuge from the day-to-day incompetencies is sought . . . a board is found. This is it . . . this is where I belong. [**www** CI7:1 , emphasis ours]

Although hacking continues to be a fairly specialist activity, excessive internet use is not just a problem for hackers. Along with cybersex/porn, the idea of 'internet addiction' has actually become a central feature of public anxieties about the nature of CMC and the negative impact of the internet on offline social life. Recall from Basic Theory: Unit 4, one of the two main allegations commonly leveled against CMC is that it's necessarily antisocial, sucking people into cyberspace and drawing them away from 'proper' relationships in the 'real' world. In fact, like cyberporn, the whole idea about 'internet addiction' has been something of a moral panic (see Box C16:5 on p. 145).

MORAL PANIC: ADDICTION AND COMPULSION

BOX CI7:1 STUDENTS ARE THE WORST?

A multi-campus study by psychologist Keith Anderson found nearly 10 percent of internet-using college students spend enough time online that their usage meets the criteria for dependence. Compared with the average internet user's fifteen minutes/day, students typically spend 100 minutes/day online. However, a small group of students spends more than 400 minutes/day. College students are particularly susceptible to excessive internet use because of easy accessibility and also, according to Anderson, because 'the sense of security afforded by the anonymity of the internet provides some students with less risky opportunities for developing virtual relationships'. (*APA Monitor on Psychology*, May 2001[**www** CI7:2)]

In the 1990s there was something of an 'online rush' as the internet became more and more popular in many countries. In an article for *CMC* magazine entitled 'I'm online, you're online', CMC scholar Steven Jones (1996) noted how the idea of addiction soon became a part of people's experience of the online rush:

> Internet addiction seems to be catching on as the latest version of public fear of technology. Given the numerous warnings throughout the twentieth century about computers, television, and movies, it seems a medium cannot achieve widespread use without sowing fear among various groups that it will be addictive.

What he's saying is that internet 'addiction' isn't so much about the technology but about the choices people make concerning their social interaction online and offline. Recall from Basic Theory: Unit 3 the fears around the telegraph and the hysteria which typically accompanies the emergence of any new technology. Just as the telegraph caused an uproar in the nineteenth century, the internet caused similar fears that we would no longer communicate FtF. However, most of the people who panicked (or are still panicking) weren't exactly certain what addiction was in the first place. Indeed, there have been numerous definitions offered for the notion of addiction itself, and one of the biggest problems with the idea of 'internet addiction' is likewise a lack of definitional clarity. How much time must be spent online daily? Are there particularly addictive activities?

There's clearly a need to establish some objective, measurable criteria for assessing excessive internet use. One important point of reference in analyzing the concept of 'addiction' is the American Psychiatric Association's *Diagnostic and Statistical Manual of Mental Disorders* (known as *DSM*). For psychiatrists and clinical psychologists, the *DSM* is the professional reference for assessing psychiatric and psychological disorders. Which is not to say, however, it's without problems. In fact, some scholars question the validity of the *DSM*, arguing it's an outdated, ideology-driven text that should no longer be used to diagnose people. Nonetheless, it continues to be an influential document and many clinicians find it a useful point of reference. ◎ In particular, there are two notions relevant to people concerned about excessive internet use: addiction and compulsion.

◎ There's actually been a lot of discussion about the validity of the DSM – whether it's actually a reliable indicator of psychological well-being. Follow some of this controversy by reading *Dump the DSM* [**www** C17:3] and a counter-argument [**www** C17: 4].

ADDICTION

Whatever reservations people may have about the *DSM*, it's worth seeing what the most recent version has to say about **addiction**. Interestingly, the *DSM* categorizes addiction under the general category 'Substance Dependence', the main diagnostic criterion for which is a maladaptive pattern of substance use, leading to significant psychological impairment. Within any given year, this impairment is manifested by at least three symptoms from a list of conditions including withdrawal, loss of control over the substance, and continued consumption of the substance despite adverse consequences. Immediately, we see a problem here with applying the term 'addiction' to internet use, since the term is properly reserved for bodily and psychological dependence on a physical substance – and not a behavioral pattern. With a certain amount of good humor, Joseph Walther and Larry Reid (2000: 114) critique the way that 'addiction' has been associated with internet use (see Box C17:2).

BOX CI7:2 ARE YOU AN 'ACADAHOLIC'?

Do you feel as if you spend a lot of time reading and writing, but you need to spend still more? Do you ignore family members in order to concentrate on theories, research, or lectures? Do you postpone personal activities just to eke out a few more minutes for revising a manuscript? If so, you may be an acadaholic – someone who is addicted to academe.

Of course, 'acadaholism' isn't a real disease. But some scholars have claimed that internet addiction is – using criteria very similar to those we invented for acadaholism.

COMPULSION

Along with associating 'addiction' to internet use, **compulsion** is similarly connected with CMC. Compulsion is a different, but related, technical term, used by the DSM to describe any repetitive behaviors, such as hand-washing and checking on things over and over again. It's thought the purpose of such behaviors is to prevent or reduce anxiety, rather than provide gratification or pleasure. In many cases, people with compulsive tendencies feel driven to perform the behaviors to prevent a perceived 'dreaded situation'. Compulsions are excessive and, most importantly, interfere significantly with people's lives and personal relationships. It is this capacity for an excessive activity to seriously disturb people's usual or daily functioning which, in some respects, makes it a more relevant notion in the case of excessive internet use.

INTERNET ADDICTION DISORDER: VALID OR NOT?

The fact that the American Psychiatric Association has never officially recognized 'internet addiction' hasn't stopped scholars studying excessive internet use and trying to establish it as a proper 'disorder'. Most of this research emerged in the mid-1990s, when the label 'internet addiction' started popping up in both academic research and the popular press – particularly in the form of **Internet Addiction Disorder**. ◎

◎ Have a look also at what the American Psychological Association has to say on the matter: **www** C17:15.

Ironically, so-called Internet Addiction Disorder (IAD) actually began as something of a joke when, in 1995, psychiatrist Ivan Goldberg posted his 'official' diagnostic criteria for IAD to the *Psychology of the internet* (see an excerpt of Goldberg's posting in Box CI7:3). Goldberg cleverly based his criteria on the APA criteria for substance abuse:

BOX CI7:3 INTERNET ADDICTION DISORDER

These are some of the main diagnostic criteria which Goldberg jokingly proposed in 1995. Internet Addiction Disorder is recognized as:

A maladaptive pattern of internet use, leading to clinically significant impairment or distress as manifested by the following:

(a) Tolerance defined by markedly increased amounts of time on internet to achieve satisfaction.

(b) Withdrawal symptoms: anxiety, obsessive thinking about what is happening on the internet, fantasies or dreams about internet, voluntary or involuntary typing movements of the fingers.

(c) A great deal of time is spent in activities related to internet use (e.g., buying internet books, trying out new web browsers, researching internet vendors, organizing files of downloaded materials).

(d) Important social, occupational, or recreational activities are given up or reduced because of internet use.

That Goldberg intended his diagnostic criteria as a joke was subtly communicated by inclusions of the word 'humor' in the web address for his webpage about IAD. Several months later the truth came out in a *Wired* magazine article (Brown, 1996) which quoted Goldberg as saying:

> It's all bullshit . . .There's no such thing as internet addiction. The internet is about as addictive as work. Sure, there are workaholics, but they're simply working to avoid the other problems in their lives.

Despite the intended humor of Goldberg's posting, the press ran with the concept of this new addiction. Academic and mental health researchers, fueled by Goldberg's criteria and press coverage, followed suit. Parents nervously analyzed children's activities and time spent online. People even started talking about 'cyberwidows' – women whose partners had become hooked on the thrills of life online. Organizations and corporations profited from 'internet addiction' fears, developing tracking software for keeping tabs on 'addicts'.

'Addiction' is clearly a popular term with lay people and scholars because of its medical cachet and because it made the issue of excessive internet use sound more dramatic or serious. One manifestation of the medicalization of excessive internet use was also the establishment of therapeutic and self-help centers to 'treat' peopled addicted to the internet. For example, Kimberly Young founded the Center for Online Addiction which continues to offer online therapy [**www** CI7:5]. As a more serious attempt to define and measure so-called 'internet addiction', Young also developed her own diagnostic criteria (Box CI7:4).

BOX CI7:4 DIAGNOSTIC QUESTIONNAIRE FOR ADDICTIVE INTERNET USE

1 Do you feel preoccupied with the internet (think about previous online activity or anticipate next online session)?

2 Do you feel the need to use the internet with increasing amounts of time in order to achieve satisfaction?

3 Have you repeatedly made unsuccessful efforts to control, cut back, or stop internet use?

4 Do you feel restless, moody, depressed, or irritable when attempting to cut down or stop internet use?

5 Do you stay on-line longer than originally intended?

6 Have you jeopardized or risked the loss of significant relationship, job, educational or career opportunity because of the internet?

7 Have you lied to family members, therapist, or others to conceal the extent of involvement with the internet?

8 Do you use the internet as a way of escaping from problems or of relieving a dysphoric mood (e.g., feelings of helplessness, guilt, anxiety, depression)?

(Young, 1998)

PROBLEMATIC OR PATHOLOGICAL INTERNET USE

There's little doubt that, for a relatively small number of people, excessive use of the internet can be problematic. Like many activities in life, people can become dependent on their online activities. Most IAD studies have, however, been greatly limited by their methodology, especially in relying on self-selected research participants. ◎ For example, Young and others posted calls for participants on sites designed by and for heavy internet users. This is a bit like going into a shopping mall and asking people to come forward if they like shopping!

◎ Recall how this was also an issue with cybersex research in Central Issues: Unit 6 (p. 141).

Researchers have also tried to link 'internet addiction' with other addictive behaviors included in the *DSM*, such as pathological gambling, sexual addiction, obsessive day-trading, compulsive shopping and workaholism. All these specific behaviors or activities, say researchers, are related to excessive internet use. Many other scholars, however, have questioned the validity of 'internet addiction', and regard terms or official-sounding labels like IAD as inappropriate – especially given the lack of adequate diagnostic testing. Internet scholar Sherry Turkle (2001) makes the following case:

> The term addiction is most usefully saved for experiences with substances like heroin, which are always dangerous, always bad, always something to turn away from. The internet offers experiences in which people discover things about themselves, good and bad, usually complicated and hard to sort out. People grow and learn and discover new potential. People also discover preoccupations and fantasies that they may have never dealt with before and which may be very troubling. *If you call the internet addicting, then you have to call all powerful, evocative experience addicting* [our emphasis].

What critiques within Internet Studies and elsewhere have done is promote a more cautious approach to discussions of excessive internet use. The question always remains, by whose standards is internet use to be defined as excessive? Recent research has, therefore, tended to use labels like 'problematic' or 'pathological' to describe patterns and levels of internet use which have become debilitating and make it difficult for people to sustain their usual family and social lives or to hold down their jobs. **Problematic** or **Pathological Internet Use** (or PIU), for example, is described as 'disturbed patterns' of internet use, with symptoms like 'mood-altering' internet use, inability to fulfil major role obligations, guilty feelings and cravings for more (Morahan-Martin and Schumacher, 2000: 14).

Most studies of PIU have been conducted in the United States where the assumption is that such use (or misuse) is unhealthy. Studies in other countries like Taiwan, however, suggest PIU is instead rooted in how people relate to overall communication processes rather than to technology itself. A study of nearly 1,000 Taiwanese students by Chien Chou and Ming-Chun Hsiao (2000) suggests there's a type of pleasure for internet users, and the greater the pleasure experienced online, the greater the desire for even further use. According to Chou and Hsiao, this pleasure is found primarily in interaction with text, a sense of escapism, and relative anonymity when online. Importantly, however, another major source of pleasure is derived from interpersonal communication. In other words, what makes the internet compelling for many is person-to-person communication online.

ANTISOCIAL BEHAVIOR AND THE INTERNET

While researchers use terms like 'problematic' or 'pathological' internet use, empirical evidence to establish that such disorders exist remains limited. One interesting finding by researchers Janet Morahan-Martin and Phyllis Schumacher (2000: 26) is that for some problematic users the most important draw to CMC is online anonymity and the possibility for identity play. For users who go online to seek emotional support, chat and play very interactive games, the internet is 'socially liberating, the Prozac of social communication.' ◎

◎ The pros and cons of the internet's liberation potential are discussed in Basic Theory: Unit 5 (p. 62) and Central Issues: Unit 2 (p. 99).

This implies that people exhibiting **antisocial behavior** are better at communicating in virtual rather than real worlds. Recall from Basic Theory: Unit 4 the controversial claim by Robert Kraut and colleagues (1998) on the negative impact of CMC on offline communication and social interaction (p. 46). Kraut *et al.* concluded that increased internet use was associated with decreased FtF social interaction and increased depression and loneliness. From what you've seen in Basic Theory: Units 4–6, however, this finding flies in the face of claims that CMC is inherently social, facilitates sociality and even enhances it. Social psychologist Tom Tyler (2002: 204), for example, asserts that people tend to work CMC into their social 'tool-kit' – which also holds FtF, telephone, and traditional postal communication. Recall also from Basic Theory: Unit 6 how James Katz and Ron Rice have argued that CMC actually facilitates social involvement and generates social capital.

BOX CI7: 5 THE INVISIBLE MOUSE

Based on their long-term research program, James Katz and Ron Rice (2002) say the following. There are 'activities that can take place only in cyberspace or at least in computer-assisted environments and put into perspective the enormous richness and diversity of activities that are taking place in cyberspace'. Although it's not always easy to see what the social benefits are of millions of individuals spending time online, nonetheless all this individual human energy and interpersonal communication activity is having a tremendous impact on social life, creating a great deal of social involvement and collective social capital. It is, Katz and Rice argue, all about the workings of the 'invisible mouse'.

Israeli psychologists Yair Amichai-Hamburger and Elishiva Ben-Artzi (2003) have also challenged the kinds of antisociality allegations made by Kraut and colleagues – in particular, the idea that internet use leads to loneliness and social isolation. While Kraut *et al.* argued the internet *causes* loneliness, however, Amichai-Hamburger and Ben-Artzi suggest it's really only people who are already feeling lonely and perhaps more isolated who spend large amounts of time online. Thus it's not the technology *per se* which explains online behavior patterns but rather factors related to users themselves – and also the uses to which they put the internet. Amichai-Hamburger and Ben-Artzi argue the internet is 'not to be written off as an unhealthy intrusion to be avoided, but rather, for certain people, if used in the right way, it has the potential to enhance well-being' (p. 79). ◎

◎ Remember also from Basic Theory: Unit 5 the study by Lynne Roberts and her colleagues which found how CMC can enhance shy people's offline well-being (p. 62).

The truth of the matter is that, especially in the United States, scholars and journalists alike have been caught up with the wider debates about the decline in public engagement and perceived loss of community. (Remember our discussion in Central Issues: Unit 3 about nostalgic yearnings for 'traditional' community.) US scholar Robert Putnam is author of a widely read book, *Bowling Alone* (2000), on the decrease of civic participation. We're sure these concerns are also being felt in other parts of the world as well. Nonetheless, the important issue is whether it's really the internet's introduction that's declined civic connection. In fact, research on social interaction in the Global South indicates the introduction of television has greatly reduced a sense of civic engagement (Hooghe, 2002; Mutz *et al.*, 1993). Needless to say, the picture is a complex one, as the following commentator explains:

> For every story about internet addiction leading victims to ignore their families and become withdrawn, antisocial, and depressed, there is a countervailing example of a person who has found a support group, employment prospects, or a community of like-minded topical enthusiasts through the net. (Goodman, 2001)

A CASE STUDY: ONLINE GAMBLING

Recall from Central Issues: Unit 6 our discussion of cybersex/porn. Some researchers argue these are some of the most compulsive aspects of the internet and are activities which account for large amounts of CMC. Another online activity commonly thought to be addictive is interactive gaming. Robert Kubey and his colleagues (2001) found heavy leisure-related use by 'internet-dependent' university students, including online games, had a detrimental effect on academic performance. In fact, some game-developers are playfully explicit about intentions to *promote* addictive behavior: creators of the *Age of War* MUD [**www** CI7:6], for example, announce they addict players 'for their own enjoyment'.

After public concerns about pornography, one of the most hotly debated compulsions is **online gambling**. Paul Bellringer, director of GamCare, a UK-based organization that monitors the social impact of gambling, believes online gambling poses a special threat to those who already have problems controlling gambling habits.

Some online gambling sites report they promote responsible behavior by tracking users to monitor excessive activity. However, most critics express concern that online gambling has become particularly problematic in recent years, drawing government monitoring and increasing public involvement (see Box CI7:6)

BOX CI7:6 BETTING ON WAR, PLAYING AT WAR

The subject matter of some gambling activity is also sometimes a concern. For example, in 2003 there was a public outcry in Britain and the United States over people placing online bets about the invasion of Iraq. Several gambling sites were reported to have exploited the international situation by allowing participants to place bets on when the conflict would start, when it would end, how many people would be killed, how long it would last, whether it would get UN support and what countries would support the action [**www** CI7:7]. As with the gambling sites, the main concern was that these games were easy to find and use, and that they promote antisocial and even fanatical behavior [**www** CI7:8].

Capitalizing on the problem – perceived or real – of online gambling, some organizations offer online counselling and chat forums to help those desiring control. For example, New Zealand-based Gambling Problem Helpline [**www** CI7:9] offers free email counselling to New Zealand residents. The website includes discussion boards for online gamblers and families to develop supportive communities. And, again, where there are help groups there are bound to be diagnostic criteria. In this case, the Canadian Direction de la Santé Publique (Public Health Department) in Quebec offers the test in Box CI7:7. As with Young's text in Box CI7: 4, if respondents recognize one or two behaviors they would be considered 'symptomatic', three or four would classify them as 'problem' gamblers, and five or more would be diagnosed 'pathological'.

BOX CI7:7 A SCREENING TEST FOR GAMBLING PROBLEMS

A gambler who is at risk presents one or several of the following behaviors:

1 Are you constantly preoccupied with past gambling or planning the next venture, or thinking of ways to get money with which to gamble?
2 Do you need to gamble with increasing amounts of money in order to achieve the desired excitement?
3 Have you made repeated unsuccessful efforts to control or stop gambling?
4 Are you restless or irritable when attempting to cut down or stop?
5 Do you gamble to escape from problems or an unpleasant frame of mind?
6 After losing money gambling, do you often return another day to get even?
7 Have you ever lied to others to conceal the extent of involvement?
8 Have you ever committed illegal acts such as forgery, fraud, theft, or embezzlement to finance gambling?
9 Have you jeopardized or lost a significant relationship, job, or educational or career opportunity?
10 Do you ever rely on others to provide money to ease a financial situation caused by gambling?

(Direction de la Santé Publique, 2002)

WHAT TO MAKE OF IT ALL?

This brings us back to our earlier discussion critiquing assumptions that alleged 'addicts' don't know how to adequately communicate FtF. Recall from Basic Theory: Unit 6 O'Sullivan and Flanagin's suggestion that we need to contextualize CMC and avoid simplistic explanations for complex social interactions. It's clearly important to recognize, as illustrated by Chou and Hsiao (2000), the strong pleasurable, interpersonal communication aspect to CMC. Ultimately, these studies reveal we need to expand our understanding of social interaction to include CMC as ordinary behavior, rather than as deviant, addictive and compulsive.

In Basic Theory: Unit 6 we also discussed the notion of 'embedded media' and the importance of considering not just the principles and theory but also the daily 'realities' of CMC. One reality is the time-consuming nature of CMC, as psychologist Patricia Wallace (1999: 171) attests:

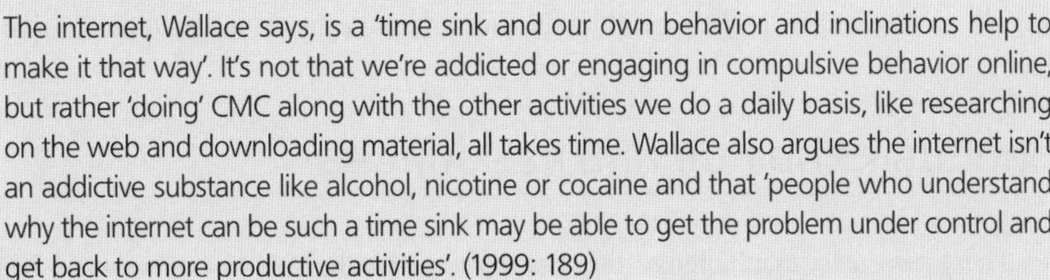

BOX CI7:8 THE INTERNET IS A 'TIME SINK'

The internet, Wallace says, is a 'time sink and our own behavior and inclinations help to make it that way'. It's not that we're addicted or engaging in compulsive behavior online, but rather 'doing' CMC along with the other activities we do a daily basis, like researching on the web and downloading material, all takes time. Wallace also argues the internet isn't an addictive substance like alcohol, nicotine or cocaine and that 'people who understand why the internet can be such a time sink may be able to get the problem under control and get back to more productive activities'. (1999: 189)

Actually a great deal of what we do online today *is* productive, useful and healthy. And more of what we're expected to do, as scholars and professionals, for example, involves the internet. Think about university life less than a decade ago. Few students communicated with instructors online. Few submitted course papers as email attachments. Now these activities are required and they're ordinary. (For more see Focus Areas: Topic 7.) Most of the time, ordinary people do fairly ordinary things online and the internet is just incorporated (or embedded) into everyday communication.

Let's wrap up some issues covered in the Central Issues strand that relate to this discussion. We'll also push forward some ideas to encourage critical reflection about CMC. First of all, as presented in Central Issues: Unit 1, it is important to remember being online as generally a good thing, a privilege those in the Global North take for granted. Think, for example, about young people in Sarajevo in Central Issues: Unit 1, who were able to develop relationships with other young people outside south-eastern Europe in ways not possible through more traditional communication channels. Second, we can avoid polarized arguments about the phenomenon surrounding CMC. Think about Unit 3, for example, and debates about whether online communities are either all-bad or all-good. A critical reflection of online communities helps increase understanding of human communication, both online and off. Third, we should avoid sweeping judgements and generalizations about the impact of the internet, as evidenced in Units 4–5. Finally, and most importantly, we ought to always focus more on how CMC creates spaces to develop identity, relationships and communities.

By focusing on CMC within this frame we can, for example, look at the complexity of interpersonal attraction in Unit 6 critically, rather than succumb to media sensationalism.

Finally, recall how Joseph Walther and Larry Reid (2000: 114) created an addiction to academia. They're making an important argument: that it's possible to fashion and fetishize a phenomenon. However, they argue, 'We must avoid launching a technological witch-hunt instead of conducting substantive research about whether the net causes addiction or dependence.' Instead we can examine how the internet is embedded in our lives and how it affords a space to enact ordinary types of day-to-day activities and communication.

REVIEW

In this unit, we started by examining so-called disorders, including internet addiction and problematic or Pathological Internet Use (PIU), before turning to examine public debates about them in the press, the academy and among the health professions. We also considered how problematic the notions of 'addiction' and 'internet addiction' really are. We then turned to evaluate the related allegation that CMC is necessarily antisocial, raising the matter of offline antisocial tendencies and patterns of online socialization.

STIMULUS READINGS AND RESOURCES

Note: These two articles challenge the assumption that the internet necessarily has a detrimental impact on social interaction:

Walther, J.B. and Reid, L.D. (2000). Understanding the allure of the internet. *Chronicle of Higher Education*, 4 February 2000, pp. 114–15.

Tyler, T. (2002). Is the internet changing social life? It seems the more things change, the more they stay the same. *Journal of Social Issues*, 58 (1), 195–205.

Note: The next two articles provide localized but also international perspectives on so-called internet addiction:

Amichai-Hamburger, Y. and Ben-Artzi, E. (2003). Loneliness and internet use. *Computers in Human Behavior*, 19, 71–80.

Chou, C. and Hsiao, M-C. (2000). Internet addiction, usage, gratification, and pleasure experience: the Taiwan college students' case. *Computers and Education*, 35, 65–80.

IDEAS FOR FURTHER DISCUSSION AND INVESTIGATION

1 Review the chapter and think about the debate whether 'Internet Addiction Disorder' exists. Think about your own use of CMC. Does it have addictive characteristics? Now search on the web for online therapy sites. Analyze them for quality, reputation and discretion. Would you engage in online therapy? Why or why not?

2 Take the questionnaire in Box CI7:4. How did you score? Has your perception of your CMC activity changed? Do you feel like an addict now? How do you think Young's research has made people feel about their CMC activity?

3 One of the best-known discussions about the negative impact of the internet on offline communication started with the paper 'Internet Paradox' by Robert Kraut and colleagues [**www** CI7:10]. Arrange with two (or more) people in your class to summarize the main points and then those made in subsequent papers which respond to it: La Rose *et al.* (2001) [**www** CI7:11] and Kraut *et al.* (2002) [**www** CI7:12]. What appears to have been the final outcome of this debate? Can you find another example where scholars have criticized the 'Internet Paradox' study?

4 Examine some online games and gambling sites (for example, **www** CI7:13 or **www** CI7:14). What stands out as potentially addictive? Is it easy to find these sites? How do you think online gambling differs from RL gambling? Think about the allegation that internet use can be antisocial and additive, and how that relates to gambling. You could start by taking the screening test for gambling problems in Box CI7:7. Compare your scores on that test with the one in Box CI7:4. Then look at the discussion boards at the Gambling Problem Helpline website to see how gambling 'addicts' and their families articulate their concerns to others online.

STRAND 3

APPLY: FIELDWORK

'FREEDOM WITH RESPECT TO THOSE IN POWER'

What does Pierre Bourdieu mean when he says that the third pillar of intellectual life is 'freedom with respect to those in power' (see p. 4)? At first glance, it could mean giving people in power respect and freedom. However, what we think Bourdieu means is that we should always be free to make up our own minds rather than listen only to what powerful people tell us. This means anyone in a position of authority, like in government, the media or religion. In fact, it also means authority figures in education. One of the ways of doing this is to apply your knowledge and to use your own privilege and power responsibly. It's not enough to have the tools, it's knowing how to use them that counts.

This strand involves a number of tasks designed to build core practical and technical skills, as well as involving you in hands-on, experiential investigations about the nature of CMC. We encourage you to reflect on your own experience of CMC and its influence on your life. It's only by *doing* CMC that you can really know what it's about. It's also only by applying what you have already *learned*, *critiqued* and *explored* that you can be sure that you have understood.

In this strand, you have the chance to construct your own online identity, to make your own relationships online, and build your own sense of online community. These activities represent precisely the kind of independent search for knowledge that Bourdieu is talking about – thinking for yourself, finding out for yourself, and creating something for yourself.

NOTE FOR COURSE LEADERS

This Fieldwork strand has been specifically designed to get students applying some of the basic theory and critical awareness encouraged in earlier strands. The tasks here are not comprehensive lesson plans. Different course leaders will obviously have different priorities and areas of expertise. We also recognize that you will have your own teaching style and expectations regarding learning outcomes and assessment. For this reason, we are offering frameworks and stimulating suggestions, but also leaving lots of room for you to make the materials and methods your own.

Each Fieldwork Task will have its particular technical and practical considerations. While we are not assuming every course leader will have extensive technical support, we do assume that there will be available basic computing facilities for individual students and reasonable opportunity for them to access the freeware needed, say, for Fieldwork Tasks 4 and 5. You will also see that we propose one or two Task Readings in most cases and, wherever possible, have selected those which are on the internet.

TASK 1

SEARCHING AND RESEARCHING ON THE INTERNET

MAIN OBJECTIVES

- Identify the main information sources on the internet.
- Learn how best to use the main online search tools.
- Critique the credibility of online information.
- Apply this knowledge in a case-study task.

TASK READING

Murphy, P. (2002). A 21st century challenge: preparing 'cut and paste' students to be 'information literate' citizens. *Teaching Learning and Technology Center*. Available (15 April 2003) online: <http: //www.uctltc.org/news/2002/04/feature.html>[**www** FW1:1].

SEARCHING ON THE INTERNET

The main objective of this practical unit is really to find out about finding out. As the first task reading by Paula Murphy, a learning technology specialist, points out, most students have already used the internet to find out about leisure pursuits (recording music online, shopping, and so on) But, she points out, there's a difference between searching for popular information and conducting academic research. 'In essence,' Murphy says, 'students don't know what they don't know.' With your help, this unit will explode that myth!

INFORMATION GATHERING

According to popular discourse, we're living in the 'Information Age'. One of the ways the internet has revolutionized our lives is by making more information available to more people than ever before. However, just because information is available doesn't mean it's worth something. There's a lot of rubbish out there. What's important is how you assess online information and test it for its credibility and usefulness.

www For weblinks and resources visit the CMC website at <www.sagepub.co.uk/resources/cmc>

Before we get to looking at how to grade information, we'd like to identity some of the main information sources which you may find helpful. (Remember what we said in Basic Theory: Unit 2, you may already know a lot about this so please bear with us.) Of course, as you can see in Box FW1:1, there are all sorts of reasons why people turn to the internet for information. Depending on what you want to find, you will need to use one or more different sources. Most people find it useful to use several sources at the same time.

BOX FW1:1 DIFFERENT INFORMATION FOR DIFFERENT PURPOSES

Among other things, people seek information online to:

- get an overview of a subject they know nothing about (e.g. the mapping of the human genome);
- find factual information (e.g. statistics about the latest internet demographics);
- keep up to the minute (e.g. following an ongoing political crisis);
- balance different points of view from different sources (e.g. following the same political crisis by visiting news sites around the world);
- test a hypothesis or theory (e.g. are women paid less than men in some jobs in another country?).

For the purposes of internet and CMC research, some of the key information sources which we recommend you use are the following:

1 *Mailing lists.* Major list (or 'e-conference') management organizations include: Listserv [**www** FW1:2], JISCmail [**www** FW1:3] and Majordomo [**www** FW1:4]. You can also search on the web for mailing lists, for example, About.com offers a useful resource page on Mailing List Directories [**www** FW1:5]. Another well known directory is Topica [**www** FW1:6].

2 *Newsgroups.* Usenet/newsgroups and bulletin boards have played an important part in the history of the internet and continue to offer themselves as valuable resources for a wealth of diverse information. You may need technical support in accessing these, but otherwise a good starting place is Google's online listing [**www** FW1:7].

3 *Online news sources USA Today* [**www** FW1:8], *South African Post* [**www** FW1:9], *BBC News* [**www** FW1:10], *The Australian* [**www** FW1:11], *South China Morning Post* [**www** FW1:12], *Egypt Today* [**www** FW1:13], *The Times of India* [**www** FW1:14].

5. *Electronic journals, books, and reports*. See our recommendations in the Resource Materials section of the CMC website.

6. *Reports by major international, government, and professional organizations*. By no means the only ones, examples of large, internet-related organizations which might be useful are: The World Wide Web Consortium [**www** FW1:15], the Internet Society [**www** FW1:16], the World Summit on the Information Society [**www** FW1:17] and, in the United States, the National Telecommunications and Information Administration [**www** FW1:18].

7 *Commercial internet research sources*. The best-known commercial research resources offering the latest facts and figures about the internet are Cyberatlas [**www** FW1:19], Nua [**www** FW1:20] and Internet.com [**www** FW1:21]. It's important to remember that these organizations usually present data taken from other sources, so make sure you always cite the original source.

Sometimes commercial sites are also promoting their own agendas, so be critical of their figures and claims.

Obviously, an effective researcher also has to consider carefully whether online sources are in fact more appropriate, relevant or useful. For example, if you were looking at the sort of lives women were leading in the 1950s, it might be much more productive to look at print sources like books or original newspapers, and even to interview people. It's always important, therefore, to combine different types of sources to make sure you have the topic covered in enough depth. The internet is never the last word on anything.

INFORMATION GRADING

It's strange how the same people who would never say, 'It must be true – I saw it on TV,' fail to question the credibility of information on the internet. Equally, just as you wouldn't use a twenty-year-old book to provide information about a current issue, so you wouldn't trust the meanderings of an eccentric setting up a webpage from an attic somewhere about a topic beyond his or her knowledge and experience.

Remember that there are political decisions behind what is included and what is excluded in information offered online, or anywhere for that matter. A good way of testing this is to look up a current news item, preferably involving controversy of some kind. Both sides of the debate will publish their point of view online and it's interesting to analyze what each chooses to leave out or to include, depending on whether it serves their argument or not. There is no such thing as neutrality online. For each topic there's always more than one point of view and to be an effective researcher you can't afford to listen to only one side of the argument.

The other thing to look out for is the currency of the information. What's put up on the internet remains there unless someone removes it or updates it. Always make a note not only of the date on which you visited and retrieved information from the site but also the date on which the site was created and/or updated, which usually appears somewhere.

BOX FW1:2 CREDIBILITY AND CURRENCY CHECKLIST

Here's a useful checklist when researching online:

- Does the site represent the voice of an organization or of an individual?
- Is the author's identity declared and authentic? (E.g. is the site 'signed'?)
- Do you trust the authorship? Why?
- How many times has the site been visited, if indicated?
- Where, in your view, may the author be 'coming from'?
- What can you gauge about the political standpoint of the site?
- Does the site reflect a sufficiently broad awareness of the topic under discussion?

- Does the factual information the site offers appear to be based on reliable sources?
- Is the site current? Could there be more recent data elsewhere?

If you would like to find more information about the issue of credibility online, we can recommend an excellent resource at Stanford University in California which looks at how people actually assess the credibility of websites [**www** FW1:22].

INFORMATION RECORDING

Very briefly, it's imperative that you acknowledge your sources – online and offline – by citing them correctly. It is unacceptable and illegal to steal someone else's work just because a paper, an article, or an image is on the internet or web. It is plagiarism. ◎

◎ The same goes for images and photos you use say, on a homepage – acknowledge their source and maybe include a weblink.

You must also reference all online materials using proper academic conventions. You can always check the American Psychological Association's style guide if you are unsure about this [e.g. **www** FW1:23]. In the meantime, you could look at our own list of references (p. 236 onwards) to see how we do it. In particular, notice how we always give the date on which we retrieved an online document and a full URL (i.e. web address) of the *exact* page from which we retrieved it.

SEARCH TOOLS: GETTING WHAT YOU WANT

Now that we've considered issues related to the evaluation of information, we'd like to tell you how you can actually go about getting the information in the first place! For most of us this entails a search engine, and the ones we recommend are these:

- Yahoo! [**www** FW1:24]
- Google [**www** FW1:25]
- Excite [**www** FW1:26]
- AltaVista [**www** FW1:27]
- Dogpile [**www** FW1:28]

There's not a lot to be said about these different search tools other than to draw your attention to the difference between:

- *Subject directories* like Yahoo! which organize online information into categories.
- *Search engines* like Google, Excite and AltaVista which are based on catalogues of keywords in websites and webpages.
- *Meta-search engines* like Dogpile which run searches by searching other search engines.

Most experienced internet researchers know that it's always worth running your search on more than one search engine – perhaps starting with a meta-search. For a comprehensive listing of many other different search engines, you might like try BlueAngels [**www** FW1:29].

BOX FW1:3 OUR TOP SEARCH TIPS

1. Be as specific as you can be and be sure to spell correctly.
2. Phrase your query in the language of the page you are looking for (e.g. don't use slang when searching for academic information).
3. Stick with lower-case letters unless you really want to specify a search for capital letters (e.g. *technology* will return *technology* and *TECHNOLOGY*, but searching for *TECHNOLOGY* will sometimes only return *TECHNOLOGY*).
4. Type a plus (+) or AND in front of a word to make sure your search term is included.
5. Type a minus (–) or NOT and the search term will be excluded.
6. Put whole phrases and people's names in "quotation marks" (e.g. *"computer mediated communication"* will make sure you get pages which are about CMC rather than pages which randomly contain the words *computer* or *communication* or *mediated*).
7. Use * for a wildcard query (e.g. *cyber** will return *cyberspace, cybersociety* and *cyberculture*).
8. Use OR to look for either or both of two concepts (e.g. when searching for information about communication and the law you could enter *legal OR forensic*)

More often than not your search engine will rank results for relevance and specificity. However, the main thing to keep remembering about search engines is that they know the content of pages but not the meaning or importance, which is why *you* have do the discerning. In addition to the credibility and currency checklist in Box FW1:2, we use what we call a 'hierarchy of legitimacy' as a rough way of sifting through the hundreds of pages usually returned by a search engine. In other words, for academic research purposes, we prioritize sources for reliability something like this:

- academic sources
- professional organizations
- government and other public bodies
- commercial research sites
- etc. . . . >
- personal homepages as a last resort!

One other very useful indicator of legitimacy is simply to look at the domain name which appears in the web address – for example:

www.name.edu.au	an educational institution in Australia
www.name.ac.uk	an educational institution in the United Kingdom
www.name.edu	an educational institution in the United States
www.name.com	a commercial enterprise
www.name.co.za	a commercial enterprise in South Africa
www.name.gov	a governmental agency in the United States
www.name.org	a non-profit or non-governmental organization
www.name.net	an internet service or organization

RESEARCHING *ABOUT* THE INTERNET

Searching on the internet is one thing, doing research *about* the internet is of course something different. As we discussed in Basic Theory: Unit 1, this is a growing field of scholarly inquiry. In fact, as you carry out your work in the Focus Areas we hope you'll be making many of your own observations, raising your own questions and drawing your own conclusions about the way the internet has had an impact on different areas of human communication. The idea is that you start to get a feel for actually *doing* internet research yourself. If you want to know more about conducting internet research, you could start by looking at these excellent resources:

Hewson, C.M., Yule, P., Laurent, D. and Vogel, C.M. (2003). *Internet research methods: A practical guide for the social and behavioural sciences*. London: Sage.

Hine, C. (2000). *Virtual ethnography*. London: Sage.

Jones, S. (ed.). (1999). *Doing internet research: Critical issues and methods for examining the net*. London: Sage. ◉

Mann, C. and Stewart, F. (2000). *Internet communication and qualitative research: A handbook for researching online*. London: Sage.

◉ You may remember that Steve Jones is one of the co-founders of the Association of Internet Researchers (AoIR) [**www** FW1:30].

TASK AND FIELDNOTES

Thinking about the idea of moral panic from Central Issues: Unit 6, identify a current controversy or burning issue that seems to be worrying society at the moment. (It doesn't have to be about the internet or CMC.) Now imagine that you're a journalist working for a major newspaper. Your senior editor has just asked you to explore the possibility of a lead article about this subject in the Sunday edition. Your job is to put together a summary of the major angles and details of this issue. The deadline is tomorrow morning.

Use a number of online methods and sources to start preparing the report. The tools and resources you use should include a search engine and a meta-search engine. The sources should include:

- mailing lists
- online news sources
- reports from government bodies
- reports from professional organizations

In order to prepare a report which will be useful to your editor, you will also need to gather a wide spectrum of information and views from all sides of the issue, including:

- statistical facts
- expert views
- official statements

- personal points of view
- statements by concerned organizations

Fieldnotes: While conducting this investigation, make some short fieldnotes about the process and the outcome. For example, how easy were the different sources to locate and use? What were the quality and credibility of information which they offered?

TASK 2

ONLINE COLLABORATION: DOING CMC, DISCUSSING CMC

MAIN OBJECTIVES

- Explore ways of collaborating online, either one-to-one or in groups.
- Practice skills in building and maintaining an online relationship.
- Discuss some of the issues and ideas covered in the book.
- Critique the differences between online and offline collaboration.

ONLINE COLLABORATION

In all the different Focus Areas (starting on p. 197) such as health, education, the law and politics, you can be sure that online collaborations are taking place more and more these days. Companies are no longer competitive if they do not exploit all the potential of communications technology. Journalists in remote regions of the world send reports and images back online to their editors. Designers attend the top fashion shows, make quick sketches and send them back to their manufacturing companies so that production can begin immediately on all the latest designs. Doctors across the globe share life-preserving information with each other via cyberspace. Hundreds of thousands of people across the world are engaged in distance education, working with tutors and seminar groups online. In many cases, the people working together in these instances never have the chance to meet face-to-face. Their relationship is carried out entirely by CMC. In fact, anyone entering the work force these days, in whatever career, needs to know how to collaborate productively online.

The idea behind this Fieldwork Task is to ensure that you experience first-hand the potential, and the pitfalls, that online collaborations offer. (Remember, as Pierre Bourdieu tells us, nothing is ever all-good or all-bad.) We have had extensive experience ourselves of working with students in online collaborations between Europe (e.g. the United Kingdom, Russia, the Netherlands), the Americas (e.g. Mexico and the United States),

www For weblinks and resources visit the CMC website at <www.sagepub.co.uk/resources/cmc>

Africa (e.g. Kenya) and the Middle East (e.g. Dubai). We've also spent a lot of time seeing what makes a CMC collaboration successful, and this Fieldwork Task emerges from that experience. ◎

◎ With colleagues, authors Alice Tomic and Laura Lengel designed and continue to run the successful Frontera Project [**www** FW2: 1].

TASK

Depending on how your course leader wants to do things, you're going to carry out an online collaboration which involves working with an individual or group preferably not already known to you. Over a period of several weeks (e.g. during the term or semester), you need to exchange views and comments on specified discussion points. The easiest collaboration is between individuals using one-to-one email exchanges. However, to make the collaborative project more interesting and rewarding, we recommend using Mailing Lists (i.e. group emailing), or chatrooms (see Fieldwork: Task 4), or online bulletin boards. If your institution supports virtual learning environments such as Blackboard, FirstClass or WebCT, you'll be able to set up a bulletin board quite easily. Alternatively, you may try a free, web-based board service such as ezboard [**www** FW2:2], Assembly [**www** FW2:3] and QuickTopic [**www** FW2:4].

Once the technical side of things has been set up, the rest is up to you! Remember, there's no clear agenda here other than for you and your online partner/s to move through a series of discussion points in order to *do* some CMC – to get a feel for what it's like to bounce ideas off one another online.

SCHEDULE OF DISCUSSION POINTS

Discussion Point 1 Who am I? Who are you?

Establish contact with each other by introducing yourselves. In order for the project to work, it's important to build the right foundations, so this first part of the online discussion will be relatively extensive. For example, write a 500 word portrait of yourself, trying to give your counterpart/s a comprehensive idea about who you are. Subsequent, shorter exchanges can focus on expanding this description through strategic questioning of each other about specific aspects of identities.

Discussion Point 2 Unpacking stereotypes

The mass media often create stereotypical representations of different groups of people which inevitably affect the way we see the world. Discuss with your partner what the dominant media stereotypes are of each other's cultural backgrounds (e.g. gender differences, state or regional differences, national differences). Ask these questions:

- To what extent, in your view, are these stereotypes 'true' and where do they have their origins?
- Does new technology allow people to transcend socio-economic class, gender and sexuality, race, ethnic origin and physical disability?

Discussion Point 3 Haves and have-nots?

Thinking about what you learned in Central Issues: Unit 1, explore with your partner these questions:

- What do you each understand by the term 'digital divide'? Do you think there is a difference between students and 'ordinary' citizens in terms of access to computer technology?
- Which way does the information gradient flow? In other words, which countries produce information via computer technology and which countries just receive? Is it always a one-way flow?

Discussion Point 4 Digital citizens?

In thinking about what it means to be a 'digital citizen', ask these questions:

- What are the implications of electronic networks for the development of personal, professional and political relationships across national boundaries?
- Does being a digital citizen distance people from the 'lived' (as opposed to the 'virtual') experiences of social life and interaction?

Discussion Point 5 Global village?

The 'global village' is a very popular but problematic term. Discuss with your online partner/s the following questions:

- Will the internet homogenize the world into a consumer-driven, Western or American-style culture? Have you come across evidence of any resistance to this?
- What potential does technology really offer for democracy and civil society to increase dialogue and manage global conflicts?

Discussion Point 6 Global language?

Thinking about the issues and statistics covered in Central Issues: Unit 2, what do you think about the following questions?

- Is it a good thing to have a 'lingua franca' or world language being used on the internet? What are the political implications of this?
- What other languages are represented on the internet and what kind of information is made available in these languages? What conclusions do you draw from this?

Discussion Point 7 Thinking about CMC

As a way of starting to round off your online collaboration, ask these questions about this first-hand experience of CMC:

- What communication barriers have you come across during your online discussions with each other? What have you found frustrating and what have you found satisfying?
- Have you found yourselves more or less willing to disclose personal information? If so, why? If not, why not?

Discussion Point 8 Reflections and goodbye(?)

Finish off your online collaboration by reflecting together on the process and outcome. Ask these questions:

- Have you learned anything new about yourself and your counterpart/s during the process?

- Can you imagine staying in touch with each other – either online or offline?
- If you were to do it again, what would you choose to do differently?

FIELDNOTES

While conducting this investigation, make some short fieldnotes about the process and the outcome. For example, in thinking about the process, ideas from Discussion Points 7 and 8 will be really useful. Your fieldnotes on this occasion should be a journal-like reflection on how the whole thing went from your point of view. It can be very frank (expressing satisfaction at the success of the project or referring to specific frustrations and disappointments). The fieldnotes could be presented to your course leader along with a record of your exchanges with your partner throughout the different Discussion Points.

BOX FW2:1 ASSESSING THE SUCCESS OF YOUR COLLABORATION

- Did you work strategically to establish a sound relationship with your partner(s) from the outset?
- Were you sensitive and responsive to your counterpart's contributions (e.g. by giving feedback and encouragement)?
- Did you engage with the Discussion Points in an informed and reflective way, showing evidence of critical thinking?
- How much reference did you make to the Task Reading and ideas from elsewhere in the book?

NOTE FOR COURSE LEADERS

Although it is possible to carry out a collaboration between participants in the same school or university but in different classes or departments, or in the same town but at different institutions, this Fieldwork Task provides a much richer opportunity for learning if the collaborating partners/teams are geographically separated. The wider the distance between the participants (in terms of cultural background, language and geography) the greater the potential for learning.

The potential for variations on this task is also wide-ranging. ◎ Again, we've left space for you to adapt this for your own purposes. For example, one very productive option is to have students working towards a jointly created website, then providing a summary of their online negotiations and exchanges. In Box FW2:2 we offer a series of practical and pedagogical tips based on our own experiences of running classroom-based online collaborations. Beyond these, one further bit of advice worth special mention is the need to allow students enough time for this task; implicit in the collaboration is a process of self-development and reflection which cannot be squeezed into two weeks.

◎ One thing you may like to consider is setting up a blog – either just for your class to use, or to share with their online collaborators.

BOX FW2:2 TIPS FOR RUNNING ONLINE COLLABORATIONS

- Establish clear objectives and learning outcomes for the project.
- Plan carefully in terms of viable computer access for all parties, compatible equipment/software and adequate technical support.
- Decide whether communication is to be synchronous or asynchronous and ensure everyone understands any time differences between locations.
- Be aware that different institutions have different class schedules (e.g. one place may meet twice a week for an hour and a half, the other may have only one weekly session).
- Ensure that the first few communications are used for 'chat' to establish who each person is and to create the possibility of a relationship being built before work starts on any assignments.
- Establish a clear assessment policy for all those participating to aid student motivation and ensure that dedicated work gets the recognition it deserves (e.g. marks for the tasks should carry equal weighting for all participants to avoid any unnecessary variation in commitment).
- Clarify the procedure for students' reporting on progress or problems to the course leader at regular intervals.
- Set clear deadlines to be observed by everyone participating.
- Establish accountability in all participants (e.g. what happens if a team at one end works terribly hard but gets very little response from their collaborative partners?).
- Encourage students to record (and report) 'failures', disappointments and frustrations calmly and objectively in fieldnotes.
- Capitalize on such 'failures' to test students' ability to troubleshoot, making constructive criticisms/suggestions and getting more out of their partner/s.

TASK 3

CREATING A WEBPAGE: HTML AND WYSIWYG EDITING

MAIN OBJECTIVES

- Grasp the basics of HTML and WYSIWYG web-editing.
- Consider some key design issues in creating webpages.
- Explore opportunities for publishing a personal homepage.
- Experiment with the construction of your own online identity.

CREATING A WEBPAGE

If you're not on the web yet, yikes!

If you're not on the web, you're finished.

If you're not on the web, you're nowhere.

If you're not on the web, you don't exist.

If you're not on the web, you're dead.

These are all genuine slogans from organizations offering their services to help companies and individuals create websites of their own. Obviously, these people have a special interest in making us feel like we're 'finished', 'nowhere' or 'dead' if we don't have a presence on the web. Nonetheless, for all the hype and hysteria about the internet, one thing which can't be disputed is that the internet and web are revolutionary in enabling ordinary people like you and us to publish our ideas, and to promote ourselves to the world in a way that has simply never been possible in the history of human communication and the media. Being able to address so many people (*potentially* thousands and even millions) used to be the privilege of only the very elite, powerful and rich.

www For weblinks and resources visit the CMC website at <www.sagepub.co.uk/resources/cmc>

In spite of the heavy-handed warnings above, you don't *have* to have a webpage or a fancy website. However, knowing how webpages work and being able to cast a sensible opinion about what makes a website good or bad is a part of most people's working lives these days. If you end up running your own business or organization, you'll find it even more important. Besides, the only way to really understand the role of webpages in CMC is to have a go yourself at creating an online presence.

TASK

◎ Somewhat confusingly, a personal homepage can be just a single webpage or it can be an entire website made up of many webpages. What's more, a homepage isn't always 'personal' either; sometimes a homepage is just another name for the portal (or front) page of a business or institutional website.

If you don't know how already, you need to create your own personal homepage. ◎ This task is where you'll probably be parting company with some of your colleagues. You may already have learned how to create a good webpage. In fact, you may already be maintaining quite a sophisticated website, never mind a single page! Alternatively, you may have done an introductory course some time ago and pretty much forgotten everything. Of course, you may also be one of many people who've never done anything like this at all. What we offer here is a quick overview for people who fall into the last two categories.

Creating a webpage means having to do a lot of your own hands-on experimentation, including getting to know the very simple programing language in which webpages are written. Most people learn how create webpages not through expensive lessons but through their own initiative and through trial and error. We think you'll be surprised how easy it really is.

HTML AND WYSIWYG EDITING

Open up your browser (e.g. Netscape Navigator or Internet Explorer), select View and then Source (or Page Source). This will immediately reveal the original programing code which lies beneath each and every webpage. The code is called HTML (Hypertext Mark-Up language) and is what's often called *plain text*. It's a bit of a dog's dinner! The magic of browsers is that they convert all this dull computer code into colour, spatial arrangements, images and varying font sizes – what's called *rich text*. To make sure the browser knows exactly what to display, and *how* to display it, HTML uses a variety of different commands (or 'tags'); for example, <B> tells the browser to start displaying text in bold, while </B> tells it to stop using bold.

You need to learn how to write HTML to build your webpage and there are two ways to do this: the hard way and the easy way. The hard way means manually entering the HTML code into a simple text editor (e.g. Notepad with all Microsoft systems). Once you're ready to view your code through a browser, you just save the text file with an .htm or .html extension so that the browser knows it's a webpage file. Even if it is the hard way, we recommend you start off learning to write some HTML this way. There are masses of really excellent tutorials available for free on the web and so we don't want to reinvent the wheel [see Weblinks FW3: 1–3]. However, Box FW3:1 has just a few pointers to get you going.

BOX FW3:1 STARTING OUT WITH HTML TAGS

Type the following into a text editor:

```
<HTML>
<HEAD>
<TITLE>My personal homepage</TITLE>
</HEAD>
<BODY>Welcome to my personal homepage.</BODY>
</HTML>
```

The <HTML> and </ HTML> tags let the browser know that this is the beginning and end of a webpage file. The <HEAD> and </HEAD> tags identify the heading and everything inside these two tags will appear as part of the heading. In between the <BODY> and </BODY> tags you then type in everything you want displayed in the main part of your webpage.

Save your simple text file with an .htm or .html extension (e.g. name the file *webpage.html*). Next, open this new file in your browser and you should see the words 'My Personal Homepage' in the blue header at the very top and the words of welcome in the main screen.

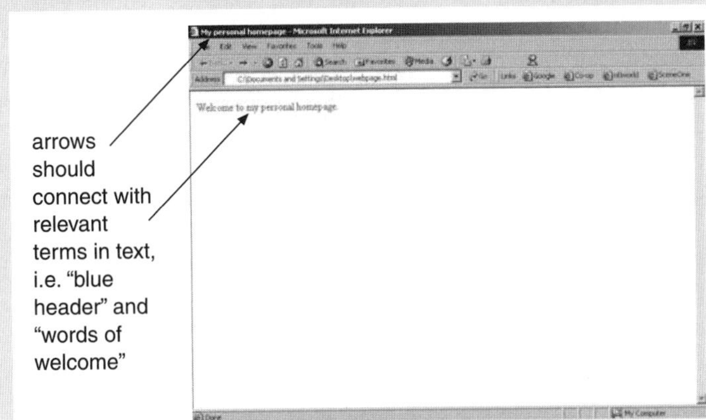

FIGURE 15

My Personal Homepage

Now use the following tags and see their effect on your emerging webpage. Notice how the line break and paragraph break do not travel in pairs.

<CENTER></CENTER>	*to center something*
 	to insert a line break
<P>	*to insert a paragraph break*

Once you've grasped the very basics of writing HTML this way, you can pretty much forget all about it! There's an easier way to create a webpage using software which writes all the HTML code for you. This is called WYSIWYG editing because the software allows you to type up your webpage like a word-processed document and **W**hat **Y**ou **S**ee **I**s **W**hat **Y**ou **G**et. In other words, while you type and format your text, the editor enters all the tags 'beneath the surface'. You then toggle (i.e. switch back and forth) between the editor and your browser, saving changes in the editor and hitting the Refresh (or Reload) button in the browser to see how the webpage is coming along.

Two of the best known WYSIWYG editors are Macromedia's Dreamweaver [**www** FW3:4] and Microsoft's FrontPage [**www** FW3:5]. They're expensive to buy and, unless your institution already makes one of them available, we recommend you use Netscape's Composer. This is a less sophisticated editor built into the Netscape Communicator package, but it's all available for free from the web [**www** FW3:6]. What's also great about Composer is that there are tutorials online for helping you to use it effectively [**www** FW3:7–8].

It always takes a bit of time to work out what you can do with WYSIWYG editors, but we suggest you just have a go experimenting with whatever options are available – especially inserting images, links to external sites, and perhaps even a table for helping to arrange your material nicely on the screen. Again, most people learn through simple trial and error.

DESIGNING YOUR WEBPAGE

Once you've started creating your webpage, and as you get more confident with using a WYSIWYG editor, the temptation is to use every available option: multiple text and background colors, multiple fonts and typefaces, loads of bullets and moving images. It's great fun, sure, but remember, someone will be reading your webpage. This is why you need to think carefully about issues of design. Keep thinking about how it's going to look for a reader – what's easy to read (e.g. black text on a white background) and what's not (e.g. yellow text on a red background). The idea is to have people want to know more, not to make them feel nauseous!

◎ See [**www** FW3:12–16] to find out about Javascript or Flash, and also more advanced information about HTML.

There are plenty of guides on the web written by people who've had time to discover what works and what doesn't when it comes to web design. [We recommend **www** FW3:9–11.] Some of the advice is quite elaborate and covers cutting-edge developments like JavaScript and Flash technology. ◎ However, most of the design tips are much more straightforward and make a lot of common sense (Box FW3:2).

BOX FW3:2 TIPS FOR DESIGNING A GREAT WEBPAGE

These are the top tips suggested by Jennifer Kyrnin [**www** FW3:2]:

- Know your audience.
- Keep your pages short.
- Use tables of contents.
- Keep images small.
- Use web colors.
- Avoid lots of text.
- Check your spelling.
- Keep links current.
- Annotate your links (i.e. explain briefly what they're about).
- Put contact information on your pages.

Even if what *you* see is what *you* get, other people may not get what you see – in more ways than one. Different browsers always convert webpages differently; your readers may also have their browser settings different from yours. Another important consideration is that browsers can't always display all the fancy fonts and colours which your WYSIWYG editor offers. In which case, regardless of the colours you use, *Navigator* and *Explorer* will just select the next best alternative. ◎

◎ On the CMC website, the Task 3 weblinks page shows the colour 'cube' (or palette) for Netscape Navigator to give you an idea of the relatively restricted choice of colors compared with all the options available on a WYSIWYG editor like Dreamweaver.

In order to keep your pages short, you'll probably need to create more than one webpage and have internal links between the pages. This is the beginning of a website. Our advice is to create an electronic folder and store all the HTML and image files related to your website in one place. (It's common practice to use *index.html* for the welcome page.) So your website could have five different HTML files and be mapped something like Figure 16:

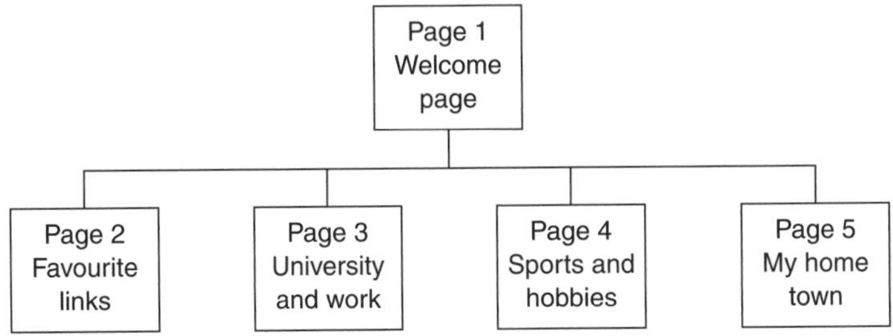

FIGURE 16

Your website could have five different HTML files

In creating your personal homepage, you'll also want to search the web for fun stuff like pictures, buttons, wallpaper and moving images; you could start with **www** FW3: 17–19. Remember to try and keep things stylish. It's also good netiquette to ask permission to use things if permission hasn't already been given, and to protect yourself from infringing copyright by acknowledging your sources. (Remember what we said about online ethics in Central Issues: Unit 1, see also p. 166.)

PUBLISHING YOUR WEBPAGE

Once your webpage is ready, you'll naturally want to load it on to the internet so that it becomes a proper page on the world wide web. You have three options available to you, really, and this is where you're going to need your course leader's help.

- You can arrange through your institution to load your homepage on to their main server. Most universities these days encourage their students to start publishing on the internet and will offer you space on their main computing system for free. Find out what's available to you.
- It's quite possible that your internet service provider at home will also offer space on one of their main computers. Nowadays this is often included as part of people's general telephone or cable packages.
- You may prefer to pay a small fee of about US$10 (or less) to have a commercial site like Tripod or Anglefire or Geocities host your webpage [**www** FW3:20–2]. One great advantage of these is that they also offer basic web-editing resources as part of the deal.

FIELDNOTES

There are no fieldnotes worth keeping for this task – the personal homepage is evidence enough of your having tried to work things out for yourself. Remember, you may find this all much more difficult than some of your colleagues. Just take your time and don't be afraid to explore and experiment. It'll be a long time before you'll be able to put together a website like Coke's [see **www** FW3:23].

BOX FW3:3 EVALUATING YOUR WEBPAGE

Your course leader may or may not decide to assess your webpage as part of the marks awarded for the class. Either way, we think you might like to consider the following while you're creating your webpage:

- Have you demonstrated a basic grasp of HTML editing?
- Have you inserted some images?
- Have you created a hypertext link to some external sites on the internet?
- Have you managed to create any internal links?
- Have you thought about design issues such as layout and colour?
- Have you used text-formatting (e.g. font size and alignment)?
- Have you shown a reasonable attempt at projecting an online identity?
- Have you shown some imagination and creativity?

NOTE FOR COURSE LEADERS

Research continues to highlight the myth of the 'net generation' and the idea that young people nowadays are necessarily skilled and comfortable with computers and the internet (see Thurlow and McKay, 2003). In fact, we are often surprised how few of our students know much about creating their own webpage. As a consequence, it's always difficult to find a balance in supporting the range of expertises which students have. This factor, coupled with the technical support needed, makes Task 3 one of the more time-consuming and intensive ones in terms of student support. On the plus side, those students for whom this is a totally new skill are always amazed at how easy it really is.

TASK 4

MAKING CONVERSATION: ONLINE CHAT AND MESSAGING

MAIN OBJECTIVES

- Participate in at least one public chatroom over a period of a week.
- Identify key aspects of interaction in online chat or messaging.
- Make fieldnotes responding to key questions and recording your impressions.
- Apply what you know about computer mediated language and discourse.

TASK READINGS

Herring, S. (1999). Interactional coherence in CMC. *Journal of Computer-Mediated Communication*, 4 (4). Available (15 April 2003) online: <http://www.ascusc.org/jcmc/vol4/issue4/herring.html> [**www** FW4:1].

Werry, C.C. (1996). Linguistic and interactional features of Internet Relay Chat. In S. Herring (ed.), *Computer-mediated communication: Linguistic, social and cross-cultural perspectives* (pp. 47–64). Amsterdam: Benjamins.

These 'classic' readings by Christopher Werry and Susan Herring are two of the few examples where scholars have sought to address in such an explicit manner the linguistic and discursive features of online chat. They're also useful also because they both consider the traditional, text-based chat environments offered by IRC.

MAKING CONVERSATION ONLINE

One of the most interactive opportunities offered by the internet is real-time (or synchronous) chatting with friends and with people you might never otherwise have met. Most people find this exciting and rewarding, although only in direct proportion to the time and effort they're prepared to invest in getting to know people and how the technical systems work. This Fieldwork Task is closely related to Central Issues: Unit 4, where we

www For weblinks and resources visit the CMC website at <www.sagepub.co.uk/resources/cmc>

examined and critiqued the notions of netlingo and netspeak. The idea here is to get online and explore first-hand some of the issues raised about multilingualism, language change and folk linguistics. As you do this, you also have the chance to reflect on basic CMC theory such as the complexities of impression management, anonymity and disinihibition discussed in Basic Theory: Units 4–5. Although you're free to use whatever chat environment you like, we recommend that you have a go with one of the most traditional, text-based chat systems supported by the internet: Internet Relay Chat – or just IRC.

WHAT IS IRC?

Internet Relay Chat was originally developed in 1988 by a Finnish computer whiz called Jarkko Oikarinen [see **www** FW4:2 for a history]. Basically, IRC is a synchronous, multi-user, text-based chat technology. People connect to *servers* (i.e. large computers) supported by different networks (or 'nets', i.e. families of servers). These servers are all over the world. Once connected to a server, it's possible to join a *channel* (i.e. a chatroom) for talking publicly in groups, or privately with just one other person. There are lots of networks with hundreds of servers and literally thousands of channels. There's also no limit to the number of people who can be on a channel at any one time. This all means there's one heck of a lot of people busy chatting with IRC at any time!

The way all this is done is to use what's called a *client* (i.e. a small computer program) which can be downloaded for free from the internet. You then run this program to connect to a server on one of the IRC nets. Because it's one we've used many times ourselves and trust, we suggest mIRC [**www** FW4:3], which is easy to download [see **www** FW4:4], has a user-friendly appearance and also offers lots of really helpful advice about how to use the program [**www** FW4:5], as well as background information about IRC more generally [**www** FW4:6]. ◎

◎ mIRC is shareware written by Khaled Mardam-Bey. This means it can be downloaded on a free thirty-day trial. If you decide you'll continue to use mIRC, you're asked to register your copy.

There are other good guides to IRC and we especially recommend David Caraballo and Joseph Lo's *IRC prelude* [**www** FW4:7]. Although IRC can be fun, Caraballo and Lo do offer the following point of netiquette: 'IRC is not a "game", and we highly recommend you treat people you meet with the same courtesy as if you were talking in person or on the phone'.

TASK

BOX FW4:1 SCREEN SHOT OF MIRC

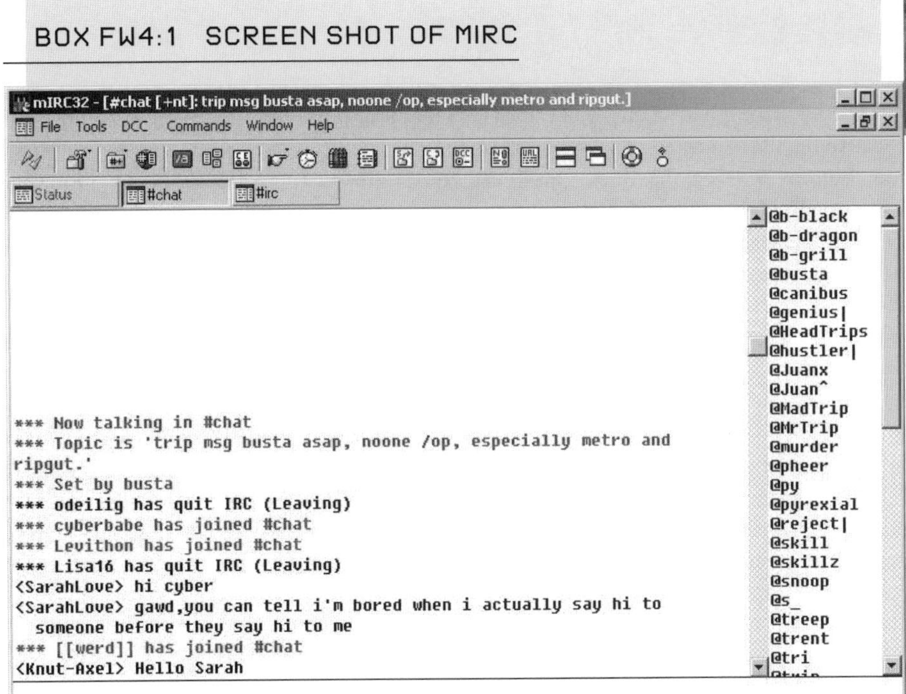

FIGURE 17 Screen shot of mIRC

Start by familiarizing yourself with mIRC. From the CMC website you can download our worksheet which covers the general layout of the mIRC environment together with the main commands you'll need [**www** FW4:8]. Much of what you need, however, is already here in Box FW4:2.

BOX FW4: 2 SOME BASIC IRC COMMANDS

Most channel names start with '# '. All IRC commands start with '/ '. Anything that doesn't begin with '/ ' will appear as a message. Try these for starters:

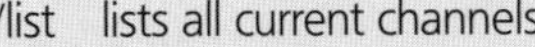

/list lists all current channels

/join to join a channel

/part to leave a channel (same as leave)

/nick changes your nickname

/whois displays information about someone
/query starts a private conversation
/ignore removes output from specific people

Of course the joy of a client like mIRC is that you don't have to type the commands because the user-interface has the familiar toolbars, buttons and windows, etc. The first four buttons will be the ones you'll use most often: Connect/Disconnect, Options, Channels Folder, and List Channels.

Over the period of about a week, we recommend that you spend some time trying out IRC (or your usual chat space or even instant messaging). Connect to one of the many IRC servers on the DALnet network. ◎ Started in 1994 as an alternative to the overburdened networks of the time, DALnet has grown into a vibrant community and is widely regarded as the most 'friendly' of the major IRC networks [www FW4:9].

◎ In addition to DALnet, other major networks are Undernet, NewNet and Efnet – the original IRC network, with over 12,000 channels and regularly with 32,000 people at once.

Make a note of what kinds of channels there are, before actually joining a channel. You'll need to find a good nickname for yourself, and it'll have to be original too, because of the thousands of people using IRC. (Sometimes using a number is one way to make it more unique.) Try not to be just a 'lurker' (i.e. all watching and no chatting) but engage with people and get involved in some decent chat. You'll need to search around for a busy channel and, even then, give things a bit of time so you can form a reasonable impression.

INSTANT MESSAGING AND WEB-BASED CHAT

Depending on what your course leader recommends, you may just prefer to run the same kind of analysis using chat spaces which are more familiar to you. For example, you could make some interesting comparisons between Werry's descriptions of a traditional CMC genre like IRC with instant messaging services like MSN Messenger [www FW4:10] or ICQ [www FW4:11]. The same goes for web-based chat spaces such as Yahoo! Chat [www FW4:12] – used by many people these days, given the convergence of the internet and web (see Basic Theory: Unit 2).

AUDIO CHAT

If you're feeling adventurous, you could think about chat spaces which offer a more multimodal kind of CMC. For example, sign up for one of Yahoo!'s Voice Chats [www FW4:13] – you'll need to download their free application. Alternatively, you could try joining Audio-Tips [www FW4:14] which interestingly, we think, states the following:

> We are real people with real names because we have found that using real names fosters a more productive environment. We ask that no nicknames be used on our site.

Or you could try the US-based Iraq Voice [www FW4:15], which presents itself as 'Your home away from home' for Iraqis abroad. Both these two chat environments raise all sort of additional issues related to community and identity online. Once again, how do they compare with text-only chat?

BOX FW4:3 STOP PRESS! SOCIAL RESPONSIBILITY OR CYNICAL PROFITEERING?

Just about the time we were getting this book ready to go to print, Microsoft announced that it had taken the controversial decision to close all of its MSN chatrooms in Britain [see **www** BT6:3]. The reason, said Microsoft, was to protect children from adult abusers. The real reason, say others, had more to do with profit. In other words, chatrooms weren't making any money for MSN.

Have a look also at the Guardian newspaper article entitled *The myth of Satan's web* **www** [BT6:4]. This incident has special relevance for Basic Theory: Unit 3, Central Issues: Unit 6 and Fieldwork: Task 4. However, ask yourself, what are the implications of Microsoft's decision – not just for chatrooms but for CMC generally and for the future of social interaction on the internet? What does it tell you about the relationship between technology and society, the struggle between capitalist and democratic values in cyberspace, and about the ways ordinary people choose to interact online?

Yes, this is the same box as in Basic Theory: Unit 6 (p. 79) – we felt it was worth repeating here!

FIELDNOTES

Whatever chat environment you choose to work with, make fieldnotes describing your online communication experience. Also comment on how you felt it tied in with the Task Readings and some of the ideas you've read about elsewhere in the book. In writing up your fieldnotes, think about the questions listed in Box FW4:4.

BOX FW4:4 FIELDNOTE QUESTIONS

- What sorts of channels are there? For example, what themes are covered?
- What naming-practices can you identify? Are people using fantasy nicknames or their own names – or a mixture of both?
- How easy is it to pretend to be someone else, do you think?
- What sorts of things are occupying people's attention in these spaces? In other words, what are they chatting about?
- Do you find evidence of much advertising? What about people directing you to commercial websites?
- Is there evidence of people using other CMC channels? For example, does anyone invite you to their personal homepage?
- Is chat equally divided between participants?
- What are your overall impressions of IRC?

BOX FW4:5 ASSESSING THE SUCCESS OF YOUR RESEARCH ACTIVITY

- Have you spent a reasonable length of time online?
- Can you make good connections with one or both of the task readings?
- Can you make connections with CMC central issues and basic theory?
- Have you used your own ideas and shown signs of critical thinking?
- Do you have well chosen examples to highlight the points you're making?
- Have you responded to some or all of the questions in Box FW4:4?

NOTE FOR COURSE LEADERS

Because it's not web-based, IRC really gives students a chance to familiarize themselves with the kind of CMC which much of the literature is based on. However, because it's not web-based it may *look* more unfamiliar. In fact, some students may find it more challenging than others getting to grips with the software. Having said which, even though it looks like it may be complicated, this isn't necessarily so. Students need only know the very basics of mIRC to be able to get going.

If you haven't tried IRC yourself before, we recommend you start by printing off mIRC's FAQs sheet, which is very comprehensive [**www** FW4:16]. Also, one of the best ways of running an introductory session with students is to set up a dedicated channel for your class. (A channel is automatically created as soon as the first person joins it.) Get the students to join the channel and begin by chatting to each other as a group, and then introduce them to DCC (Direct Client to Client connection or private chat).

It may also be that the security measures taken by your IT department make it more difficult to load up the mIRC shareware. Some people are nervous about the virus threat that mIRC can pose.

TASK 5

BUILDING COMMUNITY: METAWORLDS AND VISUAL CHAT

MAIN OBJECTIVES

- Participate in a virtual reality environment for at least a week.
- Critique the graphic representation of individuals and community spaces.
- Make fieldnotes responding to key questions and recording your impressions.
- Apply what you know about online relationships and community building.

TASK READING

Rossney, R. (1996). Metaworld: avatars could be the next interactive revolution. Just don't let them steal your head. *Wired* magazine, issue 4.06. Available (15 April 2003) online: <http://www.wired.com/wired/archive/4.06/avatar.html> [**www** FW5:1].

Taylor, T.L. (2002). Living digitally: embodiment in virtual worlds. In R. Schroeder (ed.), *The social life of avatars*: *Presence and interaction in shared virtual environments* (pp. 40–62). Berlin: Springer. Copy also available (15 April 2003) online: <http://social.chass.ncsu.edu/~ttaylor/papers/Taylor-LivingDigitally.pdf> [**www** FW5:2].

Although not a scholarly piece, Robert Rossney's magazine article offers an early perspective on metaworlds, and it's worth comparing your current experience with his fairly excited predictions. The piece by T.L. Taylor is concerned specifically with a vZones metaworld such as the one discussed in this task.

BUILDING COMMUNITY IN METAWORLDS

We noted in Basic Theory: Unit 2 how the landscape of cyberspace is changing all the time and how the nature of CMC is being impacted by the increasing use of multimodal technologies. One of the best, and most accessible, manifestations of this is Virtual Reality Environments (VREs), which combine the fantasy dimensions of traditional text-based

www For weblinks and resources visit the CMC website at <www.sagepub.co.uk/resources/cmc>

genres of MUDs with the widely popular activity of text-based chat. These hybrid genres are often referred to as *metaworlds* or simply *visual chat*. Although they've only recently become more sophisticated and popular, the first fully networked visual metaworld, called Habitat, was actually developed by LucasFilm Games back in 1985 – see [**www** FW5:3] for a very brief historical overview of metaworlds.

The idea behind this Fieldwork Task is for you to discover in practice what it means to join one of these graphical communities. We're pretty sure you'll enjoy yourself – especially if you've never done anything like this before. However, we also encourage you to reflect critically on your experience. When we were exploring online identities in Central Issues: Unit 2, it was clear that one of the things people have often enjoyed about CMC was its potential for make-believe and identity play, although not without qualification. In Central Issues: Unit 3 we also examined some of the common misconceptions about online communities – keep an eye on these too.

TASK

In this Fieldwork Task you're going to need to sign up to a metaworld. There are several well known metaworlds available, such as Active Worlds [**www** FW5:4] and Worlds.com [**www** FW5:5]. Bruce Damer's Avatars website lists many different metaworlds, not all of which are active, along with some useful background and links [**www** FW5:6]. The metaworld we recommend is vZones [**www** FW5:7] because it's one we've been using for several years with our own students. Once you get the hang of things, it's also very easy to use. In particular, we use their metaworld called newHorizones, and the small program needed to run newHorizones can be downloaded for free [**www** FW5:8].

WHAT IS VZONES?

BOX FW5:1 VZONES IN THEIR OWN WORDS

When you join the vZones, you become a digital person and meet other people from around the world. You can talk, gesture, walk around and explore . . . play games, win prizes, buy, sell and just have fun. You'll make friends . . . maybe meet a friend for life. In the vZones, anything is possible! vZones has more than 3 billion permutations you can choose from. You can choose your body shape and size, your clothing, the color of your clothes and skin, your head, hairstyle, hats, glasses . . . you name it. You can be a human, a Faerie, a Sorcerer, Troll, Elf, Animal . . . and more. ◎

◎ At the time of preparing this book, vZones had a really neat flash presentation with an avatar introducing visitors to what it's all about. The presentation (459 kb) pops up automatically when you click through to the vZones homepage.

Like most metaworlds, vZones allows people to meet, chat and play in real time. Although vZones isn't truly 3D, it produces a 3D effect by using detailed background images as well as a series of orientation and action commands for your online persona – or *avatar*. Your avatar is superimposed over these backgrounds (known as zones), and any chat text you type appears in the form of a speech bubble in a blank space above. You can move your avatar from one zone to the next and each time the background updates almost immediately, although sometimes taking a moment to upload on your screen. You can also make basic gestures and facial expressions (e.g. smiling, grimacing, waving, jumping and even levitating!). The avatars of any other participants currently in the same zone will also appear on the screen in front of you. And that's when the social interaction begins.

WHAT IS AN AVATAR?

BOX FW5:2 VZONE AVATARS IN THE GARDEN ZONE

FIGURE 18 vZone avatars in the garden

One of the first things you'll need to do when registering to use newHorizones is to select an avatar for yourself – what vZones refers to above as a 'digital person'. In Central Issues: Unit 2, we quoted Mark Dery and Sherry Turkle, who spoke about 'disembodiment' and 'incorporeal interaction'. Well, an avatar is your chance to become embodied and corporeal again! At least, virtually. Bruce Damer describes an avatar as 'your body double in cyberspace'.

In actual fact, the word 'avatar' comes from ancient Sanskrit and means a divine incarnation – in other words, the earthly manifestation of a god.

When you first enter newHorizones you'll stand out (like a sore thumb, actually) because all newbies are given pretty much the same body – either male or female. One of the main things you're going to want to do really quickly is change your appearance. There's a token system in vZones which is how you can buy changes of clothes and hair color, gifts for people, things for your apartment even! You start with a fifty-token credit which you'll need to withdraw from an ATM (cash machine). After that, the longer you spend online the more tokens you'll earn. Our students enjoy finding their own way round, but are also glad of vZones' guide for newbies [**www** FW5:9]. Your best bet is to politely strike up an acquaintence with someone and they may be willing to show you around.

FIELDNOTES

In selecting and then constructing your avatar, reflect on Goffman's theories about impression management (Basic Theory: Unit 4) and the presentation of self (Central Issues: Unit 2). In Basic Theory: Unit 5 we also discussed the idea of anonymity in terms of 'freedom from constraints' and 'freedom from responsibility'. How do you think the graphical (or visual) environment of vZones impacts on how people feel and behave towards each other? Together with the questions in Box FW5:3, these are the kinds of critical issues you'll want to think about when preparing your fieldnotes.

BOX FW5:3 FIELDNOTE QUESTIONS

- What do you make of the choice of bodies and physiques available?
- What kinds of avatars are people choosing? What motivates their choices, do you think?
- What do you make of the different zones, e.g. their selection, content and depiction?
- How does having an avatar make you feel? Does it make you feel differently about your relationships with other participants?
- What sense of play and gender performance do you witness?
- What kinds of props (i.e. objects like flowers, sunglasses, teddy bears, etc.) are people using? What do they add to interaction?
- What is your overall impression of the communication in this metaworld compared with text-based chat like IRC?

BOX FW5:4 ASSESSING YOUR RESEARCH ACTIVITY

- Have you spent a reasonable length of time online?
- Can you make good connections with one or both of the Task Readings?
- Can you make connections with CMC central issues and basic theory?
- Have you used your own ideas and shown signs of critical thinking?
- Do you have well chosen examples to highlight the points you're making?
- Have you responded to some or all of the questions in Box FW5:3?

NOTE FOR COURSE LEADERS

It has been our experience not only that students have great fun exploring virtual reality chat spaces like vZones, but it is also the first time many of them ever experience what it is really like to feel engaged with, and even committed to, an online community. vZones is a commercial venture and there is a registration fee – at the time of writing this book,

US$10.95 a month for the entry-level environment newHorizones. It's worth remembering that vZones is a commercial site and, as such, it's subject to the vagaries of the marketplace. In other words, like The Palace – a very popular metaworld which ceased in 2001 – these ventures do sometimes close down.

If you are thinking of using vZones with a large class then it is advisable – and courteous – to make contact with the administrators of vZones beforehand (davida@vzones.com). They may even be able to offer advice and help with getting the most out of your time with vZones. In the past, we have also arranged with our local technical experts to download the vZones application in advance and make it readily available to students via our institutional computing networks. Having said which, many students prefer to download it on to their own computers anyway.

TASK 6

CONSTRUCTING IDENTITY: PERSONAL HOMEPAGES AND WEBCAMS

MAIN OBJECTIVES

- Conduct an analysis of personal homepages for online identity construction.
- Consider how the marginalized can develop identity and community online.
- Make fieldnotes responding to key questions and recording your analyses.
- Apply what you've learned from Central Issues: Unit 2.

TASK READING

Chandler, D. (1998b). *Personal home pages and the construction of identities on the web.* Available (11 April 2003) online: <http: //www.aber.ac.uk/media/Documents/short/webident.html>[**WWW** FW6:1].

This excellent paper by Daniel Chandler offers many fascinating ideas for analyzing personal homepages. The material in this Fieldwork Task is obviously also closely linked with Central Issues: Unit 2.

CONSTRUCTING IDENTITIES ON THE WEB

Charles Cheung (2000) talks about the opportunity that personal homepages give for the reflexive presentation and narrativization of the Self. Along these lines, Daniel Chandler describes them as being like the bedroom walls of teenagers covered in posters, snapshots, sports insignia, etc. Meanwhile, Robert Burnett and David Marshall (2003 – Chapter 4) say personal homepages are like old-fashioned mantelpieces where people used to display all their knick-knacks and postcards.

WWW For weblinks and resources visit the CMC website at <www.sagepub.co.uk/resources/cmc>

BOX FW6:1 WELCOME TO MY HOME PAGE!!!!!!!!! I KISS YOU!!!!!

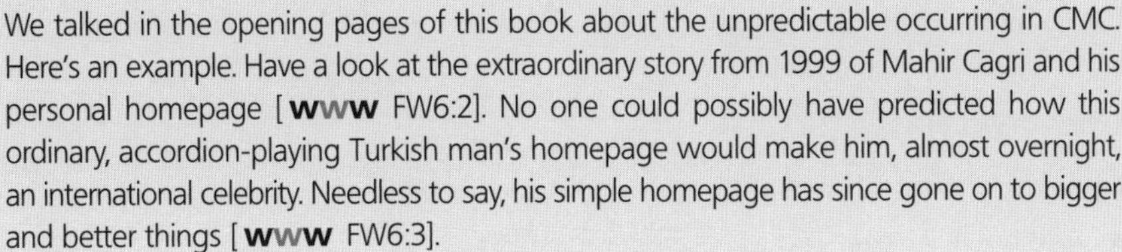

We talked in the opening pages of this book about the unpredictable occurring in CMC. Here's an example. Have a look at the extraordinary story from 1999 of Mahir Cagri and his personal homepage [**www** FW6:2]. No one could possibly have predicted how this ordinary, accordion-playing Turkish man's homepage would make him, almost overnight, an international celebrity. Needless to say, his simple homepage has since gone on to bigger and better things [**www** FW6:3].

With personal homepages, the boundaries between what's public and what's private are blurred in a way which is quite unique in the history of communication technologies. As Burnett and Marshall also say, the web is both powerful and intimate at the same time. Like a hybrid of televisions and telephones, it's both mass communication and interpersonal communication. In fact, from the point of view of CMC, what's important about these pages is that they're social interaction. Even if it's not immediate or obvious interaction, the people creating personal homepages are *in communication* with their audience – however big or small.

Personal homepages undoubtedly offer the chance to self-disclose otherwise hidden aspects of ourselves. As such, they are shaped by their authors, but also shape their authors in turn. They give people a sense of being able to validate themselves. Having said which, as we suggested in Basic Theory: Unit 2, sometimes people don't appear to have worked out who their audience is when they're building their homepages. As Chandler puts it, they may think that they're having their 'fifteen minutes of fame' when what they're actually doing is creating a fan club of one! ◎

◎ In the 1960s pop artist Andy Warhol famously said that every one of us will one day have fifteen minutes of fame. Click on high-school teacher Marc Hummel's homepage [**www** FW6:4] to see how your fifteen minutes are already trickling away!

TASK

The idea behind this task is really straightforward. Depending on how much time your course leader wants you to spend on this, and depending on their preferences in terms of content, you'll need to examine a range of different personal homepages to consider how they're representing and constructing the identities of their makers. All these homepages will tell you something about what people think about who they are, the stories they want to tell about themselves. In particular, you should try to analyze them following the guidelines proposed by Daniel Chandler in the Task Reading.

BOX FW6:2 THE *BRICOLEUR*'S WEB KIT

Using the metaphor of a *bricoleur*, Daniel Chandler identifies a number of criteria for analysing personal homepages.

Types of activity:

- *Inclusion*. What different ideas and topics are included?
- *Allusion*. What ideas and topics are being referred to?
- *Omission*. What's left unsaid or is noticeable by its absence?
- *Adaptation*. How are materials and ideas added to or altered?
- *Arrangement*. How is everything organized on the page?

Types of content

- personal statistics and biographical details;
- interests, likes and dislikes;
- ideas, values, beliefs and causes;
- friends, acquaintances and personal icons (e.g. celebrities).

Types of structure

- written text;
- graphics – whether still or moving – and other artwork;
- sound and/or video (e.g. associated webcams);
- short screenfuls to long scrolls of text;
- single page or many interconnected pages;
- separate windows or frames;
- an access counter (i.e. number of people who've visited);
- a guestbook;
- links for other pages (e.g. a 'cool links' section);
- an email button or chat button.

In terms of the types of personal homepages which you could look at, we have several suggestions.

PROFESSIONAL HOMEPAGES

One idea is to start by looking at the range of professional and/or personal homepages of the top CMC scholars in our 'Who's Who' guide on the CMC website. In this instance, focus on the balance they choose to strike (or not) between their public and private lives. What do you make of they way this is done?

PERSONAL HOMEPAGES

Another exercise is to select any first name and do a random search through the extensive listings of personal homepages based at Yahoo!'s Geocities [www FW6:5] or AOL's Hometown [www FW6:6]. For example, search for the homepages of everyone called Tommy. They may all have the same name, but it's interesting to see how totally different their homepages are – obviously!

MARGINALIZED PEOPLE ONLINE

You've already come across the claim that the internet potentially gives a voice to groups of people who are normally excluded or underrepresented in society. One suggestion, therefore, is to consider how members of such groups are using *personal* homepages to communicate, assert and construct their social identities. For example, you could choose one of the following minority groups to explore either as individuals or in a group: immigrants, Muslims living in the West, expatriates living overseas, the disabled, people who've suffered from racial harassment, the unemployed, prisoners, drug addicts or victims of domestic violence. Using Geocities [www FW6:5] or Hometown [www FW6:6], use these social labels as search terms for identifying a selection of personal homepages. An alternative is to choose a similar group from Yahoo!'s directory of *Groups and cultures* [www FW6:7].

SPECIAL CASE STUDY: GAY PEOPLE IN CYBERSPACE

Daniel Chandler (1998b) pinpoints gay people's personal homepages as a special example of the issues he's discussing. Perhaps more so than for other groups, the internet has been a powerful opportunity for gay men and women and gay young people. Although many of us are privileged to live in societies where people understand that prejudice and hate are unacceptable nowadays, gay people continue to be marginalized, suffering tremendous discrimination and, often, even violence. Consequently they are often also isolated, especially while growing up, and so the internet offers a safe environment for 'coming out' to themselves and perhaps others, for discovering that they're not alone and for seeking support. ◎ Run a similar search as above, using 'gay man', 'lesbian' or 'gay teen' as your search terms.

◎ A cover feature [www FW6:8] by Jennifer Egan for the *New York Times* gives an excellent insight into how gay teens can be empowered through CMC.

BOX FW6:3 ONLINE IDENTITY/ INFORMATION RESOURCES FOR GAY PEOPLE

Looking further afield, beyond personal homepages, you may also like to consider how 'gay identity' is being constructed and protected through a diverse range of online resources available for gay men and lesbian women:

- Gay.com [www FW4:9]
- Queer Resources Directory [www FW4:10]
- The Gay and Lesbian Review [www FW4:11]
- QueerTheory.com [www FW4:12]
- LGBT Philosophy Site Index [www FW4:13]
- National Coalition for Gay, Lesbian, Bisexual and Transgender Youth [www FW4:14]

WEBCAMS

With faster internet connections and more sophisticated technology, the use of webcams has been a growing aspect of CMC and life online. Instead of looking at personal homepages, therefore, you could look at a range of personal webcams, trying to apply some of Chandler's ideas to webcams. Anything you do here is breaking new ground. At the time of preparing this book we could find virtually no examples of scholarly writing about the role of webcams in CMC. There are a number of good webcam directories such as WebCam World [**www** FW6:14] which also has a listing of their top-100 webcam sites. For some reason, webcams have become especially popular with young women, such as UK CamGirl [**www** FW6:15]. Why do you think this is? (Refer to Central Issues: Unit 5.)

FIELDNOTES

Using the bricoleur's web kit in Box FW6:2, make fieldnotes to record your analyses of the personal homepages you visit. You may like to discuss your ideas in pairs or small groups. As well as referring to Central Issues: Unit 2, you'll probably want to make reference to your own experience of creating a webpage from Fieldwork: Task 3. Consider also the types of questions outlined in Box FW6:4.

BOX FW6:4 FIELDNOTE QUESTIONS

- What aspects of their identity are people choosing to foreground? Are these aspects similar to, or different from, those you would prioritize in your own homepage?
- How homogeneously do groups appear to be representing themselves? Do you get a sense of a community emerging in these pages? If so, how or where?
- How does what you see in these homepages tie in with what academic commentators have said about the 'unique' opportunities in CMC for identity play?

Questions specifically related to marginalized people:

- To what extent are marginalized people presenting issues related to their status as a social-political minority group?
- What opportunities do you feel are offered by the personal homepage for the assertion of minority rights?
- How fair do you think it would be to decide what it means to be a member of that specific minority group based solely on the personal homepages pages you have seen?

BOX FW6:5 ASSESSING YOUR RESEARCH ACTIVITY

- Have you spent a reasonable length of time online?
- Can you make good connections with one or both of the task readings?
- Can you make connections with CMC central issues and basic theory?
- Have you used your own ideas and shown signs of critical thinking?
- Do you have well chosen examples to highlight the points you're making?
- Have you responded to some or all of the questions in Box FW6:4?

STRAND 4

EXPLORE: FOCUS AREAS

'RESPECT FOR THE COMPLEXITY OF PROBLEMS'

What we've done in this strand is focus on a selection of topics for your own research and project work. Each topic offers you a brief account, a snapshot if you like, of key concerns and developments in a major communication domain. With the basic theory and critical perspectives you already have, it's now your turn to explore further. Exploration is not just about information gathering, it's also about evaluating that information using your critical judgement. This is your opportunity to be a CMC researcher and to find out what's new in cyberspace.

At first you may feel a bit swamped by all the material that's out there. The most helpful thing to remember, from page 4, is Pierre Bourdieu's fourth pillar of intellectual life: 'respect for the complexity of problems'. Anything to do with human behavior and culture is unavoidably complex. Remember, also, CMC is always changing, with new users, new technologies and new insights. This strand requires you to be adventurous, flexible, and critical. Knowledge is not about finding the facts or the 'right' answers, it's about asking interesting questions.

You may also feel a little uncertain about what to do. We recommend that you lean heavily on Fieldwork: Task 1, which gives lots of advice about researching and searching on the internet. Basically, you need to find out as much as you can about the topic of your Focus Area, and identify the current facts, issues and challenges. In particular, ask yourself these important questions:

- How is CMC being used in this communication domain?
- How does basic CMC theory help explain what's going on?

- What is happening in terms of identity, relationship, and/or community?
- What central issues, like inequality, language and gender, emerge in this area?
- Looking beyond your own country, what is the international perspective?

NOTE FOR COURSE LEADERS

Unlike the more in-depth analyses of the Basic Theory and Central Issues units, this strand includes nine thematic snapshots designed to lead students into thinking about different communication topics in CMC. In doing so, they are also encouraged to start *applying* the knowledge and critical and practical skills being acquired from the Basic Theory and Central Issues units and Fieldwork tasks. In fact, students should be actively looking to make links with key issues.

We have deliberately designed this strand to be as flexible as possible. Over the years we have ourselves experimented with a range of options. For example, students may be asked to tackle just one Focus Area topic or all of them, with the topics being approached in no particular order. Assessment of students' progress is also a matter for you to decide. For example, students can work individually or in small teams. They can work towards a class presentation or written coursework. In fact, rather than writing a traditional academic paper, students might be encouraged to write a professional report. This could even be presented as a webpage/website, encouraging them to share their research and writing with a wider online audience.

TOPIC 1

POLITICAL COMMUNICATION IN CMC

THE POLITICAL POWER OF ONLINE COMMUNICATION

Consider this. You live a mile away from your 'neighbors', perhaps even from family members, yet you're forbidden to speak to them on the telephone, to write them a letter, or visit them personally. You're on the island of Cyprus, which is divided into Turkish and Greek sectors. Separating you from your neighbors are barbed wire barricades, UN peacekeepers and a buffer zone, where trespassers are reported to have been murdered. If you wanted to meet face-to-face, you'd have to fly out of the Greek or Turkish sector to somewhere like Athens or Istanbul and then fly back into the other sector. The frustrations and heartache are enormous. Despite all the obstacles, however, you can send emails to each other. You *can* be in touch.

The internet has certainly afforded some dramatic new opportunities to connect with others in politically charged situations. It frees people to communicate across national borders without having to travel or show a passport. It sometimes allows people living under repressive governments to express their views more easily. Through CMC you can reach a wide audience across the world, speaking for an underrepresented group, or challenging authority. You can report events on the ground, which may conflict with how they're being reported in the mainstream media.

Clearly, CMC is both political *and* politicizing, because it may be used to confront the authority of governing powers, and to resist dominant social, cultural and political ideologies. Increasingly, in recent conflicts, the voices of individuals online from war-torn territories provide an alternative perspective to the major, predominantly Western news media. Importantly, therefore, CMC allows us to view current events from more than one perspective. It can also serve both to politicize us and to enable us to participate more actively in political processes.

www For weblinks and resources visit the CMC website at <www.sagepub.co.uk/resources/cmc>

PARTICIPATION AND RESISTANCE

On the one hand, politicians can set up official information sites, on the other hand, CMC can be used to subvert and resist government authority. In terms of the first category, there are instances of so called *e-democracy*, when governments, elected officials, media, political organizations and citizens use the internet to engage in debates about the processes and practices of governance. It's increasingly common to find both government and commercially funded sites which encourage political involvement online as a way of getting more people actively involved in national politics. In the United States, for example, there's the Institute for Politics, Democracy and the Internet [**www** FA1:1].

On the other hand, cyberactivism too is a powerful example of politicized and politicizing CMC. Cyberactivists use email, listservs, newsgroups, IRC and the web to address a large audience and communicate with their network of supporters. It's in this way that repressed minorities can build resistant communities online. Cyberactivitists use CMC to promote human rights, animal rights, environmental issues, and the rights of marginalized communities. Their goals are to organize people around these issues, and attempt to create social change. ◎

◎ Some cyberactivists have chosen to take direct action to shut down dominant discourse and organizations. For example, within the first week of the 2003 Iraq war, 1,000 websites, including military sites in the United States, were allegedly hacked by anti-war activists.

Researchers have found that online communication can indeed help increase political awareness, participatory democracy, mutual tolerance and more open, peaceful dialogue between people. But many are still excluded from this promising scenario. Disempowered people in disempowered places like poor often think their voices are not adequately heard – whether through traditional or computer-mediated means. While there are numerous e-democracy sites and organizations in rich nations, much more can be done to create online spaces for those on the margins to engage in the opportunities for that enhanced freedom, equality, justice, democracy and autonomy promised by the internet.

PORTAL BOX

A Portal Box is a kind of lucky-dip or grab-bag selection of weblinks to lead you to more facts and issues about the topic area. Remember, this is just a starting point – the rest is up to you.

www FA1:2 Center for Technology in Government
www FA1:3 Political Communication Resources
www FA1:4 E-democracy Resource Lists
www FA1:5 DoWire – Democracies Online Newswire
www FA1:6 iafrica political room
www FA1:7 Greenpeace Cyberactivist Community
www FA1:8 Samoa Chat – Politics Board
www FA1:9 Institute for Democracy in Eastern Europe
www FA1:10 Essential Information Mailing Lists
www FA1:11 World Movement for Democracy

While you explore the weblinks from the Portal Box, and in addition to the key questions from the strand introduction (see pp. 197–99), keep in mind the following additional questions. What range of views have you come across regarding political communication in CMC? Which views have you found most convincing and why? What did you find most interesting? What didn't you understand? What would you like to know more about?

BOX FA1:1 INFORMATION TARGETS

Think about targeting the following areas of information:

- facts and stats
- scholarly issues
- international perspectives
- popular treatments (such as newspapers, popular cultural forms)
- professional concerns

BOX FA1:2 EVALUATING THE SUCCESS OF YOUR RESEARCH

- *Research breadth.* Have you done a reasonable amount of researching?
- *Research quality.* Have you used academic and other appropriate sources?
- *Organization.* Have you clearly identified the main issues and concerns?
- *Good examples.* Have you found relevant case studies and examples?
- *Your own ideas.* Have you been original and critical in your thinking?

TOPICAL READINGS

Duque, A. (2001). New media as resistance: Colombia. *Leonardo*, 34 (4), 333–4.

Internet activism (2000). *The International Journal on Grey Literature*, 1 (3), 99–106.

Staeheli, L.A., Ledwith, V., Ormond, M., Reed, K., Sumpter, A. and Trudeau, D. (2002). Immigration, the internet, and spaces of politics. *Political Geography*, 21 (8), 989–1012.

TOPIC 2

LEGAL COMMUNICATION IN CMC

A GOLDEN AGE FOR LAWYERS

Back in the early days of CMC, W. John Moore (1992), in his article 'Taming cyberspace', wrote: 'The golden age of cyberspace is drawing to a close . . . but the golden age for lawyers is just dawning'. A decade after the Golden Age of cyberspace ended, the Golden Age for lawyers is still shining. Since cyberspace isn't governed by national boundaries, and international law hasn't really caught up yet, all sorts of interesting legal issues online are still turning up month by month, even week by week. Lawyers, both nationally and internationally, are having a hard time keeping up! This is one area where we're all made aware of the dynamism of this particular cultural revolution. Data protection laws have long ago been enacted to protect the individual but 'cyberlibel', 'cybersquatting', online scams, hacking into bank accounts, and intellectual property concerns, are all keeping the net legal experts busy.

ONLINE LIBEL

Flaming isn't just aggressive, sometimes it's potentially libellous. Generally speaking, laws for online publication are similar to print laws. With the increase in online publication, it follows that there will be an increase in online libel charges (hence 'cyberlibel'). Given the recent legislation in the area of cyberlibel, it may be wise to take note of how some CMC can land you in court.

www For weblinks and resources visit the CMC website at <www.sagepub.co.uk/resources/cmc>

BOX FA2:1 TO CLAIM LIBEL

To claim libel, a claimant needs to prove four things. The statement must:

- have clearly identified the claimant;
- have lowered the claimant in society's view;
- have been published by the person being sued to a third party or the public;
- be provably false.

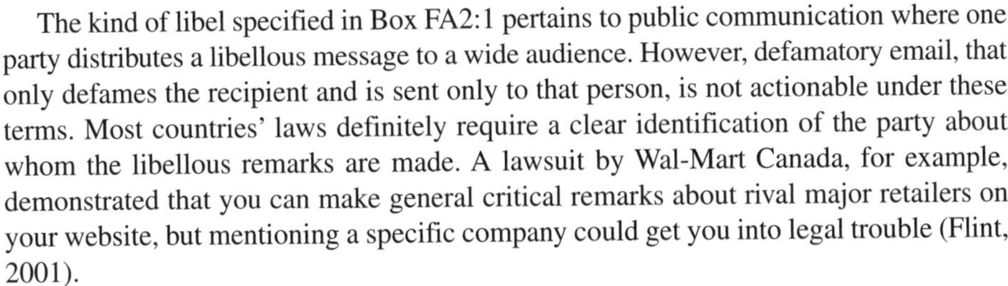

The kind of libel specified in Box FA2:1 pertains to public communication where one party distributes a libellous message to a wide audience. However, defamatory email, that only defames the recipient and is sent only to that person, is not actionable under these terms. Most countries' laws definitely require a clear identification of the party about whom the libellous remarks are made. A lawsuit by Wal-Mart Canada, for example, demonstrated that you can make general critical remarks about rival major retailers on your website, but mentioning a specific company could get you into legal trouble (Flint, 2001).

So who is held legally responsible: the author of the libellous comment or the internet service provider disseminating the comment? In a landmark British defamation case against a major internet service provider, the courts found that ISPs were to be liable if they were *aware* of defamatory content carried over their system. This has not been the case in the United States, however, where the courts ruled that ISPs are not responsible for material transmitted over their servers [**www** FA2:1].

CYBER-CRIME AND INTERNET FRAUD

Picture this: you are at your computer terminal, checking email, and an oddly typed message in your in-box asks for your assistance in 'freeing' a huge amount of money which is being 'held' by an undemocratic regime in Africa. You're promised a percentage of the cash as a reward – an amount that could reach millions – but only if you assist in the 'liberation' of the money by having it transferred into your bank account.

When this email scam flourished the 1990s, most people had never received a message from Nigeria. Spam was less usual in those days, too. The plea and the plan seemed authentic. The exotic nature of the message led many in Europe and North America to take note seriously and respond. The now infamous 'Nigerian email scam' is one of the longest-running international scams ever. The scam has completely drained many people's bank accounts. Gullible victims have reportedly even gone to Nigeria, where they may have been subject to further extortion, beatings and murder. In 2001, the Internet Fraud Complaint Center reported that 2,600 people had filed complaints about the scam – of those, sixteen reported losses totalling US$345,000 [**www** FA2:2].

CYBERSQUATTING DISPUTES

Although less common than it was before, another type of questionable practice is known as 'cybersquatting'. This entails people buying domain names using well known brand or celebrity names in the hope of subsequently selling them to the companies or people who probably should have secured them in the first place. In many cases of cybersquatting with high-profile domain names like 'harrypotterbooks.org', 'bbcnews.org', and 'madonna.com', the domain names were transferred back to those who had pursued them through the courts.

Internationally renowned movie director and producer Steven Spielberg filed a claim against a small internet firm in India over the name of its website. Spielberg's legal team claimed the Indian company's domain name 'dreamworkzweb.com' was too similar to DreamWorks, Spielberg's own production company. The Indian company was asked to forfeit its domain name or face litigation (Reddy, 2002). However, other legal experts have thought otherwise. In 2001, the World Intellectual Property Organization, an international body which deals with such disputes, judged in favor of a certain Mr A.R. Mani, when lawyers supporting the leading fashion design house Armani claimed the company should have the right to own the domain name armani.com. So, in some cases, the 'little guy' wins!

PORTAL BOX

A Portal Box is a kind of lucky-dip or grab-bag selection of weblinks to lead you to more facts and issues about the topic area. Remember, this is just a starting point – the rest is up to you.

www FA2:3 Stand, UK civil rights organization
www FA2:4 Cyber Rights and Cyber Liberties
www FA2:5 Partnership for Civil Justice
www FA2:6 Whole Lotto stealing going on
www FA2:7 IFCC Internet 2001 Fraud Report
www FA2:8 Internet Law and Policy Forum
www FA2:9 Internet Corporation for Assigned Names and Numbers (ICANN)
www FA2:10 Uniform Domain Name Dispute Resolution Policy (UDRP)
www FA2:11 Bitlaw
www FA2:12 Africa Law Institute

While you explore the weblinks from the Portal Box, and in addition to the key questions from the strand introduction (see pp. 197–99), keep in mind the following additional questions. What range of views have you come across regarding legal communication in CMC? Which views have you found most convincing and why? What did you find most interesting? What didn't you understand? What would you like to know more about?

BOX FA2:2 INFORMATION TARGETS

Think about targeting the following areas of information:

- facts and stats
- scholarly issues
- international perspectives
- popular treatments (e.g newspaper articles)
- professional concerns

BOX FA2:3 EVALUATING THE SUCCESS OF YOUR RESEARCH

- *Research breadth.* Have you done a reasonable amount of researching?
- *Research quality.* Have you used academic and other appropriate sources?
- *Organization.* Have you clearly identified the main issues and concerns?
- *Good examples.* Have you found relevant case studies and examples?
- *Your own ideas.* Have you been original and critical in your thinking?

TOPICAL READINGS

Cucereanu, D. (2001). Cyberlibel cases before the European Court of Human Rights: estimating possible outcomes. *Netherlands Quarterly of Human Rights*, 19 (1), 5–20.

Flint, D. (2001). Why does only Wal-Mart Canada suck? *Business Law Review*, 22 (2), 36–40.

TOPIC 3

ORGANIZATIONAL COMMUNICATION IN CMC

WORKING IN A MEDIATED WORLD

Consider this situation. Two people have a date. The following day, they have an email conversation, and in one of the messages the woman (whose identity has been protected) refers to the previous evening's romantic activities in subtle but evidently sexual terms. The man, a lawyer called Bradley Chait, forwards her email to four of his colleagues at the London law firm Norton Rose. The colleagues, in turn, forward the email on again. Hours after Chait forwarded the message, it had spread from Norton Rose to other London law firms, then made its way round the world, travelling as far as New Zealand. Some days later, at least two websites had developed about the story, including reader polls, news updates and chat forums. The woman, who understandably thought that her email was for Bradley Chait only, was forced into hiding to avoid harassment from people contacting her after having read the information online. Chait used his office's network to forward the email, as did his colleagues, who then forwarded it on again. The management of Norton Rose launched an internal disciplinary hearing during which Chait and his colleagues were threatened with dismissal for misusing company time and space, and for implicating the company in a case of sexual harassment.

This is just one way in which the rules and norms of workplace communication are having to be rethought in light of the internet. In fact, some researchers argue that CMC has had more significant impact on the workplace than many other arenas, revolutionizing the way we work and interact with employers and colleagues.

A VERY DIFFERENT WORKPLACE

The ability to work in 'virtual teams' has created a very different type of workplace from only a decade ago. Real-time web-conferencing, complete with virtual whiteboards, is becoming more and more common. Telecommuting too is on the increase. We now have

WWW For weblinks and resources visit the CMC website at <www.sagepub.co.uk/resources/cmc>

the ability to connect with colleagues in other office sites, whether it be down the road or on the other side of the globe – sometimes working with colleagues we've never even met FtF. Around the world, and in many different languages, telework organizations promote the idea of working from anywhere [**www** FA3:1]. The increase in workplace CMC – and especially Computer Supported Collaborative Work (CSCW) – also has an impact on how individuals experience and value work in other areas of their lives. Many employees, for example, telecommute from home in order to balance their work and family lives, blurring the boundaries between work and home (Edley, 2001). This may be seen as either a positive or a negative development.

BIG BROTHER'S WATCHING: SURVEILLANCE AND PRIVACY CONCERNS

Employees' internet use can always be monitored. A study by the Privacy Foundation in the United States found that 27 million employees around the world, or about one-quarter of the online global workforce, have their internet use or email under continuous surveillance [**www** FA3:2]. For example, in the United States, 14 million employees are supposedly being monitored by their employers. Not surprisingly, new types of legislation are clearly needed to protect the interests of both employers and employees. The British Regulation of Investigatory Powers Act 2000 is one such piece of legislation. It allows companies to monitor online communication – and often without the consent – of employees.

Privacy is an important ethical issue. Having said which, evidence does suggest that employers are right to be concerned about their employees' online activities. Research found that, out of a survey of 1,000 employees, 64 percent used the net for non-work activity ('Cyberslackers at work', 2000). Another survey by Vault (2000), found that 84 percent of employees have sent non-work-related email and 90 percent looked at recreational websites during work hours.

Some psychologists have inferred that desktop internet access in the workplace transforms some employees – particularly those with a predilection for addictive behavior – into internet junkies (Jeffrey Stanton, 2002:56).

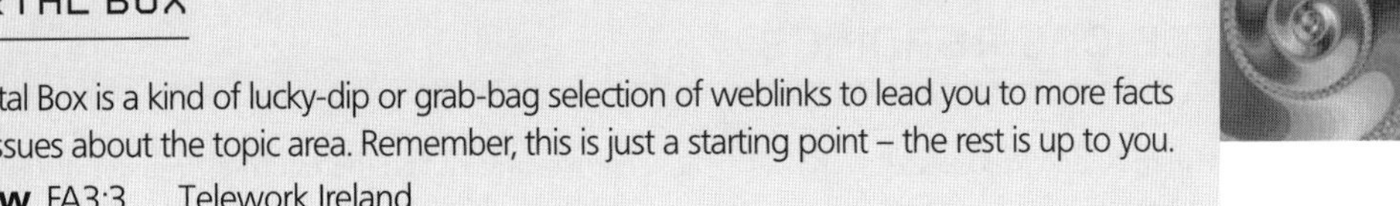

PORTAL BOX

A Portal Box is a kind of lucky-dip or grab-bag selection of weblinks to lead you to more facts and issues about the topic area. Remember, this is just a starting point – the rest is up to you.

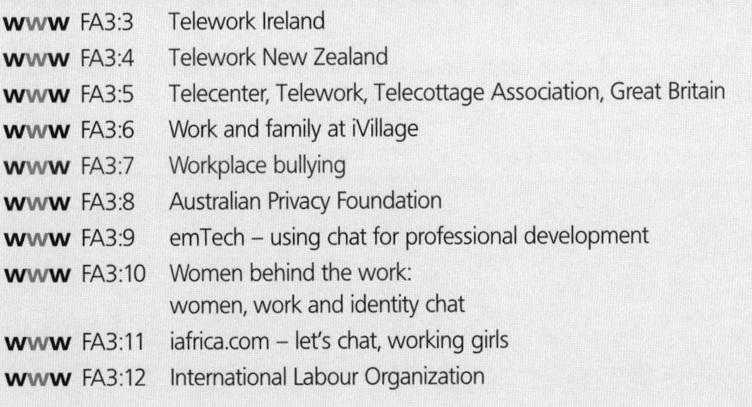

www FA3:3 Telework Ireland
www FA3:4 Telework New Zealand
www FA3:5 Telecenter, Telework, Telecottage Association, Great Britain
www FA3:6 Work and family at iVillage
www FA3:7 Workplace bullying
www FA3:8 Australian Privacy Foundation
www FA3:9 emTech – using chat for professional development
www FA3:10 Women behind the work: women, work and identity chat
www FA3:11 iafrica.com – let's chat, working girls
www FA3:12 International Labour Organization

While you explore the weblinks from the Portal Box, and in addition to the key questions from the strand introduction (see pp. 197–99), keep in mind the following additional questions. What range of views have you come across regarding organizational communication in CMC? Which views have you found most convincing and why? What did you find most interesting? What didn't you understand? What would you like to know more about?

BOX FA3:1 INFORMATION TARGETS

Think about targeting the following areas of information:

- facts and stats
- scholarly issues
- international perspectives
- popular treatments (e.g newspaper articles)
- professional concerns

BOX FA3:2 EVALUATING THE SUCCESS OF YOUR RESEARCH

- *Research breadth.* Have you done a reasonable amount of researching?
- *Research quality.* Have you used academic and other appropriate sources?
- *Organization.* Have you clearly identified the main issues and concerns?
- *Good examples.* Have you found relevant case studies and examples?
- *Your own ideas.* Have you been original and critical in your thinking?

TOPICAL READINGS

Miller, S. and Weckert, J. (2000). Privacy, the workplace and the internet. *Journal of Business Ethics*, 28, 255–65.

Stanton, J.M. (2002). Web addict or happy employee? Company profile of the frequent internet user. *Communications of the ACM*, 45 (1), 55–9. ◎

◎ This article appears as part of a special issue on the internet in the workplace.

TOPIC 4

HEALTH COMMUNICATION IN CMC

A HEALTHIER VIRTUAL [AND REAL] WORLD

What would you do if you were in an online chat session and read this posting?

* Ken Walker (Scot)	I Helo . . .have broblemd , , ,thhimk
	I I am wayin g stroke

Would you think the message was a hoax? In fact, this is a real story. Ken Walker, from Scotland, was participating in a regularly scheduled genealogy chatroom. ◎ At first the other members and the chatroom moderator (or 'systems operator'), Richard Eastman, were sceptical. However, concern escalated once Walker's chatting became even more erratic. Members encouraged Walker to stay alert and continue communicating, ensuring that he was part of a supportive community:

◎ Genealogy is all about the search for one's ancestors. It's an incredibly popular activity on the internet, with thousands and thousands of people using online information sources like Family Tree Maker at Geneology.com [**www** FA4:15] or JewishGen [**www** FA4:16].

* Ken Walker (Scot)	I i am alone
MARY L. WITTLOCK	I No you are not we are all here for you

After Walker managed to type his telephone number, Eastman contacted an international telephone operator, who provided Walker's address. The telephone operator also connected Eastman with local police. Two minutes later, an ambulance arrived and Walker was rushed to the hospital, treated, and eventually released. You can read the full transcript of this event [**www** FA4:1].

PIONEERING COMMUNITY HEALTH ONLINE

The community spirit evident in much CMC actually harkens back to early health-related CMC. In 1984 Tom Grundner and his colleagues in the School of Medicine at Case Western Reserve University, in Cleveland, USA, wanted to find an efficient way to communicate with physicians at five different medical units. To keep in constant contact,

www For weblinks and resources visit the CMC website at <www.sagepub.co.uk/resources/cmc>

Grundner set up a bulletin board and developed a program called *St Silicon's Hospital and Information Dispensary*, including 'Doc in the box', where a legitimate physician could respond to lay people's health questions.

After publishing an article in 1986, Grundner's online health resource drew international attention, including the technological support of major telephone company AT & T. Eventually the system grew from being an 'electronic hospital' to becoming one of the very first FreeNets – a fully developed electronic community, complete with a post office, library, school system and administration center, attracting six million user sessions in 1996. (See **www** FW4:2 for more background on this.)

E-MEDICINE: NEW INITIATIVES, INCREASED CONCERNS

The problem is that anyone can create a health-related website. (Dr Paul Lambden, 2000)

Developments in online health (or 'e-medicine') have not stopped since 'Doc in the box'. In fact, commentators predict that, by 2005, an estimated 88 million people in the United States alone may be using the internet for medical service and advice (Gorney, 2001). Health organizations, medical boards and physicians are developing policies to address the increase of health-related CMC. This is especially because scholars and practitioners are being faced with some important concerns about the quality of online medical resources (see the quote above by an actual doctor). Of course, it's not all bad news. There are also some important benefits to be had, such as having increased access to online medical information useful to doctors, patients and people with other health problems. The kinds of questions scholars and practitioners are therefore asking are these. What kind of information should and shouldn't be made available online? How is online health information quality to be monitored? How might patients, armed with the vast amounts of health-related information, influence their physicians' decisions over medical treatment? Is this a good thing or a bad thing?

PORTAL BOX

A Portal Box is a kind of lucky-dip or grab-bag selection of weblinks to lead you to more facts and issues about the topic area. Remember, this is just a starting point – the rest is up to you.

www FA4:3 African Networks for Health Research and Development
www FA4:4 World Health Organization
www FA4:5 HealthNet
www FA4:6 healthyplace.com
www FA4:7 parents place, chat central health
www FA4:8 iVillage health
www FA4:9 OncoChat
www FA4:10 mental health chat rooms
www FA4:11 Grief Recovery On-Line, GROWW
www FA4:12 WebMD

While you explore the weblinks from the Portal Box, and in addition to the key questions from the strand introduction (see pp. 197–99), keep in mind the following additional questions. What range of views have you come across regarding health communication in CMC? Which views have you found most convincing and why? What did you find most interesting? What didn't you understand? What would you like to know more about?

BOX FA4:1 INFORMATION TARGETS

Think about targeting the following areas of information:

- facts and stats
- scholarly issues
- international perspectives
- popular treatments (e.g. newspaper articles)
- professional concerns

BOX FA4:2 EVALUATING THE SUCCESS OF YOUR RESEARCH

- *Research breadth.* Have you done a reasonable amount of researching?
- *Research quality.* Have you used academic and other appropriate sources?
- *Organization.* Have you clearly identified the main issues and concerns?
- *Good examples.* Have you found relevant case studies and examples?
- *Your own ideas.* Have you been original and critical in your thinking?

TOPICAL READINGS

Collste, G. (2002). The internet doctor and medical ethics: ethical implications of the introduction of the internet into medical encounters. *Medicine, Health Care and Philosophy*, 5 (2), 121–5.

Potts, H.W.W. and Wyatt, J.C. (2002). Survey of doctors' experience of patients using the internet. *Journal of Medical Internet Research*, 4 (1). Available (24 February 2003) online: <http://www.jmir.org/2002/1/e5/abstract> [**WWW** FW4:13].

TOPIC 5

LIFESPAN COMMUNICATION IN CMC (I)

'SUPER YOUNG SURFERS': CHILDREN ONLINE

Charlie is woken in the morning by his mother, who gets him out of bed early so that he can have some time on the computer. He goes downstairs, crosses over to the computer and begins playing the latest skill-building game that his mother bought him that week. His sister, Anna, is already sitting at her computer, playing a different skill-build game. This may not sound unusual until we realize that Charlie is only three years old. His sister, Anna, is six. Anna's games are part of her primary school curriculum, and Charlie's are recommended by his high-end pre-school.

These days many privileged children are raised with computers in the home, so it's not surprising that one-year-olds bang away on keyboards, and that three-year-olds know how to send emails. Learning sites like Bob the Builder and Teletubbies, which have music and learning games, make computing exciting and interactive for children. The associated websites of television networks too offer games, stories, music, even online coloring.

MYTHS ABOUT CHILDREN AND COMPUTERS

Childrens' software reviewers Ellen Wolock and colleagues (1998) analyze six myths about the relationship between computers and the very young. The myths include the idea that children will be smarter if they use computers, that they will become less socialized by using computers, and that children need to become computer-literate as soon as possible in order to keep up with their peers. Marketing to the fears of these myths is lucrative. Several websites are designed to help entrepreneurs find ways of making money by creating and selling educational computer activities and games to an international market. Many companies also promote monitoring programs that promise to help parents keep track of their children's online activities. Arguably, also, this is a way to help parents control their children's online identities and social networking. With names like *I am Big Brother*, these monitoring programs threaten constant scrutiny [**www** FA5:1].

www For weblinks and resources visit the CMC website at <www.sagepub.co.uk/resources/cmc>

KIDS AND COMMUNITIES

There are numerous spaces in cyberspace where children can safely engage in online communication. For example, CBBC has a space called 'Star Chat', affording children the opportunity to email their television and online program stars, and a message board that includes 'Web Pals', boasting nearly 4,000 messages since its inception. There are a lot of spaces like this, where children can chat, play games and learn. Others, like 'Voices from Sarajevo', allow slightly older children and teens to share experiences with others and develop relationships and communities around the world in order to become politically involved.

Not only can CMC facilitate international relationships, it also has the potential to help bridge the gender gap. Some scholars argue that boys and girls would learn computing the same way and on the same level if given the chance, although males and females continue to be socially conditioned from a young age to react differently to technology. The 'digital gender divide' starts young. NFO WorldGroup reveals that the internet is now the most heavily used media by teenage boys in Hong Kong [**www** FA5:2] and it's significant that this study discusses only teenage boys. There's always a real danger of the digital gender divide simply being reinforced unless scholars and others actively seek to redress the imbalance.

WORLDWIDE YOUTH COMMUNITIES

You may have noticed that what we have said so far is based on the assumption that children have access to computers in the first place. Based at the Indian Centre for Research in Cognitive Systems, Sugataa Mitra and Viveka Rana (2001:23) conducted a cross-national study on children's exposure to CMC. They explain:

> Urban children all over the world seem to acquire computing skills without adult intervention. Indeed this form of self-instruction has produced hackers: children who can penetrate high-tech security systems. Is this kind of learning dependent only on the availability of technology?

Mitra and Rana found that children's ability to grasp technology is dependent entirely on exposure. Language, cultural background and education level did not affect how children related to CMC. These findings open many possibilities for increasing youth participation in CMC on a global scale. Websites for youth also bring the world to kids' homes and classrooms. For the *Africa for Kids* [**www** FA5:3] program, PBS sent digital cameras to children from four schools in Africa so they can share their images, text and lives with the world.

PORTAL BOX

A Portal Box is a kind of lucky-dip or grab-bag selection of weblinks to lead you to more facts and issues about the topic area. Remember, this is just a starting point – the rest is up to you.

www FA5:4 PBS Kids
www FA5:5 CBBC (Children's BBC)
www FA5:6 PBS Teacher Source
www FA5:7 FranchiseGator
www FA5:8 Control Kids
www FA5:9 MoM
www FA5:10 Teen Chat
www FA5:11 Yahoo teen chat rooms
www FA5:12 e-teen Kosovo Relief Project
www FA5:13 iafrica teen chat

While you explore the weblinks from the Portal Box, and in addition to the key questions from the strand introduction (see pp. 197–99), keep in mind the following additional questions: What range of views have you come across regarding youth in CMC? Which views have you found most convincing and why? What did you find most interesting? What didn't you understand? What would you like to know more about?

BOX FA5:1 INFORMATION TARGETS

Think about targeting the following areas of information:

- facts and stats
- scholarly issues
- international perspectives
- popular treatments (such as newspapers, popular cultural forms)
- professional concerns

BOX FA5:2 EVALUATING THE SUCCESS OF YOUR RESEARCH

- *Research breadth.* Have you done a reasonable amount of researching?
- *Research quality.* Have you used academic and other appropriate sources?
- *Organization.* Have you clearly identified the main issues and concerns?
- *Good examples.* Have you found relevant case studies and examples?
- *Your own ideas.* Have you been original and critical in your thinking?

TOPICAL READINGS

Mitra, S. and Rana, V. (2001). Children and the internet: experiments with minimally invasive education in India. *British Journal of Educational Technology*, 32 (2), 22–36.

Maczewski, M. (2002). Exploring identities through the internet: youth experiences online. *Child and Youth Care Forum*, 31 (2), 111–29.

TOPIC 6

LIFESPAN COMMUNICATION IN CMC (II)

'SILVER SURFERS': THE ELDERLY ONLINE

Helen stared at the computer screen, trying to remember how to insert the pictures that her granddaughters wanted sent by email. Helen hadn't wanted to learn to write emails, in fact, she and her husband had resisted using a computer at all, but it was the only way they could keep in touch with their tech-loving family. No one ever used the telephone any more. 'Insert, picture, choose file from list,' Helen muttered to herself, trying to remember what she'd called the picture taken that morning. 'It still isn't there,' Helen grumbled and reached for the instruction manual again. She was trying to download pictures to the hard disk . . . or was it upload? The instruction manual was confusing. Whatever happened to film cameras, anyway? It was time to link to the community at SeniorNet [**www** FA6:1] and ask for help. One of her new friends from the SeniorNet community would be able to explain it in simple terms.

Helen represents people from generations that came of age long before the computer era, those whose identities were formed without the internet and who are therefore understandably sometimes resistant to the notion of CMC. However, many elderly people, especially those who are isolated, do find themselves drawn to CMC as a means of staying in touch with family, or simply keeping up to date in their communities. ◎ The more far-flung the communities and families are, the more significant the ability to engage in CMC becomes.

◎ It's important to be politically sensitive when using labels like 'elderly', 'senior' and so on. The most acceptable label in one country is not necessarily the same for another country. Besides, what ages do they cover? How old do you have to be (or feel!) to be a senior?

THE DIGITAL AGE DIVIDE

Consider these facts:

- Two-thirds of children know more about computers and the internet than their parents (BBC, 2002).
- Only 15 percent of senior citizens in the United States have access to the internet (Lenhart, 2000).

www For weblinks and resources visit the CMC website at <www.sagepub.co.uk/resources/cmc>

- The majority of people over the age of fifty-five in the United Kingdom have never used the internet.
- Two-thirds of these people say they have no intention of ever doing so (Fielding, 2002).

Despite these rather dismal facts, the number of elderly people (or seniors) online has increased by 90 percent in just two years ('UK seniors take to the net', 2002). Going online has become a favorite hobby for retired persons in the United Kingdom. British senior citizens who have access say that being online has strengthened relationships with their family and friends, and provides opportunities to develop new relationships and communities. According to one study by the British organization Age Concern [**www** FA6:2], nearly 80 percent of men aged fifty-five or over who do go online, pursue hobbies or seek information online. By contrast, 86 percent of older women go online to connect with their family and friends (Fielding, 2002).

'BRINGING WISDOM TO THE INFORMATION AGE'

Whatever their level of interest in being online, often the first port of call is one of the growing number of dedicated websites for the elderly. A good example of these websites is SeniorNet, an international gathering place for people over fifty-five, whose slogan is 'Bringing wisdom to the Information Age'. Richard Adler (2002), writing about SeniorNet, argues that while being connected online is important to many segments of society, for seniors being connected is particularly important [**www** FA6:3]. He cites the benefits outlined in Box FA6:1 for seniors online.

BOX FA6:1 ONLINE BENEFITS FOR THE ELDERLY

Being online for senior citizens can:

- enhance communication with family and friends;
- expand opportunities for lifelong learning;
- improve the delivery of health care services;
- support independent living;
- create new options for entertainment.

BRIDGING THE GENERATION GAP ONLINE

Pioneering programs are currently in place to connect so-called 'silver surfers' to their own, and other, communities. For example, two schools in New England have developed a program to introduce older adults to the internet. Computer-literate seniors and students aged ten to twelve teach other elderly people how to use email and useful internet services. The goals of the program are to keep seniors connected with their worlds, and to bring them closer to their tech-involved grandchildren and the young teachers in the program.

Internet expert Sherry Turkle, a name you should recognize by now, sees numerous possibilities opening up through this program. She thinks that some of the best features of the program are its intergenerational aspect and that it's combined with FtF social interaction. As she says:

> There are a lot of fears that circulate about our being 'sucked into virtual reality' and taken away from our face-to-face relationships, but I think that these fears are not founded. These seniors are brought together to learn about using online resources. They should be encouraged to continue their own community both on and offline. I think that as a culture, we are just beginning to learn how to explore the opportunities on the boundary between the physical and virtual [and] how to integrate the two [**www** FA6:4].

PORTAL BOX

A Portal Box is a kind of lucky-dip or grab-bag selection of weblinks to lead you to more facts and issues about the topic area. Remember, this is just a starting point – the rest is up to you.

www FA6:5 Seniors Site
www FA6:6 Dignity Foundation (India)
www FA6:7 Helping Grandparents and Grandchildren Stay Connected
www FA6:8 iGrandparents.com, technology page
www FA6:9 Internet resources for older people (UK)
www FA6:10 Elderly Communities
www FA6:11 ElderCare Online
www FA6:12 Overseas Chinese Institute on Aging
www FA6:13 Web Wise Seniors
www FA6:14 Middle age and the elderly GLBT

While you explore the weblinks from the Portal Box, and in addition to the key questions from the strand introduction (see pp. 197–99), keep in mind the following additional questions. What range of views have you come across regarding older adults and CMC? Which views have you found most convincing and why? What did you find most interesting? What didn't you understand? What would you like to know more about?

BOX FA6:2 INFORMATION TARGETS

Think about targeting the following areas of information:

- facts and stats
- scholarly issues
- international perspectives
- popular treatments (such as newspapers, popular cultural forms)
- professional concerns

BOX FA6:3 EVALUATING THE SUCCESS OF YOUR RESEARCH

- *Research breadth.* Have you done a reasonable amount of researching?
- *Research quality.* Have you used academic and other appropriate sources?
- *Organization.* Have you clearly identified the main issues and concerns?
- *Good examples.* Have you found relevant case studies and examples?
- *Your own ideas.* Have you been original and critical in your thinking?

TOPICAL READINGS

Adler, R.P. (2002). The age wave meets the technology wave: broadband and older Americans. Available (04 April 2003) online: <http://www.seniornet.org/downloads/broadband.pdf >.

Bjørneby, S. (1999). The Seniornet Project, *ERCIM News* No. 37. Available (04 April 2003) online: <http://www.ercim.org/publication/Ercim_News/enw37/bjorneby.html>.

TOPIC 7
INSTRUCTIONAL COMMUNICATION IN CMC

EXPANDING THE CLASSROOM

Amina sits at her desk finishing her medical microbiology exam. An alarm sounds on her alert meter, reminding her that the public communication presentation begins in twenty minutes. She checks to be sure the webcam is correctly connected, so the communication class will be able to evaluate her effectively. Amina then finishes running a spellcheck on the microbiology exam, and sends her exam half-way round the world to the New England medical school she attends remotely. Her biggest challenge this semester is adjusting to real-time classes that are in a time zone eight hours behind. Amina quickly links to her home university in the UAE where her communication class is hosted, mentally going over her presentation notes.

While this example is obviously set in a hopeful future, evidenced by the student able to cross intercultural and international boundaries in a way that's economically improbable, the technology required for this type of classroom expansion already exists and is being used in many universities. You may be using similar technology if you're participating in a class using WebCT, Blackboard, or another Virtual Learning Environment (VLE).

A KEY TO LEARNING

To say the internet has had a huge impact on education is an understatement. Even studying CMC was unheard of not so long ago. Now studying CMC, and more especially using CMC, is an important way to understand how the whole process of learning is changing across many different disciplines. As stated at the start of this book, most people reading it probably won't remember the days when students handwrote their papers or used a typewriter. There was a time too when the only way to research was to walk into a library and take books off shelves. Before widespread access to the web, it took a lot more time to acquire and consume a lot less information. Technology has unquestionably

WWW For weblinks and resources visit the CMC website at <www.sagepub.co.uk/resources/cmc>

revolutionized the way students learn and the way teachers teach. In Box FA7:1 we highlight what we see as the main educational functions of CMC.

BOX FA7:1 WAYS WE ENGAGE IN CMC FOR EDUCATION

- *Communicate:* conversing with co-learners, co-researchers, instructors and experts.
- *Collaborate:* Engaging in team-learning projects, co-authoring and designing texts together.
- *Create:* using new learning tools, and finding new ways to preserve history and culture.
- *Collect:* researching data, resources, and reading materials.
- *Critique:* assessing the value of what we discover and its relevance to our purpose.

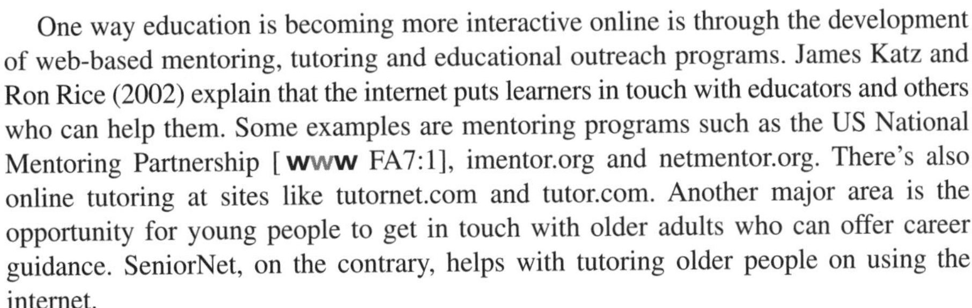

One way education is becoming more interactive online is through the development of web-based mentoring, tutoring and educational outreach programs. James Katz and Ron Rice (2002) explain that the internet puts learners in touch with educators and others who can help them. Some examples are mentoring programs such as the US National Mentoring Partnership [**www** FA7:1], imentor.org and netmentor.org. There's also online tutoring at sites like tutornet.com and tutor.com. Another major area is the opportunity for young people to get in touch with older adults who can offer career guidance. SeniorNet, on the contrary, helps with tutoring older people on using the internet.

VIRTUAL LEARNING ENVIRONMENTS

Most of the internet's early technical developments such as the first freenet were born on university campuses. Usenet, a decentralized news group network created at the University of North Carolina, is the largest collection of newsgroups in the world, with more than 30,000 topics. One of the earliest education-focused mailing/discussion lists was KIDSPHERE, created in 1989 to encourage the development of international computer networks for the use of students and teachers.

Technical developments at organizations like CERN and the National Research and Education Network [**www** FA7:2] have enhanced opportunities learning communities around the world. Additionally, virtual classrooms allow what's come to be called distance education. Critics fear this may lead to less satisfying engagement with other faculty and students and to a sense of dissociation from learning. Others who have benefited from such opportunities describe them as democratizing and part of a larger educational revolution brought about through CMC.

Virtual learning environments are another way CMC has impacted education. These systems, as mentioned at the beginning of this topic, are designed to create classroom-like environments in virtual settings, so it can be shared between a variety of different locations and in a variety of languages. VLEs thus cross national and cultural borders, as well as provide more opportunities for people who need to be able to work or learn from home. The flexibility of systems like WebCT and Blackboard encourages more non-traditional students to enter the academic world.

CULTURALLY SENSITIVE LEARNING MATERIALS

Along with the collaborative opportunities afforded through CMC, many learning initiatives encourage students' creativity. Once students create projects and learning programs, they are then encouraged to share them with other students around the world.

The Canadian SchoolNet GrassRoots Program, for example, encourages teachers to promote and facilitate effective integration of communication technology in the classroom. Canadian primary and secondary school students increase their technical communication skills by creating innovative online learning projects [**www** FA7:3]. Books Without Boundaries, a collaborative project developed by the SchoolWorld Internet Education Foundation, links Brazil, Costa Rica, Jordan, Morocco, Nigeria and Uganda, and encourages schools, businesses and organizations in the Global North to assist schools and facilities in the disadvantaged Global South. The project also encourages students to design their own books and share them with other students around the world.

PORTAL BOX

A Portal Box is a kind of lucky-dip or grab-bag selection of weblinks to lead you to more facts and issues about the topic area. Remember, this is just a starting point – the rest is up to you.

www FA7:4 European SchoolNet

www FA7:5 International Community on e-learning

www FA7:6 International Education and Resource Network

www FA7:7 epals

www FA7:8 eXplora

www FA7:9 ThinkQuest

www FA7:10 Kidlink

www FA7:11 Teachers.Net chat center

www FA7:12 Educational chat rooms

www FA7:13 Education Community: Chat Center

While you explore the weblinks from the Portal Box, and in addition to the key questions from the strand introduction (see pp. 197–99), keep in mind the following additional questions. What range of views have you come across regarding instructional communication in CMC? Which views have you found most convincing and why? What did you find most interesting? What didn't you understand? What would you like to know more about?

BOX FA7:2 INFORMATION TARGETS

Think about targeting the following areas of information:

- facts and stats
- scholarly issues
- international perspectives
- popular treatments (such as newspapers, popular cultural forms)
- professional concerns

BOX FA7:3 EVALUATING THE SUCCESS OF YOUR RESEARCH

- *Research breadth.* Have you done a reasonable amount of researching?
- *Research quality.* Have you used academic and other appropriate sources?
- *Organization.* Have you clearly identified the main issues and concerns?
- *Good examples.* Have you found relevant case studies and examples?
- *Your own ideas.* Have you been original and critical in your thinking?

TOPICAL READINGS

Dringus, L.P. (2000). Towards active online learning: a dramatic shift in perspective for learners, *The Internet and Higher Education*, 2 (4), 189–95.

Mumtaz, S. (2001). Children's enjoyment and perception of computer use in the home and the school, *Computers and Education*, 36 (4), 347–62.

TOPIC 8

VISUAL COMMUNICATION IN CMC

FROM VIRTUAL REALITY TO VISUAL REALITY

After telecommuting to work, Robert, who is visually impaired, wants to chat with friends online. He says, 'Wake up,' to launch instant messaging. With his audio screen reader he reads that Sandra's waiting for a Braille recognition program, with a scanner that reads the physical imprints of Braille. Fred talks about the new video-streaming program he is running, and Robert wonders when someone will create a technology to help the blind view films online. After all, only a few years ago Robert had no idea he'd soon be able to use a computer without the help of a sighted friend.

One of the biggest challenges for computer technology is the goal of making CMC 'user friendly'. This is often accomplished through advances in visual communication, which include improvements not only for the visually impaired but also for everyone's needs. As you know, multimodality is an increasingly important part of online communication and continues to be a major force in shaping the future of CMC. This includes visual and audio chat, webcams and virtual reality gaming. For many, it's exciting that FtF communication is being simulated online.

HUMAN-COMPUTER INTERACTION [HCI]

The connection between our sensory and cognitive capacities and technology is a central concern for the important area of scholarly activity known as Human-Computer Interaction. HCI deals with the study, planning and design of how people work and interact with computers. ◎ Researchers in HCI are concerned not only with issues of accessibility but also with usability and design. Computer display designers consider, for example, how tiny movements in our peripheral vision can distract users (Danino, 2001). HCI specialists are also aware that advances in CMC visualization make getting online more appealing and compelling for many users.

◎ For a distinction between HCI and CMC see the start of Basic Theory: Unit 3, p. 36.

www For weblinks and resources visit the CMC website at <www.sagepub.co.uk/resources/cmc>

An exciting application of this expertise is the development of virtual reality that creates visual spaces for human interaction. Webcams, voice-activated software and visual chat are synchronized with artwork to generate new 'real' space online.

NEW TECHNOLOGIES, NEW WAYS OF READING

Studies of how people read web-based material found they don't read the web as if it were a print media. This is because the web is intentionally visual, with more visible impact than in print-based text. Further, CMC allows non-print-based materials to be included, most notably, interactive materials. This means a lot is happening in a webspace, and people scan the text looking for highlighted keywords, subheadings, and short 'bytes' of information (Morkes and Nielsen, 1997).

The multimodal nature of graphical interface in CMC allows users to access more information than print media. You can look at a site, get bits of information and choose what you want to investigate. This type of reading requires a different type of attention. It requires new reading and comprehension skills, such as a new type of visual perception, the capacity to read within the visual forms available online, and the ability to negotiate the barrage of information juxtaposed with sounds and images.

Graphical User Interface (GUI) development has not only made CMC more user friendly, it's changed how we communicate on the web. GUIs are program interfaces that use the visual capabilities of computers to make programs easier to use. This helps users avoid having to learn complex command languages. Images, photos and emoticons are common enhancements, as are such basic visual characteristics as pointers and the familiar desktop. ◎

◎ Check out the first GUI, designed at Xerox PARC in the 1970s, and how Apple Macintosh popularized GUIs. The GUI Gallery chronicles the history of GUIs [**www** FA8:1].

USABILITY, VISIBILITY, ACCESSIBILITY

Designers concentrate on trying to accommodate what users are looking for in GUI usability. Researchers look at the effects of color, sound, images, and the positioning of information on webpages. Usability researchers Rakhi Rajani and Duska Rosenberg (1999) found users often fail to recognize investigative aids built into GUIs, especially regarding navigational tools. This 'banner blindness' is encountered when users searching for in-depth information fail to find the tools intended to help them access the information.

Companies have attempted to address these issues by standardizing and simplifying programs and interfaces for both web designers and web users. 'Usability guru' Jakob Nielsen, both scholar and web developer, teamed with Macromedia to create the webpage program Flash as an attempt to make business websites easier to use. Flash is one of the front runners in web development and even includes built-in support (screen readers) for accessibility for blind and visually impaired users.

Communication technologies need to address issues of accessibility for disabled persons, particularly visually impaired users. The World Wide Web Consortium (2001) estimates that more than 90 percent of all websites are inaccessible to persons with physical disabilities. Things are improving, however. For example, the European Space Agency has developed a handheld device to help blind and partially sighted people negotiate European city streets. The wearable device uses satellite technology to guide pedestrians in real time over a wireless internet connection. Another project, by the British Royal National Institute of the Blind [**www** FA8:2], attempts to highlight synthesized speech and Braille screen technologies so that the visually impaired can use computers through sound and touch.

Explore the range of visual communication in CMC and develop successful visual criteria for yourself. Choose a website that appeals to you and figure out why that is. You might want to work with a partner and share views; do you agree or disagree?

PORTAL BOX

A Portal Box is a kind of lucky-dip or grab-bag selection of weblinks to lead you to more facts and issues about the topic area. Remember, this is just a starting point – the rest is up to you.

www FA8:3 rhizome.org – new media art resource
www FA8:4 Live webcam video chat
www FA8:5 Ergoworld
www FA8:6 Everquest homepage (Korea)
www FA8:7 Accessible chat
www FA8:8 Usable Web.com
www FA8:9 Access Technology Institute
www FA8:10 Center for HCI Design, RNIB project
www FA8:11 WebWord Usability Weblog
www FA8:12 Chat rooms for disabled users

While you explore the weblinks from the Portal Box and the key questions from the strand introduction (see pp. 197–99), keep in mind the following additional questions. What range of views have you come across regarding visual communication in CMC? Which views have you found most convincing and why? What did you find most interesting? What didn't you understand? What else would you like to know?

BOX FA8:1 INFORMATION TARGETS

Think about targeting the following areas of information:

- facts and stats
- scholarly issues
- international perspectives
- popular treatments (such as newspapers, popular cultural forms)
- professional concerns

BOX FA8:2 EVALUATING THE SUCCESS OF YOUR RESEARCH

- *Research breadth.* Have you done a reasonable amount of researching?
- *Research quality.* Have you used academic and other appropriate sources?
- *Organization.* Have you clearly identified the main issues and concerns?
- *Good examples.* Have you found relevant case studies and examples?
- *Your own ideas.* Have you been original and critical in your thinking?

TOPICAL READINGS

Mazur, J.M. (2000). Applying insights from film theory and cinematic technique to create a sense of community and participation in a distributed video environment. *Journal of Computer-Mediated Communication*, 5 (4). Available (27 April 2003) online: <http://www.ascusc.org/jcmc/vol5/issue4/mazur.htm>.

Mitchell, D.P. and Scigliano, J.A. (2000). Moving beyond the white cane: building an online learning environment for the visually impaired professional. *The Internet and Higher Education*, 3 (1–2), 117–24.

TOPIC 9

NEW MEDIA DEVELOPMENTS IN CMC

MOVING THE GOALPOSTS . . .

Picture a typical day at the office. Your office is at home, but you're working with colleagues from around the world every minute of the day. You stop at McDonald's for lunch so you can have an hour of free wireless time to chat with an old friend while eating your extra-value meals. There's no need to take your laptop to the meeting downtown because you're actually wearing your computer in your eyeglasses. Sounds like the latest sci-fi adventure film? It's becoming a reality even now. While so-called 'new media' are no longer necessarily new, technological developments in CMC are happening all the time. With increasing broadband (i.e. speed of internet access), even 'newer' media such as internet radio, visual chat, webcams, voice-chat, mobile telephony and text-messaging are becoming standard for many people.

Of course, what's new media in some regions of the world may already be widely adopted in others. Text messaging (or SMS, Short Messaging Service) is one good case in point. Text messaging caught on in Western Europe and East Asia far more quickly than in the otherwise wired United States. And it's not always the countries of Western Europe, East Asia and North America that are leading the way. Interestingly, sometimes supposedly less developed countries are also quicker to adopt new technology than their more developed counterparts. This can be due to different local demands such as the need for more flexible mobile telephony. It's sometimes called 'leapfrogging' [**www** FA9:1]. Leapfrogging is frequently seen in digital technologies, particularly in the way newly industrializing nations use and develop technology. For example, adoption rates of mobile telephones and other forms of what are called 'wearable computers' or 'wearable technologies', from the time they were introduced in newly industrializing nations, have surpassed those in industrialized nations where such technologies have existed for some time.

www For weblinks and resources visit the CMC website at <www.sagepub.co.uk/resources/cmc>

BLOGS AND WIKI'S

A recent trend in CMC is the widespread adoption of 'blogging', or writing of web logs. Blogs are usually comprised of short, frequently updated postings arranged chronologically, like an online diary. While blogging isn't totally new, it's only recently become widely known. ◎ One of the key players in blogging is David Winer, who created the long-running blog called *Scripting News*. Some blogs like *Scripting News* have a serious political or social purpose. Some are public, others are private. Group blogs, used for small group communication, for families and work units, promote community and group cohesion. For example, one female blogger writes:

> I have learned that people can feel very personally connected to others throughout the world despite physical constraints. [**www** FA9:3]

◎ Some commentators suggest that Tim Berners-Lee, the 'father of the web', wrote the first weblog [**www** FA9:2].

Another trend that promotes a sense of community is what's known as a 'wiki'. Running on collaborative software, wikis allow a virtual team to build a project. Like weblogs, they can be either public or private spaces for collaborative project development. One of the best examples of wikis is the *Wikipedia* open-content encyclopedia [**www** FA9:4] where thousands of volunteers have contributed more than 100,000 articles. What's unique about a project like *Wikipedia* is that any information on it can be changed or deleted by any visitor to the site.

WIFI: THE WAY OF THE FUTURE?

Wearable computers, and what's known as 'ubiquitous computing' (or just UbiComp), are among the newest of the new in CMC. As computer hardware continues to increase in functionality and decrease in size, it becomes more and more feasible to be online all the time. Examples of 'wearables' include so-called 'smart clothing' which embeds computers into textiles. Then there are Wearable Personal Assistants – the next step after PDAs – as well as digital eyeglasses, and portable DVD players that project images and films right before the user's eyes.

One of the technological developments that will surely impact CMC is what's known as WiFi – or wireless internet connections [**www** FA9:5]. You may already be using WiFi technology if you are getting email messages on your mobile phone or handheld computer. You can download audio MP3s, making your wireless equipment more efficient than a portable and CD player, and enhancing your music collection more easily. The advent of digital XM radio and Sirius radio, now becoming standard in many automobiles, reflects how digital wireless communication is becoming everyday technology. Even McDonald's is promoting wireless internet, and began offering an hour of wireless internet with the purchase of two extra-value meals at select locations in the United States [**www** FA9:6]. In his book *Brave new unwired world* (2002) wireless technology expert Alex Lightman estimates that by 2005 there will be more than a billion wireless internet users. Mobility will be limitless. The future of CMC will rely on the wireless and stylish standards of UbiComp, allowing users to engage in CMC at any time, in any place.

PORTAL BOX

A Portal Box is a kind of lucky-dip or grab-bag selection of weblinks to lead you to more facts and issues about the topic area. Remember, this is just a starting point – the rest is up to you.

www FA9:7 Scripting News
www FA9:8 Blogger
www FA9:9 Been there . . . still there blogspot
www FA9:10 weblogg-ed collaboration central discussion group
www FA9:11 Weblog on Iran, technology and pop culture
www FA9:12 Chat about ultra-cool wireless wearables. Slashdot
www FA9:13 Wearable computing at the MIT media lab
www FA9:14 MIThril/Borglab wiki
www FA9:15 Techextreme
www FA9:16 WiFi technology

While you explore the weblinks from the Portal Box, and in addition to the key questions from the strand introduction (see pp. 197–99), keep in mind the following additional questions. What range of views have you come across regarding new media developments in CMC? Which views have you found most convincing and why? What did you find most interesting? What didn't you understand? What would you like to know more about?

BOX FA9:1 INFORMATION TARGETS

Think about targeting the following areas of information:

- Facts and stats
- scholarly issues
- international perspectives
- popular treatments (such as newspapers, popular cultural forms)
- professional concerns

BOX FA9:2 EVALUATING THE SUCCESS OF YOUR RESEARCH

- *Research breadth.* Have you done a reasonable amount of researching?
- *Research quality.* Have you used academic and other appropriate sources?
- *Organization.* Have you clearly identified the main issues and concerns?
- *Good examples.* Have you found relevant case studies and examples?
- *Your own ideas.* Have you been original and critical in your thinking?

TOPICAL READINGS

Lightman, A. (2002). *Brave new unwired world: The digital big bang and the infinite internet.* Hoboken, NJ: Wiley.

Mooney, C. (2003). How blogging changed journalism – almost [**WWW** FA9:16].

Schneider, J. *et al.* (2000). Disseminating trust information in wearable communities. *Personal Technologies*, 4 (4), 245–48.

LIST OF STIMULUS AND TASK READING

This reference list identifies all the readings recommended in the Basic Theory, Central Issues and Fieldwork strands.

AAUW (2000). *Tech-savvy: Educating girls in the new computer age.* Washington, DC: American Association of University Women.

Amichai-Hamburger, Y. and Ben-Artzi, E. (2003). Loneliness and internet use. *Computers in Human Behavior*, 19, 71–80.

Baker, A. (2000). Two by two in cyberspace: getting together and connecting online. *Cyberpsychology and Behavior*, 3 (2), 237–42.

Baker, P. (2001). Moral panic and alternative identity construction in usenet. *Journal of Computer-Mediated Communication*, 7 (1). Available (4 April 2003) online: <http://www.ascusc.org/jcmc/vol7/issue1/baker.html>.

Baron, N. (1998). Letters by phone or speech by other means: the linguistics of email. *Language and Communication*, 18, 133–70.

Baym, N.K. (2000). Chapter 4: 'I think of them as friends': Interpersonal relationships in the online community. In *Tune in, log on: Soaps, fandom, and online community* (pp. 119–42). Thousand Oaks, CA: Sage.

Baym, N. (2002). Interpersonal life online. In L. Lievrouw and S. Livingstone (eds), *The handbook of new media* (pp. 62–76). London: Sage.

Bell, D. (2001). Identities in cyberculture. In *An Introduction to cybercultures* (pp. 113–36). London: Routledge.

Berland, J. (2000). Cultural technologies and the 'evolution' of technological cultures. In A. Herman and T. Swiss (eds), *The world wide web and contemporary cultural theory* (pp. 235–58). New York: Routledge.

Berners-Lee, T. (2002). *The world wide web – past, present and future: Exploring universality.* The Commemorative Lecture 2002, Japan Prize. Available (02 November 2003) online at <http://www.w3.org/2002/04/Japan/Lecture.html>.

Brey, P. (2000). Disclosive computer ethics. *Computers and Society,* 30 (4), 10–16.

Bridges.org (2001). *Spanning the digital divide: Understanding and tackling the issues.* Available (28 March 2003) online: <http://www.bridges.org/spanning/summary.html/>.

Burnett, R. and Marshall, P.D. (2003a). Chapter 4: Webs of identity. In *Web theory: An introduction* (pp. 61–80). London: Routledge.

Burnett, R. and Marshall, P.D. (2003b). Chapter 3: The web as communication. In *Web theory: An introduction* (pp. 45–60). London: Routledge.

Burnett, R. and Marshall, P.D. (2003c). Chapter 1: Web of technology. In *Web theory: An introduction* (pp. 7–22). London: Routledge.

Castellá, V.O., Zornoza, A.M.Z., Alonso, F.P and Silla. J.M.P. (2000). The influence of familiarity among group members, group atmosphere and assertiveness on uninhibited behavior through three different communication media. *Computers in Human Behavior*, 16 (2), 141–59.

Chandler, D. (1995). *Technological or media determinism.* Available (11 April 2003) online: <http://www.aber.ac.uk/~dgc/tecdet.html>.

Chandler, D. (1998b). *Personal home pages and the construction of identities on the web.* Available (11 April 2003) online: <http://www.aber.ac.uk/media/Documents/short/webident.html>.

Chou, C. and Hsiao, M-C. (2000). Internet addiction, usage, gratification, and pleasure experience: the Taiwan college students' case. *Computers and Education*, 35, 65–80.

Cooper, A., Scherer, C. and Marcus, I.D. (2002). Harnessing the power of the internet to improve sexual relationships. In A. Cooper (ed.), *Sex and the internet: A guidebook for clinicians* (pp. 209–30). New York: Brunner-Routledge.

December, J. (1995). Transitions in studying computer-mediated communication. *CMC Magazine,* January. Available (11 April 2003) online: <http://www.december.com/cmc/mag/1995/jan/december.html>.

December, J. (1997). Notes on defining computer-mediated communication. *CMC Magazine,* January. Available (11 April 2003) online: <http://www.december.com/cmc/mag/1997/jan/december.html>.

Driskell, R.B. and Lyon, L. (2000). Are virtual communities true communities? Examining the environments and elements of community. City and Community, 1 (4): 373–90.

Escobar, A. (2000). Welcome to cyberia: notes on the anthropology of cyberculture. In D. Bell and B.M. Kennedy (eds), *The cybercultures reader* (pp. 56–76). London: Routledge.

Ferris, S.P. (1997). What is CMC? An overview of scholarly definitions. *CMC Magazine,* January. Available (11 April 2003) online: <http://www.december.com/cmc/mag/1997/jan/ferris.html>.

Guice, J. (1998). Looking backward and forward at the internet. *The Information Society*, 14 (3), 201–11.

Haythornthwaite, C. (2002). Strong, weak and latent ties and the impact of new media. *The Information Society*, 18 (5), 1–17.

Herring, S. (1999). Interactional coherence in CMC. *Journal of Computer-Mediated Communication*, 4 (4). Available (15 April 2003) online: <http://www.ascusc.org/jcmc/vol4/issue4/herring.html>.

Herring, S. (2001). Computer-mediated discourse. In D. Schiffrin, D. Tannen and H.E. Hamilton (eds), *The handbook of discourse analysis* (pp. 612–34). Oxford: Blackwell.

Herring, S. (2003). Gender and power in online communication. In J. Holmes and M. Meyerhoff (eds), *The Handbook of language and gender* (pp. 202–28). Oxford: Blackwell.

Holloway, S.L. and Valentine, G. (2003). Cyber-geographies: children's online worlds. In *Cyberkids: Children in the information age* (pp. 127–52). London: Routledge Falmer.

Howard, P.H. (2003). Embedded media: who we know, what we know, and society online. In P.H. Howard and S. Jones (eds), *Society online: The internet in context* (pp. 1–27). Thousand Oaks, CA: Sage.

Joinson, A.N. (2003a). Negative aspects of intra- and interpersonal internet behaviour. In *Understanding the psychology of internet behaviour* (pp. 53–84). Basingstoke: Palgrave Macmillan.

Joinson, A.N. (2003b). A framework for understanding internet behavior. In *Understanding the psychology of internet behavior* (pp. 163–84). Basingstoke: Palgrave Macmillan.

Jones, S. (1995). Understanding community in the information age. In S. Jones (ed.), *CyberSociety: Computer-mediated communication and community* (pp. 10–35). Thousand Oaks, CA: Sage.

Jones, S. (2002). *The internet goes to college: how students are living in the future with today's technology.* Pew Internet and American Life Project. Available (2 April 2003) online: <http://www.pewinternet.org/reports/pdfs/PIP_College_Report.pdf>.

Katz, J.E. and Rice, R.E. (2002). Involvement examples: evidence for an 'invisible mouse'? In *Social consequences of internet use: Access, involvement, and interaction* (pp. 161–200). Cambridge, MA: MIT Press.

Mehta, M. (2001). Pornography in Usenet: a study of 9800 randomly selected images. *Cyberpsychology and Behavior*, 4 (6), 695–704.

Murphie, A. and Potts, J. (2002). Theoretical frameworks. In *Culture and technology* (pp. 11–38). Basingstoke: Palgrave Macmillan.

Murphy, P. (2002). A twenty-first century challenge: preparing 'cut and paste' students to be 'information literate' citizens. *Teaching Learning and Technology Centre*. Available (15 April 2003) online: <http://www.uctltc.org/news/2002/04/feature.html>.

Murray, P.J. (1997). A rose by any other name. *CMC Magazine*, January. Available (11 April 2003) online: <http://www.december.com/cmc/mag/1997/jan/murray.html>.

Noonan, R. (1999). The psychology of sex: a mirror from the internet. In J. Gackenbach (ed.), *Psychology and the Internet: Intrapersonal, interpersonal and transpersonal implications* (pp. 143–68). San Diego, CA: Academic Press.

O'Sullivan, P.B., and Flanagin, A. (2003). An interactional reconceptualizing 'flaming' and other problematic communication. *New Media and Society*, 5 (1), 67–93. Draft version also available (11 April 2003) online: <http://www.ilstu.edu/~posull/flaming.htm.>.

Plymire, D. and Forman, P. (2000). Breaking the silence: lesbian fans, the internet, and the sexual politics of women's sport. *International Journal of Sexuality and Gender Studies* 5 (2), 141–53.

Rossney, R. (1996). Metaworld: avatars could be the next interactive revolution. Just don't let them steal your head. *Wired Magazine*, issue 4.06. Available (15 April 2003) online: <http://www.wired.com/wired/archive/4.06/avatar.html>.

Schumacher, P. and Morahan-Martin, P. (2001). Gender, internet and computer attitudes and experiences. *Computers in Human Behavior,* 17 (1), 95–110.

Spears, R., Lea, M. and Postmes, T. (2001). Social psychological theories of computer-mediated communication: Social pain or social gain? In W.P. Robinson and H. Giles (eds), *The handbook of language and social psychology* (pp. 601–23). Chichester: Wiley.

Spears, R., Postmes, T., Lea, M. and Wolbert, A. (2002). When are net effects gross products? The power of influence and the influence of power in computer-mediated communication. *Journal of Social Issues*, 58 (1), 91–107.

Sterne, J. (1999). Thinking the internet: cultural studies and the millennium. In S. Jones (ed.), *Doing Internet research: Critical issues and methods for examining the net* (pp. 257–88). London: Sage.

Taylor, T.L. (2002). Living digitally: embodiment in virtual worlds. In R. Schroeder (ed.), *The social life of avatars: Presence and interaction in shared virtual environments* (pp. 40–62). Berlin: Springer.

Thurlow, C. and Brown, A. (2003). Generation Txt? The discourses of young people's text-messaging. *Discourse Analysis Online*. Available (15 April 2003) online: <http://www.shu.ac.uk/daol/articles/open/2002/003/thurlow2002003-t.html>.

Tyler, T. (2002). Is the internet changing social life? It seems the more things change, the more they stay the same. *Journal of Social Issues*, 58 (1), 195–205.

Wakeford, N. (2000). New media, new methodologies: studying the web. In D. Gauntlett (ed.), *Web.studies: Rewiring media studies for the digital age* (pp. 31–41). London: Arnold.

Walther, J.B. (2002). Research ethics in internet-enabled research: human subjects, issues and methodological myopia. *Ethics and Information Technology*, 4, 205–16.

Walther, J.B., and Parks, M.R. (2002). Cues filtered out, cues filtered in: computer-mediated communication and relationships. In M.L. Knapp and J.A. Daly (eds), *Handbook of interpersonal communication* (pp. 529–63). Thousand Oaks, CA: Sage.

Walther, J.B. and Reid, L.D. (2000). Understanding the allure of the internet. *Chronicle of Higher Education*, 4 February, pp. 114–15.

Warschauer, M. (2003). Dissecting the "Digital Divide": A case study in Eygpt. *The Information Society*, 19 (4): 297–304.

Warschauer, M., El Said, G. and Zohry, A. (2002). Language choice online: globalization and identity in Egypt. *Journal of Computer-Mediated Communication*, 7 (4). Available (11 April 2003) online: <http://www.ascusc.org/jcmc/vol7/issue4/warschauer.html>.

Werry, C.C. (1996). Linguistic and interactional features of internet relay chat. In S. Herring (ed.), *Computer-mediated communication: Linguistic, social and cross-cultural perspectives* (pp. 47–64). Amsterdam: Benjamins.

Wynn, E. and Katz, J. (1997). Hyperbole over cyberspace: self-presentation and social boundaries in internet home pages and discourse. *The Information Society*, 13 (4), 297–328. Also available (15 April 2003) online: <http://www.slis.indiana.edu/TIS/articles/hyperbole.html>.

ALL OTHER REFERENCES

Anderson, B. (1983). *Imagined societies: Reflections on the origin and spread of nationalism*. London: Verso.

Anderson, R. and Ross, V. (2002). *Questions of communication: A practical introduction to theory*. New York: St Martin's Press.

Anthony, L.M., Clarke, M.C. and Anderson, S.J. (2000). Technophobia and personality subtypes in a sample of South African university students. *Computers in Human Behavior*, 16, 1, 31–44.

Askt, D. and Jensen, M. (2001). 'Africa Goes Online'. Available (20 October 2003) online: <http://www.digitaldividenetwork.org/content/stories/index.cfm?key=158>.

Australian National Radio (1995). *The Republic of Cyberspace*. Available (25 February 2003) online: <http://www.abc.net.au/rn/talks/bbing/stories/s10794.htm/>.

Baym, N.K. (1998). The emergence of online community. In S. G. Jones (ed.), *Cybersociety 2.0: Revisiting computer-mediated communication and community* (pp. 35–68). Thousand Oaks, CA: Sage.

BBC (2002). Parents alerted to safe surfing benefits. Available (28 April 2003) online: < http://news.bbc.co.uk/2/hi/technology/2446785.stm>.

Beckerman, L. and Nocero, J. (2003). High-tech student hate mail. *Educational Digest.* 68 (6), 37–40.

Bell, C. and Newby, H. (1971). *Community studies: An introduction to the sociology of the local community*. London: Allen and Unwin.

Bellis, M. (2002). *The history of the telephone: Alexander Graham Bell, Elisha Gray*. Available (3 June 2002) online: <http://inventors.about.com/library/inventors/bltelephone.htm>.

Biber, J.K. *et al.* (2002). Sexual harassment in online communications: effects of gender and discourse medium. *CyberPsychology and Behavior*, 5 (1), 33–42.

Blankenship, L. (1986). The Hacker manifesto. *Phrack*, 1 (7). Available (29 March 2003) online: <http://www.phrack-dont-give-a-shit-about-dmca.org/phrack/7/P07–03>.

Bodmer, C. (2001). Women are majority of online gamers. *Marketing to Women*, 14 (1), 12.

Bourdieu, P. (1998). *Acts of resistance: Against the new myths of our time*. Cambridge: Polity Press.

Brail, S. (1996). The price of admission: harassment and free speech in the wild, wild west. In L. Cherny and E.R. Weise (eds), *Wired women: Gender and New Realities in Cyberspace* (pp. 141–57). Seattle, WA: Seal Press.

Brisco, R. (2001). *Turning analog women into a digital workforce*. Available (4 April 2003) online: <http://www.totheweb.com/digitaldivide.html>.

Brown, J. (1996). BS detector: 'internet addiction' meme gets media high. *Wired News*. Available (29 March 2003) online: <http://www.wired.com/news/culture/0,1284,844,00.html>.

Burgoon, J. (1994). Nonverbal communication. In M. Burgoon, F.G. Hunsaker and E.J. Dawson (eds), *Human communication* (pp. 122–71). Thousand Oaks, CA: Sage.

Bynum, T.W. (2000). A very short history of computer ethics. Available (29 April 2003) online: < http://www.southernct.edu/organizations/rccs/resources/research/introduction/bynum_shrt_hist.html >.

Canary, D.J., Cody, M.J. and Manusov, V.L. (2003). *Interpersonal communication: A goals-based approach.* Boston, MA: Bedford/St Martin's Press.

Caplan, S.E. (2001). Challenging the mass-interpersonal communication dichotomy: are we witnessing the emergence of an entirely new communication system? *Electronic Journal of Communication*, 11 (1). Available (10 March 2002) online: <http://www.cios.org/www/ejcrec2.htm>.

Castells, M. (2000). *The rise of the network society*. New York: Blackwell.

Chandler, D. (1996). Shaping and being shaped: engaging with media. *CMC Magazine*. Available (8 April 2003) online: <http://www.december.com/cmc/mag/1996/feb/chandler.html>.

Chandler, D. (1998a). *Imagining futures, dramatizing*

fears: The portrayal of technology in literature and film. Available (15 April 2003) online: <http://www.aber.ac.uk/media/Documents/SF/sf.html>.

Chang, H-C. (2000). Reconfiguring the global society: 'Greater China' as emerging community. In G.M. Chen and W.J. Starosta (eds). *Communication and Global Society* (pp. 49–72). New York, NY: Peter Lang.

Cheung, C. (2000). A home on the web: presentations of self on personal homepages. In D. Gauntlett (ed.), *Webstudies: re-wiring media studies for the digital age* (pp. 43–51). London: Arnold.

Clark, L.S. (1998). Dating on the net: teens and the rise of 'pure' relationships. In S. Jones (ed.), *Cybersociety 2.0: Revisiting computer-mediated communication and community* (159–83). Thousand Oaks, CA: Sage.

Cooper, A., Scherer, C., Boies, S.C. and Gordon, B. (1999). Sexuality on the internet: From sexual exploration to pathological expression. *Professional Psychology: Research and Practice*, 30 (2), 154–64.

Cooper, A., Scherer, C. and Mathy, R.M. (2001). Overcoming methodological concerns in the investigation of online sexual activities. *CyberPsychology and Behavior*, 4 (4), 437–47.

Coupland, N., Wiemann, J.M. and Giles, H. (1991). Talk as 'problem' and communication as 'miscommunication': an intergrative analysis. In N. Coupland, H. Giles and J.M. Wiemann (eds), *'Miscommunication' and problematic talk* (pp. 1–17). Newbury Park, CA: Sage.

Crook, C. (1999). Computers in the community of classrooms. In K. Littleton and P. Light (eds), *Learning with computers: Analyzing productive interaction* (pp. 102–117). London: Routledge.

Crystal, D. (2001). *Language and the internet*. Cambridge: Cambridge University Press.

Cuban, L. (2001). *Oversold and underused: computers in the classroom*. Cambridge MA: Harvard University Press. Routledge.

Cyberslackers at work (2000). *Straits Times*, 28 April, p. 4.

Daft, R.L. and Lengel, R.H. (1984). Information richness: a new approach to managerial behavior and organization design. *Research in Organizational Behavior*, 6, 191–233.

Dahlberg, L. (2001). Computer-mediated communication and the public sphere: a critical analysis. *Journal of Computer-Mediated Communication,* 7 (1). Available (14 April 2003) online: < http://www.ascusc.org/jcmc/vol7/issue1/dahlberg.html>.

Danet, B. (1996). Text as mask: gender and identity on the internet. Paper presented at the conference on 'Masquerade and Gendered Identity', Venice, 21–4 February. Available (27 April 2003) online: <http://atar.mscc.huji.ac.il/~msdanet/mask.html>http://atar.mscc.huji.ac.il/~msdanet/mask.html>.

Danino, N. (2001). 'Making the Internet more accessible for users of speech'. Doctoral Consortium for Human Computer Interaction Conference, Lille, France 2001.

Darlington, R. (2002). Overcoming the digital divide: internauts and internots. Presentation to the 'Unions and the Internet' conference, Trades Union Congress, London, 12 May 2001. Available (15 February 2003) online: <http://www.rogerdarlington.co.uk/digitaldivide.html/>.

Derakhshan, H. (2003). *Weblogs, an Iranian perspective. Weblog on Iran, technology and pop culture.* Available (30 March 2002) online: <http://hoder.com/weblog>.

Dery, M. (1995). *Flame wars: The discourse of cyberculture*. Durham, NC: Duke University Press.

Deuel, N.R. (1996). Our passionate response to virtual reality. In S.C. Herring (ed.), *Computer-mediated communication: Linguistic, social and cross-cultural perspectives* (pp.129–46). Amsterdam: Benjamins.

Dibble, J. (1994). A rape in cyberspace: or, How an evil clown, a Haitian trickster spirit, two wizards, and a cast of dozens turned a database into a society. In M. Dery (ed.) *Flame wars: The discourse of cyberculture* (pp. 237–62). Durham, NC: Duke University Press. Also available (11 April 2003) online: <http://www.mhhe.com/socscience/english/holeton/chap2/dibbell.mhtml>.

Direction de la Santé Publique (2002). Gambling addiction: treatment for this health problem. *Prévention en pratique médicale.* Supplement (pp. 1–4). February. Available (29 March 2003) online: <http://www.santepub-mtl.qc.ca/Publication/pdfppm/ppmmarch02–1.pdf.>.

Doane, M.A. (1992) Film and the masquerade: theorizing the female spectator. In *The Sexual Subject: A Screen Reader in Sexuality* (pp. 227–43). London: Routledge.

Drew, S. (2001). Student perceptions of what helps them learn and develop in higher education. *Teaching in Higher Education*, 6, 43–56.

Dringus, L. P. (2000). Towards active online learning: a dramatic shift in perspective for learners. *The Internet and Higher Education,* 2 (4), 189–95.

Dyer, R., Green, R., Pitts, M. and Millward, G. (1995). What's the flaming problem? or Computer mediated communication: deindividuating or disinhibiting? In M. Kirby, A. Dix and J. Finlay (eds), *Proceedings of the 1995 HCI Conference*, Huddersfield (pp. 289–302). Cambridge: Cambridge University Press.

Edley, P. (2001). Technology, working mothers, and corporate colonization of the lifeworld: a gendered paradox of work and family balance. *Women and Language*, 24, 28–35.

Fattah, H., Paul, P. and Gitteau, J. (2002). Gaming gets serious. *American Demographics*, 24 (5), 38–43.

Fielding, R. (2002). *Silver surfers in the minority*. Available (28 April 2003) online: < http://www.vnunet.com/News/1134440>.

Fletcher, A. (2001). *The art of looking sideways*. London: Phaidon Press.

Martin, L.H., Gutman, H. and Hutton, P. H. (eds) (1988). *Technologies of the self: A seminar with Michel Foucault*. Amherst, MA: University of Massachusetts Press.

Franklin, U. (1990). *Real world of technology*. New York: Vintage Books.

Gackenbach, J. and Ellerman, E. (1998). Introduction to psychological aspects of internet use. In J. Gackenbach (ed.), *Psychology and the internet: intrapersonal, interpersonal and transpersonal implications* (pp. 1–25). San Diego, CA: Academic Press.

Gauntlett, D. (ed.). (2000). *Web.studies: Rewiring media studies for the digital age*. London: Arnold.

Geyer, F. (1996). *Alienation, ethnicity, and post-modernism*. Westport, CT: Greenwood Press.

Giddens, A. (1991). *Modernity and self-identity: Self and society in the late modern age*. Cambridge: Polity Press.

Giddens, A. (1999). *Globalization: The Reith Lectures*. London: BBC News Online. Available (21 April 2003) online at <http:--news.bbc.co.uk/hi/english/static/events/reith_99/week1/week1.htm>.

Giroux, H. (1998). *Real race talk faces hard truths and embraces justice*. Available (29 April 2003) online: <http://www.psu.edu/ur/oped/giroux.html>.

Glassner, B. (1979). *Essential interactionism: On the intelligibilty of prejudice*. London: Routledge.

Glassman, E. (2000). Cyber hate: the discourse of intolerance in the New Europe. In L. Lengel (ed.), *Culture and technology in the New Europe: civic discourse transformation in post-communist nations 4*, (pp. 273–92). Westport, CT: Ablex.

Goffman, E. (1959). *The presentation of self in everyday life*. Harmondsworth: Penguin.

Goode, E. and Ben-Yehuda, N. (1994). *Moral panics: The social construction of deviance*. Cambridge: Blackwell.

Goodman, A. (2001). *Online communities endure as platforms come and go*. Available (29 March 2003) online: < http://www.traffick.com/story/2001–04/online_community.asp >.

Gorney, M. (2001). *E-medicine: The cyber-revolution hits medical practice*. Available (26 February 2003) online: <http://www.medem.com/corporate/corporate_Addendum_A_eRiskGuidelines.cfm#doctors_company/>.

Hacker, K.L. and Steiner, R. (2002). The digital divide for Hispanic Americans. *Howard Journal of Communications*, 13 (4), 267–84.

Hafkin, N. and Taggart, N. (2001). *Gender, information technology and developing countries: An analytical study*. Washington, DC: USAID.

Hale, C. (ed.). (1999). *Wired style: Principles of English usage in the digital age*, revised version. New York: Broadway Books.

Hall, S. (1990). Cultural identity and diaspora. In J. Rutherford (ed.), *Identity: community, culture, difference* (pp. 222–37). London: Lawrence and Wishart.

Hall, S. and du Gay, P. (1996). *Questions of cultural identity*. London: Sage.

Hamilton, D.P. (2000). Web's design hinders goals of user privacy. *Wall Street Journal*, April, pp. 131. Available (14 April 2003) online: <http://www.acm.org/technews/articles/2000–2/0403m.html#item1>.

Hamman, R. (1997). *Cybersex and cyber-romance*. Special issue of *Cybersociology Magazine*. Available (14 April 2003) online: http://www.socio.demon.co.uk/magazine/1/issue1.html.>.

Hancock, J.T. and Dunham, P.J. (2001). Impression formation in computer-mediated communication revised. *Communication Research*, 28, 325–47.

Harris Interactive (2003). *Americans up in arms about spam*. Available (18 February 2003) online: <http://www.nua.ie/surveys/index.cgi?f=VS&art_id=905358690&rel=true/>.

Herron, A. and Bachman, E. (2000). ZaMir Transnational Net: Computer Mediated Communication and Resistance Music in Bosnia-Herzegovina, Croatia and the Federal Republic of Yugoslavia. In L. Lengel (ed.),

Culture and Technology in the New Europe: Civic Discourse in Transformation in Post-Communist Nations (pp. 273–92). Westport, CT: Ablex.

Harrison, S. (2000). Maintaining the virtual community: use of politeness strategies in an email discussion group. In L. Pemberton and S. Shurville (eds), *Words on the web: Computer-mediated communication* (pp. 69–78). Exeter: Intellect.

Haythornthwaite, C., Wellman, B. and Garton, L. (1998). Work and community via computer-mediated communication. In J. Gackenbach (ed.), *Psychology and the internet: Intrapersonal, interpersonal and transpersonal implications* (pp. 199–226). San Diego, CA: Academic Press.

Heinz, B., Gu, L., Inuzuka, A. and Zender, R. (2002). Under the rainbow flag: Webbing global gay identities. *International Journal of Sexuality and Gender Studies*, 7 (2/3), 107–24.

Henrickson, L. (2000). Communications technology and personal identity formation. *Educational Technology and Society,* 3 (3), 27–38.

Herring, S. (ed.). (1996). *Computer-mediated communication: Linguistic, social and cross-cultural perspectives*. Amsterdam: Benjamins.

Herring, S. (2002). Cyber violence: recognizing and resisting abuse in online environments. *Asian Women*, 14, 187–212.

Hewson, C.M., Yule, P., Laurent, D. and Vogel, C.M. (2003). *Internet research methods: A practical guide for the social and behavioural sciences*. London: Sage.

Hillier, L., Kurdas, C. and Horsley, P. (2001). *'It's just easier': The internet as a safety-net for same-sex attracted young people*. Available (11 January 2002) online: <http:// www.latrobe.edu.au/ssay/2ndpages/internetreport.pdf>.

Hillman, J. and Ventura, M. (1992). *We've had one hundred years of psychotherapy and the world's getting worse*. New York: Harper Collins.

Hine, C. (2000). *Virtual ethnography*. London: Sage.

Hoffman, E. (1998). *Lost in translation.* London: Random House.

Holmes, D. (1997). Virtual identity: communities of broadcast, communities of interactivity. In D. Holmes (ed.), *Virtual politics: Identity and community in cyberspace* (pp. 26–45). Newbury Park, CA: Sage.

Hooghe, M. (2002). Watching television and civic engagement: disentangling the effects of time, programs, and stations. *Harvard International Journal of Press and Politics*, 7 (2), 84–104.

Huff, C. (1997). The internet is a fine place for women. *Computers and Society*, 27 (4), 27.

Hughes, T.P. (1994). Technological momentum. In M.R. Smith and L. Marx (eds), *Does technology drive history?* (pp. 101–14). Cambridge, MA: MIT Press.

Hutchby, I. (2001). The communicative affordances of technological artefacts. In *Conversation and Technology* (pp. 13–33). London: Polity Press.

Huyer, S. (2001). Cited in NetCulture, World Voices on the Web: Women of the Global Village. Available (13 April 2003) online: <http://netculture.about.com/library/weekly/aa071000a.htm>.

Irigaray, L. (1993). *An ethics of sexual difference.* Ithaca, NY: Cornell University Press.

ITEA (2000). *Standards for technological literacy.* Available (5 June 2002) online: <http://www.iteawww.org/TAA/PDF/xstnd.pdf>.

Ivanic, R. (1997). *Writing and identity.* Amsterdam: Benjamins.

Jacobson, D. (1999). Impression formation in cyberspace: online expectations and offline experiences in text-based virtual communities. *Journal of Computer-Mediated Communication*, 5 (1). Available (11 April 2003) online: <http://www.ascusc.org/jcmc/vol5/issue1/jacobson.html>.

Joinson, A. (1998). Causes and implications of disinhibited behavior on the internet. In J. Gackenbach (ed.), *Psychology and the internet: Intrapersonal, interpersonal and transpersonal implications* (pp. 43–58). San Diego, CA: Academic Press.

Joinson, A.N. (2001). Self-disclosure in computer-mediated communication: the role of self-awareness and visual anonymity. *European Journal of Social Psychology*, 31 (2), 177–92. Also available (11 April 2003) online: <http://iet.open.ac.uk/pp/a.n.joinson/papers/self-disclosure.PDF>.

Jones, S. (1996). I'm online, you're online. *CMC Magazine*, February. Available (12 October 2002) online: <http://www.december.com/cmc/mag/1996/feb/last.html>.

Jones, S. (ed.). (1999). *Doing internet research: Critical issues and methods for examining the net*. London: Sage.

Kalathil, S. and Boas, T.C. (2003). *Open networks, closed regimes: The impact of the internet on authoritarian rule*. New York: Carnegie Endowment for International Peace.

Katwala, S. (2001). The truth of multicultural Britain. *Observer*. Available (16 February 2003) online:

<http://www.observer.co.uk/Print/0,3858,4306676,00.html/>.

Kiesler, S. and Sproull, L. (1992). Group decision-making and communication technology. *Organization Behavior and Human Decision Processes*, 52, 96–123.

King, S.A. (1999). Internet gambling and pornography: illustrative examples of the psychological consequences of communication anarchy. *CyberPsychology and Behavior*, Vol 2, 3. 175–84.

Kling, R. (1996). Hopes and horrors: technological utopianism and anti-utopianism in narratives of computerization. *CMC Magazine,* February. Available (11 April 2003) online: <http://www.december.com/cmc/mag/1996/feb/kling.html>.

Korenman, J. and Wyatt, N. (1996). Group dynamics in an e-mail forum. In S. Herring (ed.), *Computer-mediated communication: Linguistic, social and cross-cultural perspectives* (pp. 225–42). Amsterdam and Philadelphia: Benjamins.

Kraut, R., Kiesler, S., Boneva, B., Cummings, J., Helgeson, V. and Crawford, A. (2002). Internet paradox revisited. *Journal of Social Issues*, 58 (1), 49–74. Available (14 April 2003) online: < http://homenet.hcii.cs.cmu.edu/progress/jsiparadox-revisited.pdf>.

Kraut, R., Lundmark, V., Patterson, M., Kiesler, S., Mukopadhyay, T. and Scherlis, W. (1998). Internet paradox: a social technology that reduces social involvement and psychological well-being. *American Psychologist*, 53 (9), 1017–31. Available (11 April 2003) online: <http://www.apa.org/journals/amp/amp5391017.html>.

Kress, G. (2003). *Literacy in the new media age*. London: Routledge.

Kubey, R.W., Lavin, M. and Barrows, J.R. (2001). Internet use and collegiate academic performance decrements: early findings. *Journal of Communication*, 51, 366–82.

Lambden, P. (2000). Cited in *Internet health advice shunned*. Available (26 February 2003) online: <http://news.bbc.co.uk/2/hi/health/1069042.stm/ >.

Lauwerier, H. (1991). *Fractals: Endlessly repeated geometrical figures*. Princeton, NJ: Princeton University Press.

Lea, M., Spears, R. and de Groot, D. (2001). Knowing me, knowing you: anonymity effects on social identity processes within groups. *Personality and Social Psychology Bulletin*, 27, 526–37.

Lea, M., O'Shea, T., Fung, P. and Spears, R. (1992). 'Flaming' in computer-mediated communication: observations, explanations, implications. In M. Lea (ed.). *Contexts of Computer Mediated Communication* (pp. 89–112). New York: Harvester Wheatsheaf.

Lengel, L. (2000). Culture and technology in the New Europe. In L. Lengel (ed.), *Culture and Technology in the New Europe* (pp. 1–20). Stamford, CT: Ablex.

Lengel, L. and Fedak, D. (2004). The politicization of the internet in North Africa. In M. Prosser (ed.), *Discourse and discourse conflict in Africa*. Stamford, CT: Ablex.

Lenhart, A. (2000). *Who's not online*. Washington, DC: Pew internet and American life project. Available (28 April 2003) online: <http://www.pewinternet.org/reports/pdfs/Pew_Those_Not_Online_Report.pdf>.

Lenhart, A. (2002). *The digital disconnect*. Washington, DC: Pew internet and American life project. Available (11 April 2003) online: <http://www.pewinternet.org/reports/pdfs/PIP_Schools_Internet_Report.pdf>.

Leu, D.J. (2002). The new literacies: research on reading instruction with the internet and other digital technologies. In S.J. Samuels and A.E. Farstrup (eds), *What research has to say about reading instruction* (pp. 310–36). Newark, DE: International Reading Association.

Levin, D. and Arafeh, S. (2002). *The Digital Disconnect. The Widening Gap Between Internet-savvy Students and their Schools*. Washington, DC: Pew Internet and American Life Project.

Lightman, A. (2002). *Brave new unwired world: The digital big bang and the infinite internet.* Hoboken, NJ: Wiley.

Lockard, J. (1997). Progressive politics, electronic individualism and the myth of virtual community. In D. Porter (ed.), *Internet culture* (pp. 219–32). New York: Routledge.

Luft, J. (1970). *Group Processes:An Introduction to Group Dynamics*. Palo Alto, CA: National.

Luft, J. and Ingham, H. (1955). *The Johari Window: a graphic model for interpersonal relations*. University of California, Western Training Lab.

Mackenzie, D. and Wajcman, J. (1999). *The social shaping of technology*. Buckingham: Open University Press.

MacKinnon, R. (1997). Virtual rape. *Journal of Computer-Mediated Communication,* 2 (4). Available (11 April 2003) online: <http://www.ascusc.org/jcmc/vol2/issue4/mackinnon.html>.

Mann, S. (2001). Alternative perspectives on the student experience: alienation and engagement. *Studies in Higher Education,* 26, 7–19.

Mann, C. and Stewart, F. (2000). *Internet communication and qualitative research: A handbook for researching online*. London: Sage.

McKenna, K. (2003). Social identity and the self on the internet. Paper presented at the 'Computer-supported Social Interaction' Conference, Miami University, April.

McLaughlin, M.L., Osborne, K.K., and Smith, C.B. (1995). Standards of conduct on usenet. In S. Jones (ed.), *Cybersociety: Computer-mediated communication and community* (pp. 90–111). Thousand Oaks, CA: Sage.

Mehta, M.D. (1998). Sex on the net: regulation and control of pornography in the new wired world. In L. Pal and C. Alexander (eds), *Digital democracy: Politics and policy in the wired world* (pp. 164–79). Toronto: Oxford University Press. Also available (15 October 2002) online: <http://www/arts.usask.ca/policynut/pornnet.htm>.

Mided, J. (2000). The internet and the public sphere: what kind of space is cyberspace? In L. Lengel (ed.), *Culture and Technology in the New Europe* (pp. 63–75). Stamford, CT: Ablex.

Miller, S. and Weckert, J. (2000). Privacy, the workplace and the internet. *Journal of Business Ethics*, 28, 255–65.

Miller, V. (2000). Search engines, portals and global capitalism. In D. Gauntlett (ed.), *Web.studies: Re-wiring media studies for the digital age* (pp. 113–21). London: Arnold.

Millward, S. (2000). The relationship among internet exposure, communicator context and rurality. *American Communication Journal*, 3 (3). Available (27 August 2002) online: <http://acjournal.org/holdings/vol3/Iss3/rogue4/millward.html >.

Mooney, C. (2003). Forum: how blogging changed journalism – almost. *Post-gazette.com*. Available (29 March 2003) online: < http://www.post-gazette.com/forum/comm/20030202edmoon02p1.asp>.

Moore, W. J. (1992). Taming cyberspace. *National Journal*, 24, 745–9.

Morahan-Martin, J. (2001). Women and the internet: promise and perils. *CyberPsychology and Behavior*, 3 (5), 683–92.

Morahan-Martin, J. and Schumacher, P. (2000). Indicidence and correlates of pathological internet use among college students. *Computers in Human Behavior*, 16, 13–29.

Morkes, J. and Nielsen, J. (1997). Concise, SCANNABLE, and Objective: How to Write for the Web. Available (23 October 2003) online: <http://www.useit.com/papers/webwriting/writing.html>.

Morrison, J.L. and Oblinger, D.G. (2002). Information technology and the future of education: an interview with Diana Oblinger. *Vision*. Available (11 April 2003) online: <http://www.westminstercollege.edu/strategic_planning/infotechandfuture.pdf>.

Mulcahy, J.K. (1997). *Role playing characters and the self*. Available (26 April 2003) online: <http://beyond3sigma.loki.ws/anthro.html>.

Mutz, D.C., Roberts, D.F. and van Vuuren, D.P. (1993). Reconsidering the displacement hypothesis: television's influence on children's time use. *Communication Research*, 20, 51–75.

Natale, M. (2002). The effect of a male-oriented computer gaming culture on careers in the computer industry. *Computers and Society*, 32 (2), 24–31.

Newsom, V. (2003). Contained empowerment: a study of online feminism. Paper presented at the 'Computer-supported Social Interaction' conference, Miami University, April.

Newsom, V. and Baker-Webster, L. (2002). Cited in websites for women in technology miss something. *Women in Higher Education*, 11 (2), 7–10.

Newton, F. (2000). The new student. *About Campus*, November–December, pp. 8–15.

North, A. and Noyes, J. (2002). Gender influences on children's computer attitudes and cognitions. *Computers in Human Behavior,* 18 (2), 135–50.

NSPCC (2002). *Protecting children from sexual abuse*. Available (29 April 2003) online: <http://www.nspcc.org.uk/html/home/needadvice/protectingchildrenfromsexualabuse.htm>.

NTIA (2002). *A nation online: How Americans are expanding their use of the internet*. Washington, DC: NTIA and Economics and Statistics Administration.

Nua. (2002). African-Americans take to the net . Available (15 February 2003) online: <http://www.nua.ie/surveys/index.cgi?f=VS&art_id=905358673&rel=true/>.

O'Hagan, C. (2002). *Global universities: sowing the seeds of the future, or hanging on to the past?* Available (23 March 2003) online: <http://ts.mivu.org/default.asp?show=article&id=906/>.

O'Sullivan, P.B. (2000). What you don't know won't hurt me: impression management functions of communication channels in relationships. *Human Communication Research*, 26, 403–31.

Palme, J. (2000). *Why do people use CMC?* Available (1 April 2003) online: <http://www.dsv.su.se/%7Ejpalme/why-people-use-cmc.html>.

Parks, M. and Roberts, L.D (1998). 'Making MOOsic': the development of personal relationships on line and a comparison with their off-line counterparts. *Journal of Social and Personal Relationships*, 15, 517–37.

Parks, M.R. and Floyd, K. (1996). Making friends in cyberspace. *Journal of Computer-Mediated Communication*, 1 (4). Available (11 April 2003) online: < http://www.ascusc.org/jcmc/vol1/issue4/vol1no4.html>.

Pastore, M. (2000). *Digital divide more economic than ethnic*. Available (15 February 2003) online: <http://cyberatlas.internet.com/big_picture/demographics/article/0,1323,5901_395581,00.htm>.

Pew Report (2001). *Teenage life online: the rise of the instant-message generation and the internet's impact on friendships and family relationships*. Available (15 April 2003) online: <http://www.pewinternet.org/reports/pdfs/PIP_Teens_Report.pdf>.

Poster, M. (1990). *The mode of information: Poststructuralism and context*. Chicago: University of Chicago Press.

Poster, M. (1998). Virtual ethnicity: tribal identity in an age of global communications. In S. Jones (ed.), *Cybersociety 2.0: Revisiting computer-mediated communication and community* (pp. 184–211). Thousand Oaks, CA: Sage.

Postman, N. (1993). *Technopoly: The surrender of culture to technology*. New York: Vintage.

Postmes, T., Spears, R. and Lea, M. (2000). The formation of group norms in computer-mediated communication. *Human Communication Research*, 26, 341–71.

Potts, H.W.W. and. Wyatt, J.C (2002). Survey of doctors' experience of patients using the internet. *Journal of Medical Internet Research*, 4 (1). Available (24 February 2003) online: <http://www.jmir.org/2002/1/e5/abstract>.

Preece, J., Rogers, Y., Sharp, H., Benyon, D., Holland, S. and Carey, T. (1994). *Human–computer interaction*. Harlow: Pearson/AAUW Educational Foundation. Summary of research report available (11 April 2003) online: <http://www.aauw.org/2000/techsexecsum.html>.

Putnam, D.E. and Maheu, M.M. (2000). Online sexual addiction and compulsivity: integrating web resources and behavioral telehealth in treatment. *Sexual Addiction and Compulsivity: the Journal of Treatment and Prevention*, 7, 91–112.

Putnam, R. (2000). *Bowling alone: The collapse and revival of American community*. New York: Simon and Schuster.

Rafaeli, S. and Sudweeks, F. (1997). Networked interactivity. *Journal of Computer-Mediated Communication*, 2 (4). Available (3 April 2003) online: <http://www.ascusc.org/jcmc/vol2/issue4/rafaeli.sudweeks.html>.

Rajani, R. and Rosenberg, D. (1999). Usable? . . . or not? Factors affecting the usability of Web sites. *CMC Magazine* 6 (1). Available (23 October 2003) online: http://www.december.com/cmc/mag/current/toc.html>.

Reber, A.S. (1985). *The Penguin dictionary of psychology*. London: Penguin.

Reddy, K.S. (2002). Spielberg threatens legal action against Kerala firm. *The Hindu*. Available (28 April 2003) online: <http://www.hinduonnet.com/thehindu/2002/08/25/stories/2002082500471200.htm>.

Reid, E. (1998). The self and the internet: variations on the illusion of one self. In J. Gackenbach (ed.), *Psychology and the internet: Intrapersonal, interpersonal and transpersonal implications* (pp. 29–41). San Diego, CA: Academic Press.

Rheingold, H. (1993). *Virtual communities: Homesteading on the electronic frontier*. Reading, MA: Addison Wesley.

Rheingold, H. (1994). *The virtual community: Finding connection in a computerized world*. London: Minerva.

Rice, R.E. (1993). Media appropriateness: using social presence theory to compare traditional and new organizational media. *Human Communication Research*, 9, 451–84.

Richardson, J. (2000). *Researching student learning*. Buckingham: Open University Press.

Roberts, L., Smith, L. and Pollock, C. (2000) 'U r a lot bolder on the net': shyness and internet use. In W.R. Crozier (ed.), *Shyness: Development, consolidation and change* (pp. 121–38). London: Routledge.

Roberts, P.M. (1996). Writing layered texts: a pathway to multimedia presentations. Paper presented at ASCLTE conference, University of South Australia. Available (15 April 2003) online: < http://www.ascilite.org.au/conferences/adelaide96/papers/19.html >.

Rodino, M. (1997). Breaking out of binaries: reconceptualizing gender and its relationship to language in computer-mediated communications.

Journal of Computer-Mediated Communication, 3 (3), 000–00. Available (27 April 2003) online: <http://www.gscusc.org/jcmc/vol3/issue3/rodino.html> http://www.gscusc.org/jcmc/vol3/issue3/rodino.html>.

Rutherford, K. (2000). Internet activism: NGOs and the Mine Ban Treaty. *International Journal on Grey Literature*, 1 (3), 99–106.

Rutter, M. (1987). Psychosocial resilience and protective mechanisms. *American Journal of Orthopsychiatry*, 57 (3), 316–31.

Sachs, J.D. (2003). Visiting global public policies for sustainable development: A transatlantic dialogue. Paper presented at the Alliance Conference, Columbia University, New York, 26 May 2003. Available (26 October 2003) online: <http://www.columbia.edu/cu/alliance/>.

Santoro, G.M. (1995). What is computer-mediated communication? In Z.L. Berge and M.P. Collins (eds), *Computer mediated communication and the online classroom.* Cresskill, NJ: Hampton.

Schneider, J., Kortuem, G., Jager, J., Fickas, S.and Segall, Z. (2001). Disseminating trust information in wearable communities. *Personal Technologies*, 4 (4), 245–48. Available (11 April 2003) online: <http://delivery.acm.org/10.1145/600000/593569/00040245.pdf?key1=593569&key2=4119500501&coll=portal&dl=ACM&CFID=9797556&CFTOKEN=9896999>.

Schumacher, P. and Morahan-Martin, P. (2001). Gender, internet and computer attitudes and experiences. *Computers in Human Behavior*, 17 (1), 95–110.

Schiffrin, D. (1994). *Approaches to discourse.* Cambridge, MA: Blackwell.

Seabrook, J. (1995). Home on the net. *The New Yorker,* 16 October, Vol. 71, issue 32, pp. 66–71. Available (14 April 2003) online: <http://www.levity.com/seabrook/homenet.html>.

Shashaani, L. and Khalili, A. (2001). Gender and computers: similarities and differences in Iranian college students' attitudes toward computers. *Computers and Education*, 37 (3–4), 363–75.

Short, J., Williams, E. and Christie, B. (1976). *The social psychology of telecommunications.* London: Wiley.

Shortis, T. (2001). *The language of ICT.* London: Routledge.

Siegal, J., Dubrovsky, V., Kiesler, S. and McGuire, T. (1986). Group processes in computer-mediated communication. *Organizational Behavior and Human Decision Processes*, 37, 157–87.

Silicon.com (2003). *Is this the unluckiest spam recipient in Britain?* Available (19 February 2003) online: <http://www.silicon.com/news/500013/1/1037064.html?et=search/>.

Silver, D. and Garland, P. (2003). 'sHoP onLiNE!': advertising teen female cyberculture. In P.H. Howard and S. Jones (eds), *Society online: The internet in context* (pp. 157–72). Thousand Oaks, CA: Sage.

Simmons, J. (2001). British Council-sponsored 'World Speak' symposium.

Smith, C.B., McLaughlin, M.L. and Osborne, K.K. (1997). Conduct control on usenet. *Journal of Computer-Mediated Communication*, 2 (4). Available (15 April 2003) online: <http://www.ascusc.org/jcmc/vol2/issue4/smith.html>.

Spears, R. and Lea, M. (1992). Social influence and the influence of the 'social' in computer-mediated communication. In M. Lea (ed.), *Contexts of computer-mediated communication.* Hemel Hempstead: Harvester Wheatsheaf.

Spears, R., Lea, M., Corneliussen, R-A., ter Haar, W. and Postmes, T. (2002). Computer-mediated communication as a channel for social resistance: the strategic side of SIDE. *Small Group Research*, 33, 555–74.

Spears, R., Russell, M. and Lea, M. (1990). De-individuation and group polarization in computer-mediated communication. *British Journal of Social Psychology*, 29, 121–34.

Spinello, R. (2001). Code and moral values in cyberspace. *Ethics and Information Technology,* 3, 137–50.

Sproull, L. and Kiesler, S. (1986). Reducing social context cues: electronic mail in organization communication. *Management Science*, 32, 1492–512.

Stacey, R. (1992). *Managing the unknowable.* San Francisco: Jossey Bass.

Standage, T. (1999). *The Victorian internet: The remarkable story of the telegraph and the nineteenth century's on-line pioneers.* New York: Walker.

Stanton, J.M. (2002). Web addict or happy employee? Company profile of the frequent internet user. *Communications of the ACM*, 45 (1), 55–9.

Statistical Research (2002). *Hispanic households slower to embrace Net.* Cited in *Nua Internet Surveys.* Available (15 February 2003) online: <http://www.nua.ie/surveys/index.cgi?f=VS&art_id=905358101&rel=true/>.

Stoll, C. (1995). *Silicon snake oil.* New York: Anchor Books.

Stratton, J. (1997). Cyberspace and the globalization of

culture. In David Porter (ed.), *Internet culture* (pp. 257–75). New York: Routledge.

Surratt, C.G. (1999). *Netaholics? the creation of a pathology*. Commack, NY: Nova Science.

Tannen, D. (1996). *Gender and discourse*. Oxford: Oxford University Press.

Thompsen, P. A., and Foulger, D. A. (1996). Effects of pictographs and quoting on flaming in electronic mail. *Computers in Human Behavior*, 12 (2), 225–43.

Thurlow, C. (2001). Language and the internet. In R. Mesthrie and R. Asher (eds), *The concise encyclopedia of sociolinguistics* (pp. 287–9). London: Elsevier.

Thurlow, C. and McKay, S. (2003). Profiling 'new' communication technologies in adolescence. *Journal of Language* and *Social Psychology*, 22 (1), 94–103.

Todd, Z. and Walker, S. (2000). Multilingualism on the net: language attitudes and the use of talkers. In L. Pemberton and S. Shurville (eds), *Words on the web: Computer-mediated communication* (pp. 63–8). Exeter: Intellect.

Trillo, N. (1997). Intercultural computer mediated communication. *CMC Magazine*, January. Available (2 March 2003) online: <http://www.december.com/cmc/mag/1997/jan/triimpl.html/>.

Turkle, S. (1990). The psychology of personal computers. In T. Forester (ed.), *The information technology revolution* (pp. 182–201). Oxford: Blackwell.

Turkle, S. (1995). *Life on the screen: Identity in the age of the internet*. New York: Touchstone.

Turkle, S. (1999). Identity in the age of the internet. In Mackay and T. O'Sullivan (eds), *The media reader: Continuity and transformation* (pp.287 – 304). London: Sage.

Turkle, S. (2001). Cited in Tech Topic, *The future of the internet: Addiction, stereotypes and cyborgs*. Available (17 April 2003) online: <http://www.cybergrrl.com/tech/ttopic/art1261>.

Turner, J.W., Grube, J.A. and Meyers, J. (2001). Developing an optimal match within online communities: an exploration of CMC support communities and traditional support. *Journal of Communication*, 51, 231–51.

UK seniors take to the net (2002). Available (28 April 2002) online: <http://www.nua.ie/surveys/index.cgi?f=VS&art_id=905357796&rel=true>.

UN News Center (2001). *UN report on bridging digital divide*. Available (28 February 2001) online: <http://www.un.org/News/>.

UNDP (2001). *Making new technologies work for human development*. Available (29 April 2003) online: <http://www.undp.org/hdr2001>.

Utz, S. (2000). Social information processing in MUDs: the development of friendships in virtual worlds. *Journal of Online Behavior*, 1 (1). Available (11 April 2003) online: <http://www.behavior.net/JOB/v1n1/utz.html>.

Van Gelder, L. (1997). The strange case of the electronic lover. In D. Fallon (ed.), *Technology and society* (pp. 104–12). Chicago, IL; Coursewise

Vault (2000). *Vault Internet Use in the Workplace Corporate Survey.* New York: Vault.

Wakefield, J. (2000a). Demon verdict threatens ISPs. *ZDNet News*. Available (22 February 2003) online: <http://news.zdnet.co.uk/story/0,,t269-s2078075,00.html/>.

Wakefield, J. (2000b). Demon users banned from usenet. *ZDNet News*. Available (22 February 2003) online: <http://news.zdnet.co.uk/story/0,,t269-s2078472,00.html/>.

Wakefield, J. (2000c). UK ISPs will continue to be at a disadvantage — defamation law needs reform. *ZDNet News*. Available (22 February 2003) online: <http://news.zdnet.co.uk/story/0,,t269-s2078734,00.html/>.

Wakefield, J. (2001). Government digital divide strategy in disarray. *ZDNet News*. Available (11 April 2003) online: < http://news.zdnet.co.uk/story/0,,t269-s2086031,00.html.>.

Wallace, P. (1999). *The psychology of the internet*. Cambridge: Cambridge University Press.

Walther, J.B. (1992). Interpersonal effects in computer-mediated interaction: a relational perspective. *Communication Research*, 19, 52–90.

Walther, J.B. (1994). Anticipated ongoing interaction versus channel effects on relational communication in computer-mediated interaction. *Human Communication Research*, 20, 473–501.

Walther, J.B. (2002). Research ethics in Internet-enabled research: Human subjects issues and methodological myopia. *Ethics and Information Technology*, 4, 205–16. Available (20 October 2003) online: <http://www.nyu.edu/projects/nissenbaum/ethics_wal_full.html>.

Walther, J.B. (1996). Computer-mediated communication: impersonal, interpersonal, and hyperpersonal interaction. *Communication Research*, 23, 3–43.

Walther, J.B., and Burgoon, J.K. (1992). Relational communication in computer-mediated interaction. *Human Communication Research*, 19, 50–88.

Walther, J.B. and D'Addario, K.P. (2001). The impacts of emoticons on message interpretation in computer-mediated communication. *Social Science Computer Review*, 19, 323–45.

Walther, J.B., and Parks, M.R. (2002). Cues filtered out, cues filtered in: computer-mediated communication and relationships. In M.L. Knapp and J.A. Daly (eds), *Handbook of interpersonal communication* (pp. 529–63). Thousand Oaks, CA: Sage.

Walther, J.B. and Tidwell, L.C. (1995). Nonverbal cues in computer-mediated communication, and the effects of chronemics on relational communication. *Journal of Organizational Computing*, 5, 355–78.

Walther, J.B., Anderson, J.F. and Park, D.W. (1994). Interpersonal effects in computer-mediated communication: a meta-analysis of social and antisocial communication. *Communication Research*, 21, 460–87.

Walther, J.B., Slovacek, C. and Tidwell, L.C. (2001). Is a picture worth a thousand words? Photographic images in long term and short term virtual teams. *Communication Research*, 28, 105–34.

Watson, J. (1998). Audience: the uses we make of media. In *Media Communication: An introduction to theory and process* (pp. 60–82). Basingstoke: Macmillan.

Weil, M.M. and Rosen, L.D. (1995). The psychological impact of technology from a global perspective: a study of technological sophistication and technophobia in university students from twenty-three countries. *Computers in Human Behavior* 11 (1), 95–133.

Weinstein, L. (2002). Online gambling laws a good bet. *Wired News*. Available (29 March 2003) online: <http://www.wired.com/news/politics/0,1283,55704,00.html >.

Weiss, J. and Nance, M. (1997). *It came from . . . beyond the browser!* Available (24 March 2000) online: <http://www.cnet.com/Content/Features/Howto/Beyond/>.

Wellman, B. and Haythornthwaite, C. (eds) (2002). *The internet in everyday life*. Oxford: Blackwell.

Wellman, B. (1997). An electronic group is virtually a social network. In S. Kiesler (ed.), *Cultures of the internet* (pp. 179–205). Mahwah, NJ: Erlbaum.

Wilson, J. (1999). *Equiangular spirals*. Available (12 April 2003) online: <http://jwilson.coe.uga.edu/EMT668/EMAT6680.F99/Erbas/KURSAT geometrypro/nature&logspiral/nature&logspi.html>.

Witmer, D. and Katzman, S. (1997). On-line smiles: does gender make a difference in the use of graphic accents? *Journal of Computer-Mediated Communication*, 2 (4). Available (20 March 2003) online: <http://www.ascusc.org/jcmc/vol2/issue4/witmer1.html>.

Wolf, A. (2000). Emotional expression online: gender differences in emoticon use. *CyberPsychology and Behavior*, 3 (5), 827–33.

Wolock, E., Orr, A., and Buckleitner, W. (1998). *Young kids and computers: A parent's survival guide*. Flemington, NJ: Children's Software Revue.

Woodward, K. (ed.) (1997). *Identity and difference*. London: Sage and Open University.

World Wide Web Consortium (2001). How People with Disabilities Use the Web. Available (23 October 2003) online: <http://www.w3.org/WAI/EO/Drafts/PWD-Use-Web>.

Young, K. S. (1998). Internet addiction: the emergence of a new disorder. *CyberPsychology and Behavior*, 1 (3), 237–44.

Zickmund, S. (1997). Approaching the radical other: The discursive culture of cyberhate. In S.G. Jones (ed.), *Virtual culture: Identity and communication in cybersociety*. Thousand Oaks, CA: Sage.

INDEXED GLOSSARY OF KEY TERMS

As a brief but by no means comprehensive overview of the range of ideas and concepts covered in the book, this glossary lists all the key terms specified at the start of each Basic Theory (BT) and Central Issues (CI) unit.

addiction (CI 7, p. 150) A term ordinarily reserved by mental health workers to describe substance dependence or misuse; sometimes erroneously used to describe excessive internet use. See also **compulsion** and **Internet Addiction Disorder**.

anonymity (BT 5, p. 62) Commonly assumed to be an automatic feature of CMC because of the relative absence of visual cues, anonymity refers to a lack of 'identifiablity' – whether perceived or real, and which may have a positive or negative influence on people's behavior.

antisocial behavior (BT 6, p. 154) Behavior usually considered inappropriate by certain cultural standards; in the context of CMC, this is often applied to the impact of excessive internet use on offline social interaction. See also **antisociality**.

antisociality (BT 4, p. 47) A label which refers to the allegation that CMC is 'bad' communication because it has a negative impact on the extent and quality of offline communication. See also **asociality**.

asociality (BT 4, p. 47) A label which refers to the allegation that CMC is 'bad' communication because the quality of communication is necessarily reduced by the technological constraints of the internet. See also **antisociality**.

autonomy (CI 1, p. 91) Derives from the Greek: *auto*, meaning self, and *nomos*, law or rule. Being able to speak or care for oneself. Right to self-govern, as in a self-governing online community.

cohesion (BT 5, p. 64) The process by which any online or offline group sticks together socially and/or psychologically. Cohesion may be achieved by direct/explicit or indirect/implicit social control.

communication (BT 1, p. 17) The transactional, multifunctional and multimodal processes of social interaction by which meaning is negotiated between people.

communication imperative (BT 4, p. 51) The idea that humans are driven by their desire to communicate, usually overcoming any technological obstacles and appropriating a technology to maximize communication satisfaction and interaction.

community (CI 3, p. 108) A term which usually describes a network of people who may or may not share a geographical space, but who have common interests and values and who interact on a reasonably regular basis. Members usually also perceive themselves to be a part of a community. See also **social networks**.

compulsion (CI 7, p. 151) Any behavior consisting of unusually repetitive actions in the attempt to attain anxiety reduction such as excessive hand washing. See also **addiction**.

computer (BT 1, p. 19) Any electronic digital technology which enables the storage and manipulation of data, and interaction between people; most obviously, personal computers and the **internet**.

conformity (BT 5, p. 64) With both positive and negative implications for group behavior, this describes the tendency for individual members either to convert or comply with the prevailing opinions, attitudes and actions of a group.

convergence (BT 2, p. 28) The coming together and/or overlapping of previously separated phenomena, such as the internet and web, offline and online life, and new and old communication technologies.

cyberculture (BT 2, p. 30) A term which highlights the emergence and maintenance of customs, values, norms and other creative social practices on the internet. See also **cybersociety** and **cyberspace**.

cybersex (CI 6, p. 140) Also known as virtual or v-sex, this is any online activity driven by sexual desire and involving erotic stimulation – usually a combination of visual, textual and physical (self-) arousal.

cybersociety (BT 2, p. 29) A term which describes and prioritizes the social life and human interaction which emerge through, and are sustained by, internet use. See also **cyberculture** and **cyberspace**.

cyberspace (BT 2, p. 29) A geographical or physical metaphor for the interactive and informational context created by the internet. See also **cyberculture** and **cybersociety**.

cyberstalking (CI 5, p. 132) Often exaggerated by the media and in popular discourse, this refers to someone tracking someone else's actions online with illegitimate or malicious intent. See also **online harassment**.

deficit approaches (BT 4, p. 48) A general term for those approaches which suggest CMC – especially text-based CMC – *lacks* important qualities of face-to-face communication and so will always be inadequate or inferior.

deindividuation (BT 5, p. 63) Similar to popular ideas about a 'pack instinct' or 'group mentality', deindividuation describes how an individual's sense of self can be subsumed by the power of the group.

diaspora (CI 5, p. 133) Large-scale, geographical migration of a community, displaced from its traditional or ancestral home or country owing to political, economic or social marginalization.

digital divide (CI 1, p. 84) A popular and sometimes scholarly term which refers to the inequality between countries', regions' and groups' use of, and access to, new communication technologies like the internet.

digital gender divide (CI 5, p. 130) Extending the notion of the **digital divide**, this refers to the unequal access to, and use of, communication technology by women. In many countries the traditional patterns of gender inequality are changing.

discipline (BT 1, p. 20) An area of scholarship which tends to have its own content, a relatively distinct curriculum and prepares people for well defined careers. See also **field**.

discourse (CI 4, p. 119) The way that **language** is actually used in conversation, and the way it is shaped by the context in which it is used. See also **netspeak**.

disembodiment (CI 2, p. 99) The idea in CMC that the virtuality of cyberspace offers a unique opportunity for people to be 'liberated' from physical markers such as age, height, weight, sex, skin color, and so on. See also **identity play** and **gender masquerade**.

disinhibition (BT 5, p. 62) A reduction in people's concern for self-presentation and other people's opinion of them. The effect of disinhibition and communication can be regarded in either a positive or a negative light. See also **deindividuation**.

embedded media (BT 6, p. 75) A term used by Philip Howard to describe the way that 'new' media have become – or are becoming – such an accepted part of everyday life, being heavily relied on and often taken for granted. See also **invisible technology**.

ethics/online ethics (CI 1, p. 85) Examines how we systematize, defend, and recommend ideas about what is right and wrong, given the particular cultural context. The notion of online ethics raises concerns about issues of access, equality, privacy, ownership and power.

field (BT 1, p. 20) A loosely associated group of scholars who work on similar problems but who are not unified by a single set of concepts or methods; scholarly fields do not usually prepare people for specific career possibilities. See also **discipline**.

flames/flaming (BT 6, p. 70) An often poorly defined notion which generally describes any hostile or aggressive interaction online.

folk linguistics (CI 4, p. 120, 126) Beliefs and concerns about language (including language on the net) held by lay people rather than by academic specialists such as linguists and communication scholars.

Gemeinschaft and Gesellschaft (CI 3, p. 109) The terms proposed by German sociologist Ferdinand Tönnies to distinguish between small, intimate or rural communities, on the one hand, and large, urban societies on the other.

gender (CI 5, p. 130) Although often used as a synonym for 'sex', scholars understand that gender is more than one's biological classification as either male or female, and also refers to culturally specific ideas about masculinity and femininity, as well as sexuality.

gender masquerade (CI 5, p. 129) A heightened performance of masculinity or femininity to mask or conceal one's usual gender identity. See also **gender**.

genres (BT 2 p. 31) The different 'discourses' or patterns and styles of linguistic and communicative practice associated with the different **sub-systems** of the **internet**.

globalization (CI 1, p. 85) A complex term which commonly describes the increased mobility and interconnectedness of goods, services, labor, technology and capital throughout the world.

hybridity (CI 3, p. 114) In this context, the term is used to describe the interweaving of traditional offline communities and new online patterns of community building.

hype and hysteria (BT 3, p. 39) Two common, but extreme, reactions to new technology. *Hype* refers to excessively optimistic (or 'utopian') expectations about the ability of a new technology to improve human existence. *Hysteria* refers to excessively pessimistic (or 'dystopian') anxieties and fears about the negative impact of technology.

hyperpersonal communication (BT 4, p. 53) The idea proposed by Joseph Walther that, far from being an impoverished form of communication, CMC can in fact be even more friendly, social and intimate than face-to-face communication.

identification (CI 2, p. 97) A term which reflects contemporary approaches to identity, seen as a fluid *process* – a communication activity – rather than as a fixed, essential and one-off 'discovery'. See also **identity construction** and **multiple identities**.

identity construction (CI 2, p. 96) According to contemporary scholarship, identity is something achieved in relationship with other people; online activity can sometimes allow people to work on their identities in new or different ways. See also **technologies of the self**.

identity play (CI 2, p. 100) The notion that the **anonymity** of CMC frees people to experiment with different aspects of their identities and to pretend to be different from who they are offline. See also **gender masquerade**.

imagined communities (CI 3, p. 111) The idea proposed by Benedick Anderson that all communities are imagined if they are larger than traditional rural villages where people have almost daily face-to-face contact.

impression management (BT 4, p. 52) Erving Goffman's famous idea that people spend the greater part of their social lives forming impressions of other people and constantly trying to influence other people's impressions of them.

interactional-normative framework (BT 6, p. 72.) The framework proposed by O'Sullivan and Flanagin which looks to contextualize online behavior – particularly **flaming** – in terms of intentions and interpretations, relationships and group norms.

interactivity (BT 5, p. 66) A term proposed by Rafaeli and Sudweeks to describe the way that electronic messages relate or refer to each other; this is therefore a means by which cohesion may be achieved in online groups.

internet (BT 2, p. 28) An almost worldwide network of computers enabling the transfer of data and creating a technological system which in turn supports a number of other technologies (or **sub-systems**) such as email, bulletin boards, internet relay chat and the **web**.

Internet Addiction Disorder (IAD) (CI 7, p. 151) Preoccupation with online activity, withdrawal symptoms, obsessive thinking or fantasies about the internet. See also **addiction**.

Internet Studies (BT 1, p. 21) A broad, interdisciplinary field of scholarship concerned primarily with the social, political and economic impact of the internet; of which CMC may be regarded as a sub-field.

interpersonal attraction (CI 6, p. 139) Whether online or offline, the social and interactional processes by which people form acquaintances and become intimate with each other as possible precursors of romance and sexual activity.

invisible technology (BT 3 p. 37) A term describing technology which has 'matured' to become so embedded in, or integral to, our everyday lives that we don't really notice it any more.

language (CI 4, p. 119) A symbolic, conventional system of sounds, letters and words which are combined and used for the negotiation of meaning. See also **netlingo**.

linguistic diffusion (CI 4, p. 126) The process by which linguistic forms and practices spread from one domain to another; in the case of CMC, the spread of **netlingo** into offline life.

locality (CI 3, p. 109) A commonly used characteristic of communities, although nowadays shared geographical location is not thought to be a necessary feature of communities. See also **sociability**.

mediation (BT 1, p. 18) The social, cultural, psychological or technological processes by which communication is transmitted, channelled and filtered.

moral panic (CI 6, p. 145) A kind of mass hysteria around the perception of a threat to the moral order, often caused by false assumptions.

multilingualism (CI 4, p. 122) The use and representation of a wide variety of languages; online this dispels the myth that English is necessarily the language of the internet.

multiple identities (CI 2, p. 97) Related to the notions of **identification** and **identity construction**, this refers to the understanding that identity is not unitary; people choose to present different aspects of themselves all the time, and take on different identities throughout their lives.

netlingo and **netspeak** (CI 4 p. 124, 125) More popular than scholarly, these terms describe the different linguistic forms used on the internet (netlingo), and the ways people actually use language in online conversations (netspeak). See also **language** and **discourse**.

online gambling (CI 7, p. 155) To play a game of chance for stakes via the internet; arguably the internet use most prone to problematic dependence.

online harassment (CI 5, p. 132) The often illegal use of the internet to communicate with, or intimidate, someone online against their will, including making personal threats. See also **flames/flaming** and **cyberstalking**.

online self-presentation (CI 2 p. 102) Following the ideas of Erving Goffman, in CMC – perhaps even more so than in face-to-face communication – people may *choose* how to present themselves to others and decide what to disclose about themselves. See also **impression management**.

polarization (BT 5, p. 63) The phenomenon in group behavior whereby views or opinions tend to be intensified toward extreme positions.

pornography (CI 6, p. 143) Materials including the description or exhibition of sexual activity that might be interpreted as obscene by specific cultural standards.

privilege (CI 1, p. 83) The advantage or benefit associated with particular people, usually those in positions of power. Privilege may be either perceived or real.

Problematic/Pathological Internet Use (CI 7, p. 153) In preference to Internet Addiction Disorder, a term to indicate a level of internet use that is disruptive of normal, everyday social and/or occupational functioning.

public sphere (CI 1, p. 88) A concept used by Jürgen Habermas to describe a social setting or opportunity where informed community members may reach consensus through open debate.

reduced social cues (BT 5 p. 60) A model of CMC which focuses on the apparent reduction of static or dynamic nonverbal features and backchannels, which, in turn, disrupts social interaction, undermines social norms and increases disinhibition. See also **deficit approaches**.

sexual health (CI 6, p. 142) Health concerns pertaining to sexual well-being; owing to the sensitive nature of sexual health, information about it is often sought online.

SIDE model (BT 5, p. 67) The Social Identity Model of Deindividuation Effects argues that CMC offers participants ample opportunity to switch from personal to **social identity**, leading to the potential for greater group cohesion in CMC than in face-to-face interaction.

sociability (CI 3, p. 109) A necessary, definitional feature of community, referring to sustained social interaction between, and the shared interests of, its members. See also **locality**.

social capital (BT 6 p. 76.) A term which describes the breadth and depth of people's social lives in terms of social relationships and civic engagement. Social capital can be enhanced or increased by access to and use of CMC.

social constructivism (BT 3, p. 42) A perspective which challenges **technological determinism** by seeing technology as entirely subordinate to the way it's used in particular socio-historical, culturally specific contexts. See also **social realism**.

social identity (BT 5, p. 67) As opposed to personal identity, people's sense of themselves as being group members, which may often be based on their feelings or perceptions of group membership rather than on actual group activity. See also **SIDE model**.

social information processing (BT 4, p. 50) In response to **deficit approaches**, the Social Information Processing model proposes that, given the same investment of time and commitment, relational quality in CMC will be the same as face-to-face communication.

social networks (CI 3 p. 112) Social network theory is one way of describing the structure of relationships between large groups. The stronger and more extensive the ties between people, the more like a **community** the network becomes.

social realism (BT 3, p. 43) A perspective on the relationship between technology and social interaction which, in contrast to the perspectives of **technological determinism** and **social constructivism**, sees the relationship as a 'two-way street' – we both shape and are shaped by technology.

speech community (CI 4, p. 120) A group or community of people with shared patterns of language who are organized around the way they speak.

sub-systems (BT 2 p. 30) The 'technologies within technologies' of the **internet** which are the focus of CMC, such as emails, listservs, newsgroups, internet relay chat, instant messaging, metaworlds and personal homepages. See also **genres**.

symbolic marking (CI 2, p. 95) A strategy available for communicating personal or **social identity** by means of resources such as clothing, corporate logos and national flags.

technical affordances (BT 3, p. 42) The practical or material opportunities made possible by a technology itself; in other words, what it allows or enables people to do.

technological determinism (BT 3, p. 40) An analytical perspective which theorizes the relationship between technology and social life, as one where technology is the prime moving force behind social and psychological transformations.

technologies of self (CI 2, p. 98) A term proposed by Michel Foucault to describe the means by which people are able to construct their identities through talking and writing about themselves.

technology (BT 2, p. 25) Any device, artifact or process by which the natural or social world is modified to satisfy and extend human needs and capabilities. For CMC this usually refers to the machinery and infrastructure which supports the internet.

web (BT 2, p. 28) Supported by the **internet**, a sub-system of computer servers and standardized programming enabling the exchange of files; files are located, retrieved and 'translated' by browsers.

INDEX